BUILDING
PSYCHOLOGICAL
FITNESS

How High Performers
Achieve with Ease

Karen Doll, Psy.D., L.P.

BUILDING PSYCHOLOGICAL FITNESS
How High Performers Achieve with Ease

ISBN: 978-1-947276-06-2
ASIN: B09GJ6MSVF

Publishing and Design:

EP&C AUTHOR
P U B L I S H I N G

Ordering Information: Quantity sales. Special discounts are available on quantity purchases by corporations, associations, and others. For details, contact the publisher at the address above. Orders by U.S. trade bookstores and wholesalers.

Please contact: 561-601-9871 | info@epicauthor.com | EpicAuthor.com

First Edition

Dedication

Dedicated to my mom, Marjean DeCesare (1944–2017), who modeled and taught me Agape.

AGAPE: Ancient Greek type of love

Support for others' growth and well-being.
Commitment to alleviate the suffering of humanity.
Support the flourishing of all beings.
A selfless love that is passionately committed to the
well-being of others.

Contents

Introduction

If you want to awaken all of humanity, then awaken all of yourself. If you want to eliminate the suffering in the world, then eliminate all that is dark and negative in yourself. Truly, the greatest gift you have to give is that of your own transformation.
—Lao Tzu

I HAVE INFORMATION THAT MAY DISAPPOINT YOU. This book is not about selling you a magic elixir to immediately and permanently enhance your emotional and mental well-being. There is not one easy, universal solution to elevate psychological health.

People are struggling and want answers. Mental illness is prevalent, and we are hearing more about the challenges of mental health. Statistics support the sentiment of increasing anxiety, depression, addiction, suicide, loneliness, stress — the list goes on. Was it always this way? Are we paying more attention to mental health? I suspect many more people were suffering in silence than we realize.

When I survey groups of professionals and ask how many know someone with mental health challenges, the **yes** responses used to be about 50 percent. These days, responses have moved into 90 percent plus. My question, though, is, why isn't this figure 100 percent? Who hasn't felt anxious, depressed, sad, or overwhelmed with life demands?

INTRODUCTION

In any area of health, it's not black or white. We aren't perfectly healthy. I am generally physically healthy without illness or disease. Yet, I experience low-grade ailments that pop up from time to time, including sore feet, recovering knee injuries, headaches, and sleep challenges.

It's the same with mental health. I don't have a clinical mental health diagnosis, yet I experience anxiety on occasion and, at times, I need to work harder to manage my elevated stress levels. I can feel overwhelmed, exhausted, lonely, or sad — just like everyone else.

We are facing a new frontier of how to address mental health in a more comprehensive way. We need increased awareness, more conversation, more advanced and accessible intervention options, and more permission for people to seek help and support. It's time for talking about mental health to be as mainstream as discussing physical health.

While I believe mental health challenges have always been present, the acceleration of our modern-day pace of life has contributed to elevated stress and hurriedness. People feel chronically rushed.

I notice a heightened sense of urgency and pressure to use the time carefully. I've been plagued with this expedience, impatience, and internal urgency for much of my life, yet it is more common now for "regular" people.

Nowhere is this phenomenon more rampant than in the workplace. Professionals feel cluttered with competing demands, never-ending emails, correspondence to handle, and days jammed with meetings. It becomes a challenge to manage energy, tasks, and time when facing a relentless myriad of these activities.

According to research by Jonathan B. Spira, two-thirds of employees feel that they have less time to complete their day-to-day tasks. Meanwhile, 94 percent of employees feel overwhelmed by information overload to the point of incapacitation.[1]

INTRODUCTION

Recent trends show that over half of U.S. employees feel unable to enjoy paid vacations — and for a good reason. The thought of dealing with more work upon their return dissuades them from taking time off.

Technology has contributed to this rapid pace of change. It has impacted our work and home lives more than any other modern factor. It also continues to reshape the future of work. Modern-day forward-thinking leaders have pondered the effects of this accelerated change and the transformation that it heralds for people. Technology offers convenience and a multitude of ways to connect, yet we haven't caught up with how to fully use it in a healthy manner.

People are having trouble keeping up with life and work demands. Worse yet, people experience increased distress by even fostering the **feelings and thoughts** that they are unable to keep up with. It can have an adverse effect on employees and their lives.

This brings us to an issue of managing mental health — stress. A heightened pace of life correlates with higher stress. People who spend extensive hours at the office are at a greater risk of mental and physical ailments that could be avoided. If stress persists and is not managed properly, it takes a toll on health and overall well-being. Excessive demands and stress pose adverse effects on people physically and mentally. Given the volatile, uncertain, complex, and ambiguous (VUCA) state of our work environment, people are experiencing chronic stress and burnout.

The COVID-19 pandemic has played a huge role in heightened stress just the same. The initial phase of the pandemic was difficult for people and businesses in several ways. Childcare, isolation, joblessness, and other challenges affected nearly everyone to varying degrees. It is an understatement to say that people's mental health took a severe hit during this time. Anxiety and stress were heightened due to lockdowns and the life changes that came afterward.

People have lived under severe stress due to the pandemic and reported higher stress levels prior to the initiation of the infamous health crisis. However, there is a slight caveat. While many people may feel the extra stress and anxiety due to COVID-19, it's a wonder if these circumstances simply pushed many **just** over the line.

Researchers have begun actively investigating the stress and fear that this pandemic has multiplied. It has compounded figures for mental health and will continue even as it subsides. The U.S. Census Bureau reports that 42 percent of the population suffers from depression and anxiety, which is a marked increase since previous reports. Data reveals disturbing trends on the global scale as well. Experts suggest that returning to baseline numbers will be challenging in the coming years, given the scale of damage the pandemic has left in its wake. Fear and isolation may continue to raise these numbers, acting as a catalyst.

COVID factors aside, there has become a mismatch between work-life demands and our overall capacity to cope, so much so that the statistics of burnout and stress are higher than they've ever been. Chronic stress has negatively affected people's minds, bodies, and immune systems.

A few common current concerns include health, difficulty in concentration, sleep disruption, distractibility, social isolation, work performance/academic productivity gaps, financial stress, job security, and lifestyle changes.

The statistics are there to support the feelings:

- In May 2019, the World Health Organization recognized burnout in the ICD-11 as an occupational phenomenon.[2]
- Seventy-seven percent of respondents experienced burnout in their current job.[3]
- The CDC reported a significant increase in anxiety and depression in 2019–2020 and 2020–2021.[4]
- Deaths associated with alcohol, drugs, and suicide took the lives of 186,763 Americans in 2020, a 20 percent one-

year increase in the combined death rate and the highest number of substance misuse deaths ever recorded for a single year.[5]

- In 2019, 96 percent of managers experienced burnout.[6]
- The American Institute of Stress indicates that 80 percent of workers experience stress on the job.[7]
- In a 2020 global study, 75 percent of employees felt more isolated since the pandemic.[8]

We don't have to look far to find suffering. This is one reason I wrote this book. People are looking for solutions to address the struggle. I don't have an answer. Yet, I've written this book to provide accessible ideas, interventions, and ways people can improve mental health.

Building Psychological Fitness is for anyone who wants to elevate their mental health, thrive, and flourish in their lives. It also aims to help high-achieving professionals succeed and be at their best without unnecessary distress and overwhelm. In this book, you will learn how to care for your mental health, feel less stressed, and be effective.

WHAT IS PSYCHOLOGICAL FITNESS?

I use the term to capture mental and emotional well-being while embracing the whole person, mind-body connection. Psychological fitness is effective self-management, including healthy thinking and effective emotional processing.

Being psychologically fit will positively impact your performance, well-being, and how you respond to stress. Building your psychological fitness also includes developing coping skills, enhancing social connections, and community involvement.

WHAT IS THE IDEAL STATE?

In research for this book, I interviewed many high-achieving, successful professionals who have demanding lives. I inquired about the current state of their lives, including well-being, mental health, stress levels, and life challenges. I also asked, what would be better? What is your ideal state? Most answers revolved around how they **felt**. Most expressed that they wanted to **feel better, feel less stressed, feel more balanced, feel equanimity, feel lighter, freer, happier, etc.**

◇◇◇

Equanimity is the capacity to let your experience be what it is without trying to fight it and negotiate with it. It's like an inner smoothness or frictionlessness.[9]
—Jeff Warren, author

◇◇◇

The most common response? At one point, 27 people in a row landed on "I want to feel AT EASE." They seek a life of continuing to be challenged, striving, achieving, and pursuing their lofty goals, WITHOUT the unnecessary drain, strain, and distress. They don't want to compromise or sacrifice their standards, yet the emotional drag of negative stress, a chronic feeling of discontent, and not-enough-ism is heavy. They want to thrive and flourish, be actively engaged, and leave the feelings of overwhelm, exhaustion, hurry, and self-criticism behind.

An American English definition of *at ease* involves feeling relaxed and secure, without anxiety or discomfort. In the military, the phrase *at ease* or *stand at ease* is used as a command or order given to soldiers, not to be confused with rest. While at ease allows permission for a more relaxed position than standing at attention, it is still considered a stationary drill. It requires soldiers to remain silent, stand still with their feet apart and place their hands behind their backs.

While the military command of *at ease* is not applicable for civilians, there is something to be learned. Being at ease is not about slouching, being complacent or not trying, or disengaging. Rather, it references an alert yet not constricted state of attention that allows for optimal engagement.

Consider how you can tap into an engaged and alert state without the unnecessary emotional strain.

You may not be able to directly control how long you live, yet you can take steps to **live better** while you're here. You can tap into your personal power to choose how you live now.

Key Point:

High-performing professionals want to **achieve** AND feel **AT EASE**. This book offers steps you can take to live better, thrive, and flourish without unnecessary distress.

I provide science-backed interventions to enhance the mental capacity necessary for you to respond to life's challenging circumstances. You will find evidence-based practices to foster well-being and resilience and experience less stress and strain. This book will help you learn how to feel more centered, excel, and make progress without compromising your standards.

This book is for most people, whether you want a boost in well-being, you feel prisoner to your thoughts, you struggle with emotional regulation, or you're just curious to learn about mental health. Regardless of your age, occupation, or background, it applies to you.

If you need to quiet the clutter in your head or better manage your emotions, I can lead the way. If you find yourself being caught in traps of destructive thinking, you know what I mean. Unmanaged, negative thoughts can fuel anxiety and even panic.

I will provide information about what can get in the way of optimal mental health. What are the obstacles that are holding you back from thriving and flourishing? After all, understanding the problem and generating a deeper level of self-awareness is the first step.

Leveraging experiences from my work, I will help you understand the roadmap so you can find your power. I can help you identify patterns within yourself, especially consistent and intrinsic factors that you can understand to live a better future as a better version of yourself.

This book offers a catalog of options for you to circumvent your current condition, minimize pain, suffering, or excessive emotional turmoil, as well as foster growth and elevate your psychological life. This roadmap should help you navigate life challenges and provide direction like a GPS, your psychological positioning system. You can transcend injury and pain by nurturing and developing internal resources that cultivate positive mental health.

The mental health field is immensely vast and continually expanding as we speak. There are self-proclaimed personal development experts on this topic who have spoken at length and introduced their corrective measures yet may not have the necessary credentials to address mental health in a way that is based on scientific research. Some are misleading the population when science can expertly lead the way in this regard.

Be wary of experts who claim to have quick, easy solutions to address mental health or who have three simple tips to solve all your problems. That's not how it works.

INTRODUCTION

Having specialists in the realm of mental health is important due to the sophistication and complexity involved in understanding the psyche. However, be discerning of individuals who are too vehement in endorsing their one solution to be the only answer. It makes me think of the hammer and nail. If you have a hammer, everything can begin to look like a nail.

I don't want people to be misled or to think there is something wrong with them because they haven't successfully applied such simplistic tactics, or if they have, they aren't experiencing a miraculous recovery.

That is another reason I wrote this book. As a licensed psychologist, I have worked at the intersection of personal well-being and professional development. Having earned a doctoral degree in clinical psychology and studied these topics throughout my professional tenure, I can affirm there is no one easy solution to managing mental health.

It wouldn't be professionally reasonable to suggest that there is one single thing you can do to elevate your mental health. Again, I'm not suggesting that you don't do anything. I'm also not implying that it's easy because doing anything meaningful, impactful, and valuable **with consistency** is not easy.

Here are a few disclaimers. You aren't guaranteed to find solutions to permanently enhance your emotional and mental well-being in this book. Ideas and practices presented in the book are also not intended to be clinical interventions for people dealing with severe mental illness. If you are struggling with a clinical mental illness, please seek professional support.

However, you are going to find some ways that would take you down the path of self-regulation. This is going to be a steady process with proven results. What I am proposing is that there are practices and interventions you can leverage to upgrade and boost your mental health. I have been privileged to coach hundreds of professionals and have helpful examples and vignettes to highlight the power of suggested interventions.

INTRODUCTION

It can seem like things are falling apart, especially if you engage in the media frenzy of "breaking news." There are world disasters of an epic scale, violence, injustice, economic instability, poverty, natural disasters ... and more.

All things considered, there is hope! Now is the optimal time to tap into post-Covid growth. Regardless of where you are on the mental wellness continuum, you can build internal resources to mitigate the impact of your life stressors. By establishing psychological rituals, you can decrease unnecessary angst, experience relief, and foster joy, fulfillment, and mental health.

Here are a few benefits of building psychological capital:

- Thrive and perform at your best without unnecessary distress and overwhelm
- Increase energy, focus, and well-being
- Upgrade your mindset to free up cognitive capacity
- Move toward optimal mental health
- Manage stress, feel better, be more productive

I want people to understand something important. You are not deficient if you experience mental health challenges. We all do so to varying degrees. As you read this book and recognize familiar patterns, consider how your current state can be more manageable. It is well worth taking the time to understand yourself so you can develop a lifestyle that suits you and your present state. You can move toward the good life with attention, effort, and conditioning.

After you read this book, I sincerely hope that you will be willing to consider alternative perspectives, experiment with new techniques, and challenge assumptions you may have about your mental health and your circumstances. Accordingly, you can learn more about how to become a better and healthier you.

My book is also viable for people who, for some reason, are unable to seek help and services from their immediate surroundings. Too often, people facing challenges are disinclined to reach out and ask for help or highlight it publicly.

Stigma is still a problem silencing people who could be otherwise accessing support and resources. If you are inclined to suffer privately, my hope is that this book will provide some relief and help you know that you are not the only one struggling. I hope it gives you the motivation to reach out for help. If you aren't ready for that level of vulnerability, I hope it can help you recover and grow at your own pace within the privacy of your personal space.

When people are isolated, they are more inclined to resort to self-damaging behaviors that are increasingly counterproductive. In their struggle to counteract stressors, they can resort to negative coping methods that can do more harm than good. The book will help reinforce positive coping methods to help you live a more empowered life.

If you are a professional who wants to foster your well-being, happiness, and resilience, which in turn contributes to increased focus, productivity, and enhanced performance, I look forward to working with you on your journey through this book.

If you are a leader who is invested in the mental health of your team, thank you for selecting this book. You are in a role that allows you to share the message with many and lead the way in promoting your psychological fitness as well as supporting your team.

If you are a coach or mental health practitioner, you are my people, and I am honored you chose to read this book. While some ideas and research will be familiar, I believe they are worth reviewing.

I cover general constructs and research to support these principles. If the science is too much, just stick to the **key points** and **challenges**. I will propose suggestions and information. You make decisions on how you want to apply and take action. You are the only one who can change you.

There is no one-size-fits-all, special intervention or algorithm for psychological health. You are unique, and there is no one like you, so explore the options, take what's useful, and leave the rest.

◇◇

If we take good care of ourselves, we help everyone. We stop being a source of suffering to the world, and we become a reservoir of joy and freshness.
—Thich Nhat Hanh

◇◇

You train to achieve physical fitness. You can also train to build psychological fitness. You can work out and work in. LEARN. PRACTICE. TRAIN. REFLECT. LET'S GO.

Remember: You are not alone.

We are in this together. It's time to take control of what you *can* control by building your psychological capital through awareness and insight, learning, and skill development.

Part I:
LAYING THE
GROUNDWORK

CHAPTER 1:
Mental Health and Well-Being

Don't ask the world to change. You change first.[10]
—Anthony de Mello, author

BEING MENTALLY FIT, HAPPY, AND GRATEFUL FOR THINGS WE HAVE IN LIFE SHOULDN'T BE THAT DIFFICULT, RIGHT? Especially if you experience a "comfortable" life by external standards. Suffering makes sense when external tragedy has been imposed. But what if your life consists of conveniences, pleasurable experiences, and plentiful material items?

There are plenty of tangible reasons for human pain and struggle: poverty, death, natural disaster, cancer, crime, violence, addiction, trauma, abuse, and so on. Sadly, this is an incomplete list, and it seems never-ending.

What about the people who say that their life is great, but they are still struggling to find peace? The truth is that we all have our personal version of suffering. Life is arduous. Wealth, external success, and good fortune do not protect from emotional pain. Privilege is real and can serve as a buffer in many cases. Yet, it provides no guarantee for avoiding misery.

Plenty of people who experience a comfortable life experience emotional turmoil and mental health challenges. To make matters worse, they can get into a negative spiral of more distress because they feel guilty. They think I shouldn't feel like this because others have it worse. They can exacerbate their suffering, leading to a self-persecuting cycle that fuels their struggle.

Despite circumstances, managing mental health takes work, intention, and accountability. There is no self-manual. Mental well-being affects how you feel, behave, and engage with others. It's about your thoughts, feelings, and how you handle the ups and downs in your life.

The World Health Organization defines mental health as "*a state of well-being in which the individual realizes his or her own abilities, can cope with the normal stresses of life, can work productively and fruitfully, and contributes to his or her community*."[11] Mental health is an important part of well-being. It is not a binary state. The idea that mental health and illness are not separate constructs is well established.

In his 1937 studies, Psychologist Gordon Allport recognized that mental health is not black or white; he offered a continuum model providing a range of optimal mental health and mental illness at the two extremes.[12]

To encourage people rather than focus on ailments and symptoms, Dr. John Travis created the Illness-Wellness Continuum, with information on how modifying lifestyle can create movement toward the wellness end of the spectrum. He focused on improving well-being through emotional control, taking responsibility, generating insight and mindful, whole-person awareness. According to this model, wellness is dynamic and a natural life process. Wellness and illness are not either-or principles. We have the potential to move toward wellness.[13]

Multiple formats can be used to diagram a mental health continuum with varying levels of detail and precision. In this diagram, the categories assessed are mood, sense of self, focus, attitude, social, and wellness habits.

MENTAL HEALTH CONTINUUM

	Mental Illness	Languishing	Surviving	Thriving	Flourishing
Mood	Very Anxious, Panic	Anxious, Distressed, Anger	Agitated, Impatient	Positive, Happy	Cheerful, Vibrant
	Very Depressed	Overwhelmed, Despair	Worried, Nervous, Sad	Calm, Even Mood	Joyful, Centered
Sense of Self	Worthlessness, Suicidal Thoughts	Self-Flagellating, Learned Helplessness	Self-Doubt, Self-Critical	Confidence and Well-Being	Self-Optimization, Self-Efficacy
Focus	Inability to Make Decisions/ Complete Tasks	Difficulty Concentrating, Forgetful	Distracted, Procrastinates	Highly Focused	Flow
Attitude	Hopelessness, Helplessness	Apathetic, Restless, Giving Up	Negative, Cynical	Positive, Upbeat	Exuberant
Social	Disconnected	Avoidant, Isolation	Withdrawn	Normal Social Activity	Enriched Connections
Habits	Severe Sleep Disturbance	Poor Sleep	Sleep Difficulties	Sleeping Well	Healthy Sleep
	Weight Loss or Gain	Poor Appetite or Change in Eating	Mixed Eating Habits	Eating Normally	Healthy Eating Habits
	Extreme Fatigue	Exhaustion	Low Energy Fatigued	High Energy	Highly Active in Various Outlets

Access this continuum in your free psychological fitness guide here: psychfitguide.com/book

Generally, the far-right columns (green) are the well-zone in which people are healthy, thriving, and flourishing. Being in this zone typically indicates high functioning behaviors, ranging interests, and self-reports of feeling satisfied with life. Individuals feel emotionally balanced, grounded, centered, happy, positive, and focused. When we are thriving and flourishing, we feel energetic, engaged, and effective. We experience a sense of control over our well-being, and we are typically able to access internal resources to address obstacles.

◇◇◇

*"Flourishing is the product of the pursuit and engagement
of an authentic life that brings inner joy and happiness
through meeting goals, being connected with life passions,
and relishing in accomplishments through the peaks and
valleys of life."*[14]
—Lynn Soots

◇◇◇

Flourishing is not considered a personality trait that you have or not. Rather, it is a process that can be cultivated through action and practice.

According to Psychologist Martin Seligman, flourishing is beyond feeling happy; it is about feeling fulfillment in your life, accomplishing meaningful and worthwhile goals, and connecting with people at a deeper level, living a good life.[15]

Thriving and flourishing individuals experience a strong sense of self, confidence, and personal agency. They engage in healthy wellness practices with consistency.

Individuals who lie in the surviving mid-range of the continuum (yellow) demonstrate signs of distress or challenges coping, yet they are functioning in daily life. It can be easy to slip into the mid-range zone, depending on what challenges are present. Here, individuals may be in a static or stuck state. They are surviving and functioning yet experiencing more negative moods, attitudes, and a sense of self. Their wellness practices may be inconsistent, and their struggles are likely to be noticeable in their behavior.

The languishing (orange) zone is indicative of more significant signs of struggle. People in the languishing state are apt to have trouble focusing and being effective in performing daily tasks. They will often report more intense feelings of anger, irritation, overwhelm, anxiety, or distress.

LANGUISHING

Adam Grant recently resurfaced the term **languishing** to describe a common sentiment of how many are feeling these days. Languishing is a feeling of blah, meh, disengagement, and blunting of overall emotion.

Corey Keyes originally defined languishing as "**emptiness and stagnation, constituting a life of quiet despair.**"[16]

The APA describes languishing as "the absence of mental health, with the experience of apathy, lack of engagement, and overall dissatisfaction."[17] Individuals who are languishing are challenged to appreciate things previously enjoyed in life. Recent studies indicate that a majority of the workforce may currently be in a languishing state.

Individuals in the mid-range zones may feel acutely negative symptoms of anxiety or an overall malaise that is causing discomfort and lack of motivation.

On the far left, individuals in the mental illness (red) zone may be experiencing clinical symptoms and have difficulty coping with life demands. Their struggle is likely to be impacting their ability to perform in daily life. Individuals in the red zone are apt to experience more extreme forms of distress and trouble.

There is apt to be overlap in where we fall on the continuum at any given time. Mental health is a dynamic, not static, state. Our eating and sleeping habits may be healthy, yet our moods and attitudes are negative. We often shift between states and zones of the continuum.

You can experience symptoms in various color ranges at any given time. Also, people with mental illness who are successfully treated can be in the green zone. Many people successfully manage their mental condition and thrive and flourish in their lives. Those in the red zone may be individuals who are suffering from a mental condition without proper treatment and intervention.

Ideally, we want to progress into flourishing and thriving states. We want people to move from illness to wellness. Where individuals fall on the continuum can inform what level and type of intervention and treatment is needed.

Common statistics estimate:

- One in four people experience symptoms of mental illness.
- Approximately 280 million people worldwide are diagnosed with depression.[18]
- Up to 30–50 percent of people are languishing.
- More than 700,000 people die due to suicide every year. It is the fourth leading cause of death among 15–19-year-olds.[19]
- In the first year of the COVID-19 pandemic, the global prevalence of anxiety and depression increased by 25 percent.[20]

The reality is that it affects all of us. We all experience or know someone who experiences mental health challenges. Recent research by Accenture indicates that 90 percent of survey participants, or someone close to them, are impacted by mental health issues.[21] These reports are concerning and alarming. We are in a mental health hole — MENTAL HEALTH PANDEMIC. We want to avoid those in the mid-zone from sliding further down the continuum.

This is where building psychological fitness comes in. There is an opportunity to focus on prevention and mental health prehab to move people from stuck, strained, and languishing to thriving and flourishing.

It is the optimal time for individuals to invest in themselves and for organizations to invest in employees and mental health care. We need mental health and well-being vaccinations. To affect real change, we need a more preventative approach. No one can pour from an empty cup.

Psychological fitness covers emotional, physical, and mental well-being, embracing the mind-body connection. Solid psychological fitness denotes learning, the development of abilities, and the fostering of interpersonal connections, social networks, and community to support and promote one's well-being.

Mental well-being is about self-regulation, believing in yourself, having a sense of purpose and meaning, creating and sustaining healthy relationships, recognizing and managing negative emotions, coping with daily challenges, adapting to life changes, and working and living effectively.

WELLNESS VS. WELL-BEING

Wellness is an important factor in overall well-being. Wellness describes a state of health in which people have the ability and resources to actively engage in their lives, with the absence of chronic suffering or pain. Wellness practices may include healthy nutrition, physical activity, and good sleep hygiene.

While there is not a single definition of well-being, it includes experiencing positive emotion and mood, minimal negative emotion, life satisfaction, fulfillment and meaning, and effective functioning. Experiencing physical health and energy are also important components of well-being.

The Centers for Disease Control and Prevention identifies the following components of well-being: physical, economic, social, emotional, and psychological well-being, development and activity, engaging activities, work, and general life satisfaction.

HEDONIC VS. EUDAIMONIC WELL-BEING

Hedonic well-being refers to the pursuit of pleasure and the avoidance of pain. The hedonic framework started with the Greek philosopher Aristippus, who believed the primary goal in life was to maximize pleasure.

Daniel Kahneman expanded upon the framework indicating hedonic psychology focuses on happiness and the study of what "makes experiences and life pleasant and unpleasant, and is concerned with feelings of pleasure and pain, of interest and boredom, of joy and sorrow, and of satisfaction and dissatisfaction."[22]

Eudaimonic well-being is related to meaning, self-realization, and living a good life. It came from Aristotle's understanding that humans' well-being is connected to human potential. According to researchers Ryan, Huta, and Deci, well-being refers to the full functioning of the person, optimizing experiences with purpose and meaning.[23]

Eudaimonia translates closer to "flourishing" than "happiness." It entails living virtuously and experiencing a good, fulfilling life, which does not necessarily guarantee happiness in the modern sense of feeling pleasure.

HAPPINESS & SUBJECTIVE WELL-BEING

Another term is subjective well-being (SWB), named by Edward Diener. According to Diener, SWB is the scientific term for happiness and life satisfaction, thinking your life is going well. SWB is identified as "a process, impacted by internal and external causes, which, in turn, affects behaviors and psychological states."[24] Thought leaders generally agree on Diener's equation of happiness:

Positive affect − negative affect + one's view of their life situation = Happiness.[25]

CURRENT CONFUSION

We've confused ourselves in our pretend-happy, quick-fix, and drive-through society by expecting quick and easy ways to save our time and get well. We are attempting to persuade ourselves that a secret sauce will provide us with eternal happiness, joy, and prosperity, but there is none. The reality, on the other hand, is a difficult pill to swallow.

If a self-development guru claims there is a way to "jump to the good part," believe me when I say that there is no secret to experiencing consistent happiness and pleasure. We can't just skip to the good parts; we must face the difficult and unpleasant aspects of life.

According to Rory Vaden, author of *Take the Stairs*, we live in an escalator world of shortcuts.[26] We are constantly searching for the easy route. However, seeking the path of least resistance can backfire. While it is difficult to hear, Vaden reminds us that growth is in the journey and that applying discipline in any area is a perpetual process.

It takes effort to make progress. Inner work, reflection, and consistent practice will help you move forward in life. The part about doing the work may not capture your interest, but please stay with me, as there is more to it that you will find compelling.

There are skeptics who think personal development mental health practices are snake oil or quack remedies. If you are a self-proclaimed cynic and, for some reason, are reading this book, then the next part is for you. I'm telling you, if you do the practices with consistency, they'll help. I provide scientific research throughout the book, so you don't need to take my word for it.

It starts with self-awareness. How you see yourself and the attributes that make up **you** are important. Self-insight provides a foundation so you can effectively self-monitor. Personality traits, abilities, likes and dislikes, your moral code or belief system, and what motivates you all contribute to your self-image and self-identity. The more you know who you are, the more you can be the ideal you.

People who can clearly define these components of themselves are better equipped to make positive life changes. Knowing who you are allows you to live a purposeful life and form fulfilling connections, both of which help maintain emotional health. Lack of self-awareness will limit your development.

You can learn how to be more comfortable within your own skin and soul while doing the inner work to better yourself. It does not need to be either-or. You do have to believe in yourself.

Many people value themselves based on external factors and overlook the internal dimensions. Consumerism and social media tempt us to believe that we will be happy once we have a fitter body or drive a fancier car. We are surrounded by messages selling happiness if we use certain products or brands. Falling prey to this trap is tempting yet damaging and can erode your sense of self.

Many are tired of hearing about hacks for happiness or false promises that don't work that easily. Some are also weary of suggested well-being practices. This advice can sound tone deaf if you are amidst a crisis.

Here are a few comments I've heard recently from clients:

- Enough with the gratitude practices
- I'm going to poke myself in the eyes if you tell me to go to a yoga class
- I'm sick of hearing about meditation
- Telling me to change my negative thoughts isn't helpful
- I don't have time for this stuff
- I can't work out
- I have too much to do
- I can't afford coaching or therapy
- This isn't really the time for positive psychology

I understand that people feel like they don't have spare time for such activities. They're busy everywhere. With all the self-development suggestions, platforms, and the real languishing and struggling, I can understand how some would question it. You may feel like you have already tried it all, and it "doesn't work," so what's the point?

Now, for the good news, there is reason to be optimistic. You can improve your psychological fitness. There is hope that you can improve and feel better. Consider the information provided in this book to be psychological nutrients so you can enhance your mental health.

The methods presented are not intended to be prescribed treatments or interventions for mental illness because they will be insufficient and inappropriately sized for serious mental illnesses. Instead of a prescription, please think of this book as a guide and a menu of possibilities.

We can all start from wherever we are on our mental health journey and take action to make progress toward a better life — one with less distress and worry. I routinely work with high-achieving professionals who have demanding lives, yet this book was written for everyone. We can all use some help and need to take action in our mental health care.

There is vast information and suggestions for everything we could be doing to improve our mental, emotional, and physical health. The problem is not the lack of knowledge. It is the consistent practice and application of it. What is easy to do is also easy not to do.

The initial step is the beginning of all enlightenment and transformational experiences. Begin with a sense of empowerment in knowing that you can improve your life. You have the authority and capability to do so. It's important to cultivate a growth attitude in knowing that in order to change, you need to believe you can.

According to researcher Carol Dweck, a growth mindset is when people feel their abilities can be developed through devotion and hard work.[27] This perspective fosters a passion for learning as well as the perseverance required for outstanding success. Believe in yourself and tell yourself that you can learn what it takes to grow, prosper, and progress. It's possible if you practice a growth mindset.

People with a fixed mindset, on the other hand, believe their core qualities are unchangeable. When students have difficulty, teachers use the growth mindset theory to help them reconsider their thinking. They change the narrative from "I'm lousy at math" to "I don't know how to solve this problem **yet**." You can see how effective this messaging can be in encouraging people to keep going instead of quitting.

Key Point:

It is important to act and not simply think and reflect. Mood can follow your action.

Challenge:

I encourage you to make a commitment to executing suggested options because tools and methods that are not implemented are ineffective.

While there are no true shortcuts, my goal is to equip you with science-based solutions and data-driven strategies so you can experiment. Your job will include determining which practices can significantly influence your personal outcomes. For realistic benefits and compound impact, take small incremental steps. Over the course of months or years, a few habits added or removed can significantly influence your life. According to the deliberate idea of change, taking small actions every day can have a cumulative effect over time.

It is difficult to incorporate healthy habits and behaviors consistently. I hope this book inspires you to identify realistic approaches to improve your behavior and make progress. It's just half the battle if you know what to do; the rest is in practice.

◇◇

Practice isn't the thing you do once you're good.
It's the thing you do that makes you good.[28]
—Malcolm Gladwell, *Outliers*

◇◇

ACE Pillars

Action – Connect – Empower

Life is not for the faint of heart. This is a reasonable concern if you're asking how we can effectively exist in a world that is inherently unpredictable and chaotic, with many circumstances and events utterly out of our control. Many principles in this book are arranged around three pillars: the importance of taking action, connecting with people, and empowering yourself to do the work to facilitate change.

ACTION

Action is about figuring out how to choose and DO, rather than merely want. You are worth the investment, and there are ways to improve your well-being, boost your joy, improve your performance, and find more meaning in life if you show up for yourself and do the work. If you're willing, you can take control of your personal development.

We can be on the road to prospering as a community. This journey of discovery will necessitate taking time to evaluate, invent, learn, reflect, train, act, put in consistent effort, and set manageable goals.

Intake, content exploration, application, processing, and reflection are part of learning and growth. Experimenting with new ideas and repeating the cycle is a good choice. Studying, practicing, integration, conversation, reflection, and sharing are effective ways to enhance personal progress. But what are you going to do differently?

CONNECT

Inner labor requires solitude, community, and connection and is incomplete without all these facets. To help advance the ball, it is beneficial to be connected to a part of a community and employ accountability partnerships. Consider finding a companion, a team, or a book club to join that can help you enhance your journey to psychological fitness and increase your chances of success.

EMPOWER

You can begin by reminding and confirming that you can change. Surrender to any forces beyond your control. Accept this is how the world is. Empower yourself to focus on what you can control — your inner self — by grounding yourself. You can improve your life. It may not be simple, but it is doable and attainable.

◇◇

Between stimulus and response, there is a space. In that space is our power to choose our response. In our response lies our growth and our freedom.
—Victor Frankl, psychiatrist and author

◇◇

TRAINING TOGETHER WORKS BETTER

Start right now, wherever you are. Do not wait for ideal circumstances to act. Life is difficult, and we must prepare for it. It can be tempting to read, listen, learn, and be in intake mode. However, like learning to swim, you can only read about swimming for so long, and to truly learn to swim, you need to get in the water. The same applies to learning about psychological tools. For them to be fully effective, you need to act and apply them in your life.

The format of this book is scaffolding — a blend of information, constructs, frameworks, ideas, research, and suggested interventions. My hope is that some of the seeds planted will resonate to be nourished, grown, and developed by you. Maybe it will be a new thought, quote, practice, nudge, or insight. The book is a generalist model, written to provide a range of methods, practices, ideas, and options. The material is not intended to be specialized.

This book can serve as a resource guide. You don't need to read it cover to cover. You can select what areas are relevant to you and focus on those chapters only. Consider reviewing sections that tell you what you already know, as we all need reminders of how to continuously strengthen our psychological fitness.

During one of my last editing sessions, I was reviewing how nature positively impacts mental health. I paused and headed to a local trail for a 2.5-hour hike. Without that reminder, I wouldn't have done so.

Please proceed with **accountability and gentleness**. Throughout this training process, you will hopefully learn, apply, reflect, and continue to take inventory in your life. In doing so, my hope is that you observe from a state of curiosity and inquiry about your life, rather than self-persecution and judgment. The objective is to learn, enrich, and enhance how you live. Engaging in self-criticism and dwelling on what you are doing or not doing, or what you think you should or should not be doing, is not helpful.

TRAINING GUIDE

Remember, in this training guide, you are offered key points to summarize, as well as challenges to take action. These are psychological drills or mental Tabata. Engaging in these mental rehearsals and intervals can lead to psychological renovation. You can use this book as a do-it-yourself manual or access support through a coach, psychologist, counselor, trainer, or peer partner to help accelerate your progress.

Key Points:

You can make a choice to learn, enrich, and enhance your life.
Act. Connect. Empower.

Challenge:

Proceed from a place of observation and curiosity, not critical self-judgment.

Start where you are. Use what you have.
Do what you can.
—Arthur Ashe, professional tennis player

Chapter 2:
Psychological Fitness

PSYCHOLOGICAL FITNESS CONSTRUCTS

THE TERM *PSYCHOLOGICAL FITNESS* HAS BEEN PRE-VIOUSLY USED IN THE MILITARY TO ASSESS ONE'S EMOTIONAL AND MENTAL STATE IN PREPARATION FOR MILITARY ENGAGEMENT. The key foundations of psychological fitness are well-being, resilience, and self-awareness. Other psychological fitness constructs that have emerged include, but are not limited to, self-regulation, positive affect, perceived control, self-efficacy, self-esteem, and optimism. These categories all fall under general well-being and resilience models.

◇◇

Psychological fitness has been defined as the integration and optimization of cognitive processes and abilities, behaviors, and emotions to positively affect performance, well-being, and response to stress.[29]

◇◇

According to previous models, components that provide a base for psychological fitness cluster into three areas: cognitive (thinking), affective (emotion), and self-regulation. These categories are antecedents of and critical to optimal mental health.

The chapters in this book follow a similar framework. We'll cover practices for self-regulation and resilience building, including cognitive training, stress management techniques, positive psychology practices, and emotional coping skills.

MENTAL HEALTH PREHAB

You can develop psychological fitness as **preparation for responding to stress**. Developing coping strategies can enhance happiness, promote well-being, and buffer against the impact of adversity. Don't wait until you are unwell. Take a preventative approach. Being fit psychologically is greater than the absence of pathology. It is self-care, recovery, proactive promotion of mental health, and more.

HOW DO YOU KNOW IF YOU ARE PSYCHOLOGICALLY FIT?

You feel present, engaged, rested, and nourished. You will be thriving, flourishing, and grounded. You have more energy and vitality. You have self-awareness and can pause after the 'stimulus' to ensure you have a right-sized, healthy response. You feel less negativity, overwhelmed, and exhaustion.

Being psychologically fit leaves room for variations of all the above, cyclical episodes of high and low energy, as well as positive and negative emotions. You feel better than simply an absence of pain, diagnosis, or struggle. You are proactive in the pursuit of strength, well-being, happiness, and fulfillment. You build resilience, pursue challenges, grow, and stretch yourself.

The presence of mental illness doesn't preclude the experience of thriving or flourishing. People who experience symptoms of depression or anxiety can also excel, achieve, and experience a strong sense of purpose and meaning in life. Just like physical activity, the more you train, the more equipped you are to perform and recover.

Meet Finley. My client Finley self-identifies as a driven individual who values achievement. Growing up, he was an excellent student and an accomplished athlete. He attended an Ivy League college, which was his dream growing up, and he started off strong in his profession. He struggled with anxiety and realized that his harsh self-criticism was not serving him. He came to coaching looking for help.

Insights from Finley:

I wish I could have learned sooner that I could channel my drive and motivation toward developing my mental health as I did everything else. I didn't realize that you could develop skills to manage your stress the same way you trained for a sport or studied in school.

I finally realized that being so hard on myself was doing damage and that I could change some of these patterns. I now understand that my mental health isn't a fixed state. My emotions and thoughts are temporary states, and I can change them. Knowing that I can do the work to elevate my mental health has been a game changer for me.

WHAT IS IMPORTANT ABOUT PSYCHOLOGICAL FITNESS?

Developing a strong psychological state and skills needed to maintain and enhance your well-being will assist you in navigating through life. Weight, body fat, muscular tone, strength, flexibility, stamina, endurance, and other factors can all be used to assess physical fitness. What is the best way to assess psychological capital? Anxiety, depression, stress, self-esteem, satisfaction, positive connections, responsibility, and daily functioning, to mention a few, can all be used to assess psychological fitness or mental health.

BACKGROUND OF PSYCHOLOGICAL CONSTRUCTS

Psychology traditionally focused on the alleviation of pain and suffering. Post Second World War, psychologists became concerned with treating abnormal behaviors, pathology, and symptoms of mental illness. This approach was a good start, but it was incomplete.

Positive Psychology is concerned with authentic happiness, well-being, meaning, and living a good life. Martin Seligman, William James, Abraham Maslow, Mihaly Csikszentmihalyi, and Christopher Peterson all contributed to founding the field of Positive Psychology.

In the upgraded model looking at the healthier elements of the psyche, it was differentiated that the skills that enhance flourishing and thriving are going to be different than what will alleviate suffering or reduce pain.

So, what's more important, curing ailments and relieving suffering, or enhancing well-being and moving toward flourishing? Clearly, both are important. The focus of this book will be on the latter — how to move from the mid-zone to the thriving zone of the mental health continuum.

You will hopefully learn, apply, reflect, and continue to take inventory of yourself throughout this training process. The goal is to grow, learn, and improve your life. Self-criticism and dwelling on what you are doing or not, or what you believe you should be doing or not, will not help you.

Key Points:

Check in if you are doing well. Take inventory of your mental health. From time to time, we all feel stressed or worried. Anxiety, on the other hand, can be a symptom of a mental health condition, so if you're constantly worried, and it's interfering with your life, this is something you should not overlook.

Challenge:

Consider seeking the proper level of support and intervention to address your mental health concerns.

SELF-AWARENESS

◇◇◇

You find peace not by rearranging the circumstances of your life but by realizing who you are at the deepest level.[30]
—Eckhart Tolle, *The Power of Now*

◇◇◇

The more you know who you are, the more you can be the ideal you. What is self-awareness? Paying attention to and trying to learn about our own psychology; the capacity to observe ourselves and take notice of patterns within our thoughts, feelings, and behaviors. Being self-aware is critical to internal growth and becoming psychologically fit.

Psychologist Daniel Goleman popularized the concept of emotional intelligence, which, he identifies, includes the following components: self-awareness, self-regulation, motivation, empathy, and social skills.[31] Developing self-awareness is an important step toward increasing emotional intelligence: being aware of thoughts, emotions, behaviors, and triggers.

Internal self-awareness involves monitoring your inner world. External self-awareness is knowing the difference between how we see ourselves and how others see us. For optimal mental health, you want both.

How would you rate your self-awareness on a 1–10 scale?

(1 = limited   5 = average   10 = very aware)

According to studies done by Tasha Eurich, while 95 percent of people think they are self-aware, only 10 percent of people actually are self-aware.[32]

WHAT GETS IN THE WAY OF BEING SELF-AWARE?

Here are a few ideas: chronic self-judgment, self-attack, comparison, lack of self-acceptance, etc. What holds us back is often what we believe we're not, negative self-talk, the inner critic, 'should'-ing, guilt, not enough-ism, rumination, the pursuit of unrealistic expectations, and incomplete mental models and belief systems.

There is also the issue of attribution bias, the tendency for one to make perceptual errors. When we don't understand the whole context, we can make assumptions based on limited inputs. There are various types of attribution errors. For example, some individuals internalize mistakes made and externalize success.

Meet Shira. My client Shira received a promotion to become a director. She was excited yet quick to explain how she was in the right place at the right time and just got lucky. She gave credit to her boss for being supportive in advocating for her. She attributed the success to more external factors than her contribution or performance.

The problem is that when she transitioned into the role, she had a rocky start. She was left with a mess to clean up, so she had work to do. She faced a steep learning curve, and while objectively, she made good progress, she felt as though her performance was lacking. She internalized her perceived lack of progress as though she wasn't competent enough to operate at the director level. Rather than appreciating the challenges of the circumstances, she viewed herself as a failure.

Some individuals internalize successes and externalize mistakes made. **Meet Singh.** My client Singh received a similar director-level promotion. He experienced a boost in confidence because he felt he had worked hard to earn it and was able to speak to the impact he felt he had made on the team. He was proactive in advocating for himself and internalized his accolades.

He also faced challenges with his transition, as it was a big leap in scope. When discussing his obstacles, his focus was on how he was not set up for success as he moved into the role. He felt his manager wasn't as much supportive, his team wasn't doing their part, and colleagues were not getting him the information he needed quickly enough. He attributed the initial struggle to those external factors.

Key Point:

We are at risk of making perceptual or attributional errors as we interpret events.

Fundamental attribution error can explain how some individuals over-emphasize dispositional factors to explain behaviors in others and underemphasize situational factors. This cognitive bias involves making assumptions about what type of person someone is based on behavior rather than considering contextual influences.

Meet Frankie. My client Frankie becomes frustrated with team members who are late to meetings. She faces challenges in relationships because her frustration gets in the way of how she interacts with the team. She interprets their lack of punctuality as disrespectful and sees their behavior as a character problem, such as an inability to plan.

If Frankie runs late, however, she doesn't see it the same way. She has an explanation that feels sufficient to her. *I was late because of traffic*. Or, *my boss kept me in the previous meeting for too long*.

Meet Ramsey. My client Ramsey struggles with impatience. He is easily agitated and receives feedback that he can come across as aggressive and intimidating. When he experiences these negative work behaviors, he attributes it to his lack of sleep or deadline pressures. However, when Ramsey observes aggressive behavior in others, he attributes it to a character flaw.

YOUR EXPLANATORY STYLE

How you explain events, or your explanatory style, relates to your mental health and well-being because your interpretation of situations affects your emotional state. How you process and interpret an event impacts how you respond. Your explanatory style can contribute to life feeling easier or harder for you. How you explain good and bad things happening matters and affects your mental health.

Gregory McClell Buchanan and Martin Seligman describe the explanatory style as "our tendency to offer similar explanations for different events."[33] In *Learned Optimism*, Seligman identifies three components of the explanatory styles. Within each vector, one can trend toward optimistic or pessimistic. How you respond to a positive or negative event also influences explanatory style. Seligman identifies the three P's: pervasiveness, permanence, and personalization.[34]

Pervasiveness relates to whether factors impacting an outcome are global or specific/local.

Negative event: Mason interrupts you in a meeting.

Optimist thinking: Mason must be having a bad day.

Pessimist thinking: Mason is always rude.

Positive event: You met your quota at work.

Optimist thinking: I'm great at selling.

Pessimist thinking: I got lucky with that referred deal.

Permanence relates to space and whether an outcome is based on factors that are stable or unstable (changeable). Optimists tend to think that negative events are temporary and positive events are more permanent, while pessimists interpret negative events as permanent and positive situations as temporary.

Negative event: You lost your tennis match.

Optimistic thinking: He was a tough opponent; I'll try again next time.

Pessimistic thinking: I'm terrible at tennis.

Positive event: You won your tennis match.

Optimist: I'm athletic and awesome at tennis.

Pessimist: He just didn't play well today.

Personalization involves the level of personal control an individual feels they have over an outcome (internal vs. external) and who they believe is responsible for the outcome. Optimists may tend to blame people or circumstances for negative events, and pessimists may blame themselves. When responding to good events, optimists may attribute the event to themselves, while pessimists give credit away. Finding the right balance is key.

Negative event: You missed a big deadline.
Optimistic thinking: I did my part. My team didn't do theirs.
Pessimistic thinking: I'm a failure.
Positive event: You met a big deadline.
Optimistic thinking: I'm awesome.
Pessimistic thinking: The team is awesome. I didn't do much.

Seligman cautions against taking any approaches too far. Relieving oneself of full accountability in the face of negative events and blaming people and circumstances is not healthy. While these examples are simplistic, you get the idea. Negative explanatory styles can cause more distress and make negative situations feel more threatening.

Key Points:

Understanding your explanatory styles is helpful in promoting mental health. Ideally, you want to right-size your interpretation and respond to situations as healthily and accurately as possible.

Challenge:

Consider these styles and biases and how they show up in your life. You can upgrade your explanatory style and reduce biases with attention and practice.

Another challenge of developing self-awareness is that self-reflection can make us stressed, leading to excessive rumination and perpetual judgment. There is a risk of engaging in endless loops of self-inquiry. There is a difference between thinking about yourself vs. knowing yourself. Self-absorption is simply not healthy.

The process of analyzing versus understanding can also be intricate and can lead to asking the wrong questions about yourself. Reflecting from a place of inquiry rather than self-attack is more generative and constructive.

It's clear that comprehensive self-awareness doesn't occur in a vacuum. Introspection alone will only get you so far. While internal reflection is important, it's only part of the story. It requires being balanced in your self-appraisal and being proactive in seeking input from those you trust.

Self-awareness is ranked as a top indicator of leadership effectiveness. Seeing yourself clearly will contribute to the quality of your decisions, relationships, and communication. The benefits of being self-aware include clearer thinking, increased productivity, sounder decisions, more effective communication, and improved mood.

Developing self-awareness requires non-judgmental observation. What you judge, you can't understand. It requires feedback, personal responsibility, taking inventory, challenging yourself, asking WHAT, not WHY, self-compassion, and healthy detachment — not over-involvement with feelings and reactions.

◇◇

Knowing yourself is the beginning of all wisdom.
—Aristotle

◇◇

Key Points:

Enhancing self-awareness is foundational to your personal growth and success. Engaging in the dynamic, fluid process of self-discovery and self-monitoring makes a choice and change possible so you can be empowered. Increasing your self-awareness can contribute to mental health, performance, and effectiveness. It is critical to psychological fitness and approaching it from a place of inquiry and openness is best.

Challenge:

Formally or informally, consider asking people in your life, both personal and professional, for feedback. How do they view you? What do they appreciate and value about you? What can you improve or do better?

The Johari window is a model that is used in the realm of psychology to help differentiate between how we view ourselves, how others view us, and where there are discrepancies.

Consider engaging in a self-awareness-building exercise in which you will collect input from people in your life. One suggested way to conduct this informal study is to identify a list of words with personal characteristics. Select three to six words that best describe you. Offer the full list to the people you would like to collect feedback from and ask them to select three to six words that they think best describe you.

Matchup which words align with your self-description and note which are different. Sometimes, this exercise can close some gaps between recognizing your intention with what your impact on others is.

Access a Johari window tool in your free psychological fitness guide here: psychfitguide.com/book.

SENSE OF SELF

It is critical to have a healthy sense of self when developing psychological fitness. Self-concept encompasses but is not limited to self-efficacy, agency, self-esteem, and self-confidence.

The self-efficacy theory is a social learning concept developed by psychologist Albert Bandura. Self-efficacy is a person's belief in his or her ability to carry out the actions required to achieve specified performance goals. It involves a person's sense of being able to deal effectively with a particular task.[35]

According to a social cognitive school of thought, self-efficacy is one's **perceived** ability to deal with a task or situation. Agency is one's **actual** ability to deal with a task or situation. Human agency involves integrated learning and skill development, motivation, and emotion to accomplish your goal. Experiencing both contributes to mental health, and the absence of either can result in mental turmoil.

Key Points:

It is crucial to believe that your actions will have an impact. Self-efficacy and agency are skills that can be developed and strengthened. Feeling effective and *being* effective in your life activities are important components of psychological fitness and mental health.

Challenge:

Create goals for yourself that are reasonable to foster self-efficacy. It helps to experience modest victories to enhance your self-efficacy and agency.

SELF-ESTEEM

Self-esteem is defined as a person's regard and respect for themselves. A person's self-esteem is healthy if they have favorable feelings about themselves. One can have strong self-esteem for their work performance while having low self-esteem for their physical appearance.

It's also possible to feel efficacious about a skill set while having negative feelings about oneself. This is especially typical in people who have perfectionist tendencies. They may be competent and effective yet self-critical.

Self-esteem entails not only appreciating yourself but also treating yourself with love, value, dignity, and respect. Positive self-esteem is trusting in your abilities (to learn, succeed, and contribute to the world) as well as your sense of autonomy and independence. It indicates you believe that your thoughts, feelings, and views are valuable. In other words, self-esteem refers to how you feel about yourself (both inside and out), what you value in yourself, and how you interact.

It also has to do with how you believe others see, treat, and value you. Individuals who have been mistreated or who have experienced abuse, particularly as children, are more likely to suffer from poor self-esteem. Believing you are enough and having a healthy self-esteem is foundational to mental health and psychological fitness and can be enhanced. A damaged sense of self can contribute to mental health problems.

Key Points:

Self-esteem can be developed and improved, whether through your inner work, engaging in different behaviors, or through a healing, therapeutic process. Self-esteem comes from esteemed actions.

SELF-REGARD

By thinking we need to be better than we are or believing that we should be doing more than we are, we create unnecessary issues for ourselves. The goal is to have a positive attitude toward yourself. Self-confidence is another term to capture how you regard yourself and requires acceptance of yourself.

People who experience arrogance have an inflated view of themselves and can see themselves as better than or above others. People who have true self-confidence also have humility. Humility is not making yourself less than or minimizing yourself; rather, it is the absence of wanting others to see you as better than you are.

Key Points:

You can strive for more without beating yourself up. Developing inner strength and confidence in the spirit of being a better version of yourself is a healthy expectation. Self-esteem is having respect for oneself while being aware of your strengths and weaknesses. Self-regard is linked to feelings of inner strength and self-confidence. Boosting both will enhance your psychological fitness.

Challenge:

Practice reflection. How do you view yourself, your abilities, your accomplishments, and other areas of your life? Are you able to gently examine and comprehend yourself? What are your key negative and positive qualities? Aspire to be a better version of yourself. Becoming "the best" can feel unattainable.

SELF-COMPASSION

Self-compassion has become a popular area of psychological research. Chris Germer, the co-founder of the Mindful Self-Compassion program, provides this definition:

◇◇◇

*"Self-compassion involves the capacity to comfort
and soothe ourselves and to motivate ourselves with
encouragement when we suffer, fail, or feel inadequate.
Self-compassion is learned in part by connecting with our
innate compassion for others, and self-compassion also
helps to grow and sustain our compassion for others."*[36]

◇◇◇

Most people identify as being compassionate toward others. However, many don't apply the same level of compassion and grace for themselves. Patricia Rockman points out that we can get tripped up when self-compassion is confused with self-indulgence.[37] Self-compassion and self-care are not the same. Self-care refers to behaviors and activities to look after our mental and physical well-being. How we see and think about ourselves is self-compassion.

High achievers are often in need of more self-compassion. They operate with high standards and expectations, which can provide motivation and drive, yet being too self-critical can backfire and get in the way.

Psychological research confirms that individuals who have self-compassion experience mental health benefits. Leary and colleagues demonstrated that those who have a self-compassionate disposition demonstrate a strong ability to accept difficult experiences and move beyond negative feelings.[38]

Kristin Neff is a leading researcher of self-compassion. A review of studies indicates that self-compassion is linked to predicting lower levels of depression and anxiety.[39] Individuals with higher self-compassion were found to have improved relationships.[40] People with self-compassion reported stronger empathy, altruism, and forgiveness, leading to healthier relationships.[41]

If you aren't still convinced of the benefits, research also supports that people with higher self-compassion have:

- Decreased levels of the stress hormone cortisol and an ability to emotionally regulate[42]
- More optimism, curiosity, initiative, and emotional intelligence[43]
- Reduced self-criticism and vulnerability to depression[44]
- Positive health behaviors such as reducing smoking, dieting, and exercising.[45]

Key Points:

Fostering self-compassion will serve you well and help you improve your mental health, as well as how you regard yourself.

HOW YOU TALK TO YOURSELF MATTERS

Don't speak negatively about yourself, even as a joke. Your body doesn't know the difference. Words are energy and they cast spells, that's why it's called spelling. Change the way you speak about yourself and it can change your life.
—Bruce Lee, actor

Be aware of the language you use referring to yourself, including internal self-talk, as well as the language used to communicate with others. People can be self-deprecating in an effort to be funny. However, if taken too far, messages can become internalized and do damage. Caution how you speak about yourself, so you don't generate unnecessary mental upheaval.

Psychologists have been at work to understand how they can help people develop their self-compassion. Another specialty area, Mindful Self-Compassion, has emerged. Mindful Self-Compassion is a potent technique for emotional resilience that combines the abilities of mindfulness and self-compassion.

Again, self-compassion is about acceptance and gently supporting your emotional experience, especially negative experiences and feelings. Mindfulness is a non-judgmental, receptive state of mind, observing thoughts and feelings without pushing them away or denying them.

Key Point:

You can be kinder and more sympathetic to yourself when you are aware of your sentiments or experiences.

Mindfulness within self-compassion is a focused way to support you in overcoming personal suffering. Chris Germer offers how to free yourself from destructive thoughts and emotions in *The Mindful Path to Self-Compassion.*[46] Mindful Self-Compassion uses your sense of awareness and presence so you can specifically apply it to your sense of self-compassion. Neff and Germer developed a mindful self-compassion program and conducted a study to explore the impact of mindfulness on self-compassion. Participants reported significant self-compassion increases post-program, which were maintained at six-month and one-year follow-ups.[47]

A popular mindfulness program is Jon Kabat-Zinn's Mindfulness-Based Stress Reduction. His training is well known and regarded, with many studies supporting its effectiveness in treating depression and anxiety.[48]

An adapted version of MBSR is the Mindfulness-Based Cognitive Therapy program that can be applied in a clinical setting. These programs have also been proven to improve physical and mental health.[49]

Participating in such mindfulness programs not only promotes well-being but also contributes to increased self-compassion.[50]

A key component of Mindfulness Self-Compassion is allowing for self-acceptance without rumination. Kristin Neff provides the term **over-identification**, which is dwelling on negative feelings or experiences to the point that it dominates your thought process.[51]

Key Points:

- Mindfulness-based training of various sorts seems to be a key ticket to psychological fitness.
- Self-compassion is also important for mental health and well-being.
- Self-compassionate people understand that being flawed and facing life's hardships is unavoidable.
- They treat themselves with kindness and accept that no one is flawless. We are all flawed. We all go through hardships and make blunders.

- When you can recognize suffering and feelings of inadequacy are part of the human experience, you can reduce the intensity of negative emotions and increase self-compassion.

Challenges:
Mindfulness Self-Compassion Practice

- Understand what gets in the way of you experiencing self-compassion. Write down any core negative beliefs you have about yourself. What situations trigger these negative beliefs? What would your life look like without these beliefs?
- Try a simple daily mindfulness practice, bringing attention to the situations that are triggering a negative reaction in you.
- Consider some phrases that can shift your emotional reactions to your triggers. *I'm noticing my irritation. I'm going to take a minute to re-group.*
- When you feel negative about yourself, ask yourself how you would respond to a friend who thought or felt that way about themselves.

CHAPTER 2

In the spirit of promoting self-acceptance and self-compassion, consider the following passage:

◇◇◇

Everybody knows:
You can't be all things to all people.
You can't do all things at once.
You can't do all things equally well.
You can't do all things better than everyone else.
Your humanity is showing just like everyone else's.
So:
You have to find out who you are, and be that.
You have to decide what comes first, and do that.
You have to discover your strengths, and use them.
You have to learn not to compete with others,
Because no one else is in the contest of *being you*.
Then:
You will have learned to accept your uniqueness.
You will have learned to set priorities and make decisions.
You will have learned to live with your limitations.
You will have learned to give yourself the respect that is due.
And you'll be a most vital mortal.
Dare to Believe:
That you are a wonderful, unique person.
That you are a once-in-all-history event.
That it's more than a right, it's your duty, to be who you are.
That life is not a problem to solve, but a gift to cherish.
And you'll be able to stay one up on what used to get you down.
—Anonymous

◇◇◇

Key Points:

Fostering self-efficacy, self-esteem, personal agency, sense of self, self-awareness, and self-compassion all contribute to psychological fitness.

Challenge: Here are some quick ways to:

- **Increase self-efficacy:** develop specific skill sets, observe others, and set realistic goals
- **Foster agency:** focus on what you can control, reduce distractions, position yourself as a learner, reinforce a growth mindset, and get physical exercise
- **Enhance self-esteem:** reduce negative self-talk, focus on strengths, generate believable, positive self-statements, and take actions aligned with your values
- **Increase self-compassion:** when feeling self-critical, ask yourself what you would tell a friend right now.

MOTIVATION, DRIVE, AND GOALS

Since awareness and education are important components of how you can progress and develop psychological fitness, let's cover the foundations of drive, motivation, and goal setting.

SELF-DETERMINATION THEORY

Psychologists Edward Deci and Richard Ryan developed the concept of self-determination, a theory of human development addressing the inherent, positive human tendency to move toward growth. According to self-determination theory (SDT), humans have three innate needs: competence, autonomy, and relatedness. These needs must be continually satisfied for individuals to grow and thrive in a healthy way.[52]

Autonomy is experiencing a sense of willingness and choice in your actions. Competence entails effectively managing and controlling yourself and your environment and developing mastery over tasks that are important to you. Social relatedness (connection) includes feeling a sense of belonging, feeling understood, appreciated by, and connected to, relating, and caring for others.

Research indicates that having a need to direct your life, enhance your abilities, and live with a sense of purpose is fundamental to high performance. We are complex individuals who are typically not driven by only one kind of motivation. We experience various desires, goals, and ideas that inform what we want. We can also think of motivation as a continuum.

PINK'S COMPONENTS OF MOTIVATION

In *Drive*, Daniel Pink builds upon this model, asserting that the carrot and stick approach to motivation is flawed and incomplete. While an external reward may influence behavior, it does not necessarily produce motivation.[53]

He recognizes three core components of motivation, including:

1. **Autonomy**: the desire to direct our lives
2. **Mastery**: the urge to get better at things that matter
3. **Purpose**: the longing to engage in the service of something bigger than ourselves

Regardless of the specific model, experts suggest if you want to live better, you should set and attain goals conducive to meeting your needs for autonomy, competence, purpose, and connection and work in conditions that promote them.

Key Point:

When your sense of autonomy, mastery, and purpose are not aligned in your work, it can impact your level of motivation.

EFFORT IS STRONGLY ENDORSED

Experts remind us of the importance of putting **forth intentional effort and being willing to push yourself toward your goals. It indicates that** you care, and it provides meaning to your life. Being willing to work for something that is important to you will foster motivation.

THE "WHY"

According to related motivational theories, your goals and what you strive for are important to satisfy your needs and well-being, as is the process of working toward your goals and your **why.** Simon Sinek is known for his work on the power of recognizing why we do what we do. Our deeper sense of purpose can be a key catalyst for action, motivation, and behavior change. Sinek proposes that organizations communicate and create alignment with why they do what they do to foster employee engagement.

Key Point:

Reminding people of the why is one way to sustain them through obstacles and ups and downs.

ELEMENTS OF MOTIVATION

Motivation is the psychological force that promotes action, and it has been the object of scientific inquiry. It is considered the driver behind the pursuit of goals. Understanding motivation is important for advancing your psychological fitness since it impacts efforts directed toward change.

I believe that people have an inherent interest and capacity for growth, well-being, and flourishing; yet **we can get in our own way**. It can be so hard. But why?

What is Motivation?

There is no single motivation theory that sufficiently addresses the comprehensive aspects of human motivation. Nonetheless, let's cover some basic ideas.

Motivation can be described as the reason behind behaving or taking action toward a goal you need or something you are concerned about.

You can be motivated by avoiding pain, such as removing your hand from a hot stove. Or, you can be motivated to pursue pleasure, such as baking and eating a cake. It can come in a broader form, such as committing to a friend to work out at the gym every morning.

Some describe motivation as an energy or force that can spark action. Others propose that action comes first, and the feeling of motivation can follow. Motivation can be fleeting and momentary over the course of time. It can be experienced as a feeling of intense desire toward something.

It can be explained as the why behind a goal or the reason behind actions, desires, and needs. Motivation can energize and cause behavior. Leading motivation researcher Roy Baumeister sums it up well: motivation can essentially come down to wanting.[54]

Why Is It important?

Understanding motivation and learning ways to increase it is relevant because it leads to change, growth, and goal setting. It's an important and renewable resource that contributes to your ability to function, adapt, maintain well-being, and adjust to change.

You can experience intrinsic or extrinsic motivation. Intrinsic motivation is doing something for an internal reward. It feels good, and you enjoy it. Extrinsic motivation is doing something for an outside reward such as money, recognition, applause, visibility, or feedback. To maximize motivation, internal motives should be matched with external motivations.

According to researcher Edward Deci, motivation is something that people do, not something that is done to them. He reminds us that the power rests with those who act with self-determination and persistence.

Key Points:

- Motivation can lead to action and cause behavior, yet action and behavior can also precede motivation.
- It can be described as a need, drive, and internal state.
- Your motivation is a valuable commodity and can be multiplied only by action, with its impact and value determined by how you invest your attention.

◇◇

Why is it that we are all born with limitless potential, yet few people fulfill those possibilities?
—Abraham Maslow, psychologist

◇◇

DRIVE MOTIVATION

Internal motives that excite, direct, and maintain conduct are needs. They cause strivings for physiological survival, and for the development of growth and well-being, as in psychological and implicit wants and desires.

◇◇

A hungry stomach will not allow its owner to forget it, whatever his cares and sorrows.
—Homer, 800 B.C.

◇◇

Famous psychologist Abraham Maslow is associated with the term "hierarchy of needs." According to this model, people are motivated to meet basic physiological needs before moving on to higher-level psychological growth needs. While it is unclear if Maslow actually created a figure to represent this model, Maslow's hierarchy of requirements is commonly depicted as a pyramid, with varying recent adaptations and iterations.

Maslow suggested that lower-level needs be met first before moving toward higher-level wants, partially based on the premise that unmet needs motivate people. According to Maslow, not accommodating lower needs hampers growth. If someone is hungry or still seeks love and affection from others, he or she cannot become self-actualized.

Physiological demands involve the basic upkeep of the human condition and elements required for survival, including food, air, water, and sleep. The next level of safety and security includes shelter, job stability, health, and a safe environment. Lastly, social demands include belonging, love, affection, friendship, camaraderie, family, and friends.

Once your love and belonging needs are addressed, you can develop a more elevated sense of self-worth and esteem. Self-actualization is the highest level: fulfilling potential, personal growth, peak experiences, creativity, etc.

In his book, *Transcend: The New Science of Self-Actualization,* Scott Barry Kaufman provides an expanded hierarchy of needs and a roadmap to find fulfillment and purpose through becoming the best version of yourself. He describes how Maslow may not have viewed the pyramid as a linear sequence of events but rather as more meaningful, intricate, and integrated.[55]

Kaufman describes a sailboat as a new metaphor for the 21st century. He views life as integration, and it's about being a whole person, as a sailboat is a whole vehicle. The sailboat needs a structure to operate properly, yet that isn't enough. It needs a sail and a purposeful direction (growth) to go anywhere. He encourages us to move out of a deprivation mode of existence and toward growth, being driven by transcendent values that are outside ourselves.

Key Point:

Kaufman reminds us that even in this time of stress and uncertainty, we must not neglect our higher possibilities.

Challenge:

Reflect on your self-actualization. Are your basic needs met? What is missing or getting in the way of living in your true potential?

GOAL MOTIVATION

When it comes to motivation and making progress in your mental health, the topic of goals is relevant. A goal is a cognitive mental event and works as a "spring to action" that energizes and guides your activity in a purposeful manner.[56] Your internal life, including your attitude, beliefs, expectations, and self-concept, are all sources of motivation and goal pursuit, which are all influenced by your thinking.

Goals, ironically, are created by what isn't, or a gap between where you are and where you aspire to go. "If you don't know where you're going, any road will get you there" is a saying that describes the difference between having goals and not being focused on a particular outcome.

Identifying the "gap" is a key part of the developmental process and is much of the focus in coaching. Being able to identify where you are now, where you want to be, what's getting in the way, and what it costs you to remain there is all part of the journey.

You must have a level of discontent to feel the urge to want to grow.
—Idowu Koyenikan, author

Key Points:

- Goals are essential for getting things done and progressing in your professional and personal life.
- They serve as a motivator to keep on track and focused on the behaviors and tasks that lead to achieving your goals.
- Setting goals is a good place to start when it comes to development.
- Short-term, long-term, personal, and professional goals should all be included.
- While this can feel overwhelming, consider it an iterative process.
- Goal setting is a verb and state of being. You can start with where you want to be and work backward from there.
- Or you can start with today and think about where you would like to be tomorrow.

GOAL SETTING

Researchers Latham & Locke define goals as being "the object or aim of an action, for example, to attain a specific standard of proficiency, usually within a specified time limit."[57] In their studies on goal-setting, Locke and Latham worked individually and collaboratively. Locke initially published findings indicating that individuals are motivated by both setting appropriate goals and getting feedback.

In *A Theory of Goal Setting and Task Performance*,[58] the principles of goal setting are:

Clarity — In order for goals to be motivating, they need to be clear and concise. Too much complexity or ambiguity makes it confusing for people to understand.

Challenge — Goals need to be challenging at the right level to be motivating. If too far out of reach, engagement decreases.

Commitment — Goals need to be accepted and embraced by the person achieving them if they are to provide motivation. Just because a goal is proposed, it doesn't mean that an individual buys in or accepts it.

Feedback — Individuals need to understand how they are doing in their progress. They need to have timely and accurate performance-related feedback to remain motivated.

Task Complexity — Ideally, goals are established at the right level of complexity: simple, practical, and understandable.

Key Points:

Optimal motivation is most likely to occur with a healthy tension of pursuing a challenge while having the goal be reachable and relevant. Don't raise the bar more; close the gap. Make the goal closer.

MOTIVATION AND EMOTIONS

You are motivated by your emotions, thoughts, and ideas that prompt you to act in ways that will help you work toward your goals. Your feelings and motives are connected. The Latin root of the terms **emotion** and **motivate** is mot, and it means "to move." A state of arousal is involved in emotions and reasons, also driving behaviors and conduct. Sensations guiding your attention and influencing your actions are emotions.

While some reasons are biological, there is a myriad of other factors that influence motivation and behavior, including the need for achievement, social approval, and willingness to take risks. Engaging in behaviors simply because they feel good is also a motivator.

Frustration or boredom can lessen your motivation and, as a result, reduce your likelihood of acting and being engaged. Conversely, experiencing passion and desire will foster motivation. We will cover more about your emotional experience in later chapters.

Key Points:

What you require and desire has a significant impact on the direction of your actions. If you have an objective in mind and have wrapped your emotions around it, you will be more motivated to achieve it.

Challenge:

Consider a recent goal you have set and map it against the above criteria. Is it clear, attainable, challenging enough, meaningful, reasonable, and relevant? Is there a feedback loop built in to assess your progress?

CAVEATS TO MOTIVATION

There are opposing views on motivation. Other schools of thought criticize the idea of motivation overall.

◇◇

Motivation is crap. Motivation comes and goes. When you are driven, whatever is in front of you will get destroyed.
—David Goggins, author

◇◇

I think what he's reinforcing is that the **feeling** of motivation can come and go; it is fleeting. If we wait until we **feel** motivated to do hard things, it isn't enough. It makes sense that it's an insufficient strategy that isn't sustainable.

If you don't know who David Goggins is, I encourage you to check him out. His athletic achievements are mind-blowing. Reading his book, *Can't Hurt Me,* can be inspiring or discouraging.[59] While his accomplishments seem out of reach for us regular people, he reminds us of our tendency to unnecessarily limit ourselves. I'm not going to be an ultra-marathoner, yet I appreciate the reminder of not opting out of something as soon as I feel discomfort.

PSYCHOLOGY OF STOICISM

Fostering awareness and a healthy sense of detachment that lets you pull back and assess your perceptions, challenge your assumptions, and move forward with constructive action is core to Stoic teachings and important to foster your psychological fitness.

Stoic philosophy has always intrigued me. It is not only a school of thought or a set of philosophies, but it provides clear guidelines and practices to help you live a better, more enriched life. Stoicism is understood as medicine for the soul, and many principles still apply in modern life.

Many Stoic teachings by Seneca, Marcus Aurelius, and others sound like they were written recently, despite the span of centuries. People of that time experienced similar emotional challenges that are still relevant today.

The Stoics encourage us to regulate our thoughts and emotions, learn to be calm, reduce distraction, live modestly, learn from challenges, prioritize leisure, pursue a meaningful activity, value time, live virtuously, and seek moderation.

Ryan Holiday is a thought leader who applies Stoicism to modern life through his writings (ryanholiday.net). He presents lessons in a practical, applicable way. According to Holiday, life is about choices. You choose how to see things, what to say, what to think, and what kind of person you are. Stoicism is a framework for how to make better choices.

◇◇

Objective judgment, now at this very moment.
Unselfish action, now at this very moment.
Willing acceptance, now at this very moment,
of all external events. That's all you need.
—Marcus Aurelius

◇◇

Stoics believe in the power of the state of mind and reframing obstacles into opportunities, all relevant to fostering mental health. According to Stoics, there are three components to this process: perception, action, and will.

PERCEPTION

◇◇

It's not events that upset us but rather our
opinions about them.
—Epictetus

◇◇

Stoics recognize that we can influence our perceptions by pausing and clarifying what elements are in our control. There is personal power found in knowing our responses are in our control, and we decide how various circumstances impact us.

Once we distinguish what is in our control and accept what is outside of our control, we are equipped to act. Avoiding the temptation of pity and anger is key. While this sounds simple and straightforward, it's certainly difficult to execute consistently.

◇◇

The chief task in life is simply this: to identify and separate matters so that I can say clearly to myself, which are externals not under my control, and which have to do with the choices I actually control...
—Epictetus

◇◇

ACTION

Stoics are committed to disciplined choice and see the power of action. More thinking will not overcome our fear; however, movement can. Waiting until you're ready is a strategy that can get in the way and keep you stuck. **Fear often keeps us from taking on challenges.**

According to the law of diminishing intent, the longer you wait to act, the less likely you are to take initial steps. Intentional action with proper discernment works. The suggestion is not to react recklessly or impulsively, yet Stoics caution us to avoid overanalyzing. Consider the laws of inertia: once an object is in motion, it's easier to remain in motion. Taking the first step can be most challenging.

◇◇

Without action, knowledge is often meaningless.[60]
—Shawn Achor, *The Happiness Advantage*

◇◇

In this book, we will explore how to manage your perception, direct your actions properly, and understand how to accept what is out of your control. Serenity and stability are a result of your choices.

WILL

The Stoics refer to will as an inner citadel, an emotional fortress inside us. By building the fortress, you can persevere through obstacles and setbacks. Consistent with disclaimers provided in this book that well-being takes work, the inner citadel needs to be developed and reinforced.

Find hope and empowerment. These skills can be learned and enhanced with training. Internal obstacles can impede progress, so learning skills to manage these disturbances will help you overcome them.

Key Points:

According to the Stoics, you can manage your perception and interpretation of events, direct your actions properly, and understand how to accept what is out of your control to develop your mental health. By developing your inner citadel through persistence and perseverance, you can overcome setbacks and obstacles.

JOY

Joy is also an element of mental health and well-being, feeling great pleasure and happiness. The Stoics take it to the next level of describing joy as a deep state of being.

Spiritual leaders Desmond Tutu and the Dalai Lama wrote about how to find joy in a suffering world in *The Book of Joy*.[61] To foster joy, they advise not to think too much about yourself. Over-focusing on pain can make it grow. You may have heard the saying, "It's all about you and nothing about you." Becoming too self-focused restricts our perspective and can rob us of joy.

They reinforce that you do have control over your suffering by controlling how you respond to external events. The term **mental immunity** is used. You will still experience pain, but you'll be able to ward it off better. The authors suggest channeling anger and stress that comes from suffering into compassion. Whether suffering is internal or external, it can result from unmet expectations.

Key Points:

Thought leaders reinforce that you can control how you respond to external events and, therefore, your emotional suffering. By developing mental immunity, you will be better equipped to handle adversity. To foster joy amidst suffering, Desmond Tutu and the Dalai Lama suggest that you don't think too much about yourself. Over-focusing on your emotional pain can make it grow.

THE RESISTANCE

In the *War of Art,* Steven Pressfield addresses the internal enemy that can get in the way of making progress. He addresses the inner resistance that can surface with the creative process. For authors, this is known as writer's block. When a writer sits down to create a passage and feels stuck, like the words aren't coming, he calls it resistance (**self-sabotage, procrastination, fear, arrogance, and self-doubt**).

Pressfield normalizes how the resistance keeps us stuck, validating that we all experience it. He also affirms there is no easy path to overcoming it. Again, it requires inner work. He does offer hope that you can overcome inner obstacles.

◇◇

Procrastination is the most common manifestation of resistance because it's the easiest to rationalize. We don't tell ourselves, 'I'm never going to write my symphony.' Instead, we say, 'I am going to write my symphony; I'm just going to start tomorrow.'[62]
—Steven Pressfield, author

◇◇

Key Points:

You can apply the key teachings of the Stoics to develop your psychological fitness. Your actions, feelings, and thoughts are up to you. Your responses to external events are in your control. You have agency over your perceptions, how you take action, and how you persevere through obstacles. Choosing to focus on the things that are in your control will make you happier, more resilient, and **psychologically fit**.

Challenge:

In what areas of your life might resistance be holding you back? What is one action you can take to get unstuck?

GROWTH MINDSET

◇◇

We like to think of our champions and idols as superheroes who were born different from us. We don't like to think of them as relatively ordinary people who made themselves extraordinary.[63]
—Carol Dweck, author and researcher

◇◇

Is it true that talented individuals or all-star performers are born with it? The lines of thinking that you either "have it" or don't have been challenged by current thought leaders. A new paradigm suggests high achievers foster a "growth mentality" to help them succeed.

As previously mentioned, the phrase **growth mindset** was coined by psychologist Carol Dweck to describe one's belief that their qualities and abilities are adjustable and developable. In *Mindset: The New Psychology of Success*, Dweck describes the importance of the right mindset to maximize potential and leverage your strengths.[64]

Cultivating a growth mindset involves understanding that with commitment, dedication, and hard work, you can improve your capabilities and develop skills. A fixed mindset, on the other hand, is believing that talents and abilities are immovable and thus unchangeable.

A growth mindset is an appreciation that capabilities can be developed. People with a growth mindset believe in their ability to improve through effort and practice. It helps them work through obstacles when they are challenged.

MENTAL HEALTH BENEFITS OF HAVING A GROWTH MINDSET

A growth mindset enhances self-assurance, self-efficacy, well-being, and empowerment. It lowers the risk of perfectionism and promotes accountability and personal responsibility. It reduces victim mindset and blame as well as anxiety and depression. It improves resilience and fosters learning and growth.

Key Points:

How you think about your abilities, talents, and intelligence can significantly impact your life and your performance. Believing that you can develop your skills through effort and work and knowing it will make a difference will accelerate your progress.

The growth mindset is taught in schools and organizations, and the results are positive and hopeful. Fostering a growth mindset is about praising efforts, not outcomes, seeing mistakes as opportunities, not failures, and challenges as a healthy part of the learning process.

In her Ted Talk, Dweck refers to the power of "yet." She encourages educators to help children upgrade their mindset to cultivate a healthy learning process. An example of a fixed mindset is "I'm bad at reading." A growth mindset would be "I just don't understand this story yet."

Key Points:

In general, you get where you are through the integration of innate aptitude, effort, and work. You have more influence over your abilities than you think.

Challenge:

In what area is having a fixed mindset limiting you or getting in your way? (For example, I'm not an organized person. I'm not someone who works out.)

We will continue to discuss problems and issues that lead to mental health concerns as we proceed through each chapter. We will also keep exploring ways to upgrade your emotional style, thinking and behaviors, and brain function to positively impact your mental health.

The objective is to make progress in building your psychological fitness. It won't be linear, and it's playing the long game. Adapting and changing patterns of thinking and behavior is challenging, and it requires practice and training.

HOW TO FACILITATE CHANGE

◇◇

To truly actualize change, you have to engage in the work of making new choices every day. In order to achieve mental wellness, you must begin by being an active daily participant in your own healing.[65]
—Nicole LePera, author and psychologist

◇◇

Again. You enhance awareness, learn, take action, reflect, practice, train, and repeat. Next, we will learn how to effectively manage and navigate through stress... the details will be revealed in the following chapter.

Chapter 3:
Stress

WHEN WAS THE LAST TIME YOU HEARD SOME-
ONE SAY THEY WERE **STRESSED?** For me, it was
ten minutes ago. We can't talk about mental health
without addressing stress. It is a popular topic and understanding
it can help us learn how to better manage stress and use it to our
advantage when we can.

According to a recent American Psychological Association's
stress study, 66 percent of respondents have physical stress symptoms, and 63 percent have psychological stress symptoms on a
regular basis. Stress is one of the most serious health issues that
people face today.[66]

Stress comes in many forms and enters our lives from a variety
of sources. It could be anything from being in traffic when you're in
a hurry to the diagnosis of a frightening sickness. It can show up in
an argument with your partner, a job that's gone bad, the pressure
of caring for an ailing parent, or trying to pay outstanding debts.

Stress puts the body and mind on edge, regardless of what
causes it, resulting in a surge of stress hormones in the body. The
response can produce a series of symptoms, which could include
rapid heart rate, constructed breathing, dizziness, stomachaches,
tightened muscles, etc.

The human body's response to stress has been perfected for
millennia. The fight-or-flight response traditionally helped people
escape risks such as animal attacks, fires, floods, and human war-
fare. Many of those risks are no longer common to our experience.

The stress response can be triggered by any scenario that you view as scary or that demands you to adjust to a change. If not managed effectively, that can lead to problems. Stress itself isn't the problem; it's how you deal with it. It's about how you respond in the face of a stressor.

WHAT IS STRESS ACTUALLY?

NIMH defines stress as how the body and brain respond to any demand. Any challenge, whether it is a school test, job change, or traumatic event, can be stressful. Stress can be experienced as physical or emotional tension. It is our body's psychological and physiological response to a perceived or real threat. Our minds and bodies initially don't know the difference, whether it is real or perceived, distant or nearby. We can face physical stressors (illness), life changes (losing a job), social struggles (interpersonal conflict), or psychological challenges (low self-worth).

Key Points:

The stress response cycle of your nervous system that you experience is functional and healthy. It's designed to help you respond to a potential threat. It keeps you safe and serves a survival purpose. Stressors recruit your brain to respond in particular ways.

We all experience stress, ranging from positive to negative, intense to mild, acute to chronic, and temporary to long-term. Our emotional experience with stress also varies. Eustress or positive stress can act as a catalyst and motivator. Distress or negative stress represents suffering and people seeking relief.

According to the APA, there are three different types of stress, and each takes a different toll on our brains and bodies.[67]

Acute stress — You can experience acute stress in the form of daily stressors. There are work deadlines, kids' temper tantrums, interpersonal conflict, traffic, and unexpected inconveniences. You may experience symptoms such as headaches, increased blood pressure, tightness in the chest, shortness of breath, or psychological reactions (anxiety, sadness).

Episodic stress — This can take the form of extended acute stress revisited regularly: mini-crises that become exacerbated and extended. The long-term impact of episodic stress can be problematic. The negative effects accumulate and have a compound effect on your health.

Chronic stress — The APA recognizes chronic stress as stress that is constantly experienced over an extended period of time. Severe sources include abuse, neglect, poverty, trauma, or frequent emotional distress. The effect of chronic stress can lead to serious health problems.

We are equipped to handle stress for short periods; however, the impact of longer-term, chronic stress can do damage to mental and physical health. Other models of stress highlighted in child development models name three degrees of stress: positive, tolerable, and toxic.

Positive stress is indicated by brief increases in heart rate and mild elevations in stress hormones. Tolerable stress is serious, temporary stress responses buffered by supportive relationships. Last, toxic stress is the prolonged activation of stress response systems without protective relationships.

Stress can be viewed as bad rather than in its original meaning by Hans Selye as *"the non-specific responses of the body to any demand for change."*[68] The notion that stress is unhealthy and can exacerbate health problems has become part of the current global perception of stress.

With this prevailing belief, people have become stressed about stress, which is not the best stress management strategy. **Stress** has become a synonym for **distress**, a state of unhappiness and discomfort in which happiness and comfort have been abandoned.[69] When life feels chaotic, overwhelming, or terrible, people frequently claim they are stressed. Stress can cause people to experience uneasy psychological states, yet we don't need to be so extreme in how we reference it.

THE RELATIONSHIP BETWEEN STRESS AND MENTAL HEALTH

Even though numerous studies have found a correlation between stress and mental health issues, the cause for this association has remained a mystery. New research from the University of California, Berkeley, has shed more light on how stress can be damaging to one's mental health.

In a series of experiments, Biology Professor Daniela Kaufer and her colleagues discovered that chronic stress generates more myelin-producing cells and fewer neurons, resulting in excess myelin and white matter in some areas of the brain. This change disrupts the balance and timing of communication in the brain.[70]

Kaufer proposes that these changes affect connectivity in the brain. For example, people with PTSD may develop stronger connections between the hippocampus and the amygdala (fight-or-flight survival response) and lower connectivity between the hippocampus and the prefrontal cortex (area of the brain that moderates and reasons). Discovering these changes to the brain is important to advance the precision of mental health intervention protocols. Understanding how trauma and stress impact the brain and can predispose people to mental health problems can lead to improved therapies and treatments.

The incredible scientific advancement in the understanding of how our brains can change is called neuroplasticity, and we can use this to our advantage.

Neuroplasticity tells us that through mental activity and training, the physiology of our brains actually changes. This phenomenon will be referenced throughout the book.

While the general notion in our culture is that stress is bad, there's more to it. Scientists like Kaufer are learning about the nuances of stress and how moderate amounts can have benefits. Research shows that short-lived, moderate stress can improve alertness, performance, and memory.

MORE ON THE STRESS RESPONSE CYCLE

The stress response is essentially the outcome of the reaction known as fight-or-flight. Evolution has helped us with this reaction to **fight against** or **flee from** potential danger. The dynamics of the fight-or-flight reaction are as follows. A stressful event occurs, triggering the autonomic nervous system. The sympathetic nervous system is activated, flooding the body with stress hormones such as norepinephrine (adrenaline) and cortisol.[71]

This neurochemical change heightens senses and produces the physiological responses mentioned previously, tuning in awareness and causing an increase in focus, attention, and energy. The parasympathetic nervous system temporarily becomes taxed. While the response is useful, it can become overactivated, even if the actual stressor is mild.

85

GENERAL ADAPTATION SYNDROME (GAS)

Hans Selye developed this initial model to describe biological changes occurring in response to stress. Various stress response models have developed, yet they typically cover the core concepts noted here.

GAS consists of three stages: alarm, resistance, and exhaustion.

The alarm reaction stage is the initial reaction to stress. The sympathetic nervous system is activated, stimulating the adrenal glands, which release stress hormones.

During **the resistance stage,** the body attempts to repair and recover. If the stressor is minimized, the body seeks homeostasis and returns to baseline or pre-stress levels. If the stress continues, the nervous system remains activated, continuing to produce stress hormones.

Extended and prolonged stress results in **exhaustion**. Enduring stress without relief, rest, or recovery will drain mental, emotional, and physical resources and can result in illness or disease. The physical impact of prolonged stress can include high blood pressure, decreased immune system functioning, increased risk of heart disease, mental illness, and other chronic health conditions.

The opponent process mechanism explains the regulatory nature of the system. Pain and pleasure are processed in overlapping areas of the brain and work like a balance scale. When tipped, the brain seeks equilibrium. Self-regulating processes bring it back to level.

THE HISTORY OF STRESS

The concept of stress has evolved over time. For centuries, stress referenced physical tension, a physics term used to explain the elasticity of an object and its ability to withstand strain (Hooke's

Law of 1958). In Ancient Greece, Hippocrates referenced stress to describe a sickness that combined pathos (suffering) and ponos (illness), referring to incessant work.

Fast forward to modern culture. Hans Selye pioneered much of the psychology addressing stress. He wrote *The Stress of Life* and reinforced the model of stress and stressor (distinguishing stimulus and reaction).

Later, Selye differentiated two types of stress: **eustress** and **distress**. Using the Greek prefix **EU-**, (good) with **stress**, eustress was used to define good stress as opposed to bad stress. By distinguishing between good stress (eustress) and bad stress (distress), Selye set out to clarify how stress, while being a reaction to a stressor, doesn't need to be linked to negative circumstances.

DISTRESS

Most people equate "stressed out" with distress, a negative version. If you experience distress, you may often feel overwhelmed and anxious. The stressor that generated the response and the individual's interpretation will determine if the stress is experienced as eustress or distress. If you believe a stressor is beyond your control or beyond your capacity to address it, this will likely feel distressing.

The stress response is intended to be adaptive. For optimal mental health, you want a right-sized response to the incoming threat. If you are about to be hit by a car, you want your fight-or-flight system to react immediately.

Objectively, extreme negative events such as crises, death, or trauma will produce a distressing response in most, and this is functional. What you want to watch out for is having an unnecessarily distressing response to a slightly negative or neutral stressor that doesn't truly put you in danger. What feels scary may not be dangerous.

EUSTRESS

Eustress is used to describe healthy, beneficial, and constructive stress that can provide motivation in a positive way. It can offer inspiration and propel people to take action, improve, and perform well. Both eustress and distress activate the sympathetic nervous system, preparing you for a response.

In eustress, the energy provided is typically **proportionate** to what the situation requires and produces a constructive response. In distress, the activated response can be exaggerated or destructive.

Whether you feel eustress or distress will be determined by your views, beliefs, and how you interpret the situation at hand. If you feel confident in your capacity to deal with a scenario, you may experience eustress. A positive viewpoint will help you channel the energy released by the activated response into constructive behaviors. Going to college, starting a new job, or joining a club may be experienced as positive stress. You likely feel activation, alertness, and increased awareness since it is new.

HEALTH BENEFITS OF EUSTRESS

Eustress can have emotional and physical health benefits. According to researchers, it differs from distress in these ways: it lasts in the short term, energizes and motivates, is perceived as within our coping ability, feels exciting, and increases focus and performance.[72]

On the other hand, distress is characterized as longer term, triggering anxiety, exceeding coping, unpleasant feelings, decreasing focus and performance, and contributing to mental and physical problems. If someone experiences intense social anxiety, starting a new job or going to college may feel more distressing than exciting.

RELATIONSHIP WITH STRESS

Dr. Richard Lazarus developed a theory of stress appraisal, indicating that the interpretation of stressful events is more important than the actual events themselves. It is experienced when a person perceives the "demands exceed the personal and social resources the individual is able to mobilize." According to Lazarus and Folkman,

◇◇

Psychological stress is a particular relationship between the person and the environment appraised as taxing or exceeding his or her resources and endangering well-being.[73]

◇◇

Key Points:

People will find different things to be stressful. What one person views as a threat, someone else would find as a challenge. And remember, stress is not always bad. Being activated, stimulated, and engaged is healthy and keeps us experiencing a state of vitality in life.

WHY ZEBRAS DON'T GET ULCERS

Stanford professor Robert Sapolsky is a prominent researcher and wrote the popular book, *Why Zebras Don't Get Ulcers*. According to Sapolsky, if you are a normal mammal, a stressor is a challenge to homeostatic balance — a physical challenge — and the stress-response is the adaptation your body mobilizes to reestablish homeostasis.[74]

His research highlights the uniquely human experience of anticipatory anxiety. He indicates that for a cognitively complex species (like humans and other primates), the stressor is also the ANTICIPATION that a real physical challenge is about to happen. If there isn't an actual threat coming, we set ourselves up for an increased risk of stress-related disease.

We have a self-destructive way of activating the stress response with negative memories, worries, thoughts, and concerns. Sapolsky asserts this is not what it evolved for. Continuing to unnecessarily activate your stress response cycle puts you at risk for a range of health problems.

People under stress over time do not respond effectively, especially if they don't have proper time to recover. In Sapolsky's words:

◇◇

If you are that zebra running for your life, or that lion sprinting for your meal, your body's physiological response mechanisms are superbly adapted for dealing with such short-term physical emergencies. For the vast majority of beasts on this planet, stress is about a short-term crisis, after which it's either over with or you're over with.[75]

◇◇

Sapolsky points out that when we find ourselves sitting around and worrying, we are setting off our physiological alarm bells unnecessarily. We are **provoking ourselves**. And to what end? It has been scientifically well established that many stress-related diseases emerge from our self-induced, excessive stress responses.

Key Points:

We tend to provoke excessive stress responses that incur damage to our mind and body over time. Worrying doesn't control the outcome—at all.

Challenge:

- When you find yourself engaging in excessive worry and anticipation, what can you do instead?
- Make a pre-commitment to redirect your actions and thinking.
- Keep a log or record of situations that trigger your stress response cycle and assess the level of threat the stressor presents.
- Gaining this awareness can help you calibrate and right-size your interpretation and response.

MODERN SOURCES OF STRESS

Environmental, social, physiological, and psychological stresses are key origins of stress and anxiety. Weather, traffic, and pollution are environmental stresses. Competing demands for your time, interpersonal relationships, and financial issues are related to social pressures. Physiological stressors include nutrition, sleep, and physical and mental health. Psychological stressors include your appraisal of real or imagined threats and concerns in life.

We are all dealing with varying degrees of stress, overwhelm, trauma, and exhaustion. The pandemic's length is taking its toll, which could come in the form of depression, anxiety, addiction, restlessness, or boredom mixed with acute anxiety and apprehension about the future. Overwork and a scarcity of resources can also be stressful.

Our ability to think effectively or creatively is hampered when we are constantly stressed and intensely focused on an impending threat. The mechanism has developed to keep beings safe, so if they are pursued by a lion, they can react swiftly. Most of us don't have to worry about animal predators on a regular basis.

Yet, when faced with serious worries, we develop tunnel vision. Other relevant signs in our environment are often filtered out while we are hyper-aware of a few specific unfavorable ones.

Key Points:

Our brains and bodies are equipped to handle stress for short periods of time; however, the impact of longer-term, chronic stress damages mental and physical health. Experiencing constant stress restricts thinking and the ability to recognize other cues in the environment.

HOW CAN WE MAKE STRESS WORK FOR US RATHER THAN AGAINST US?

Emily and Amelia Nagoski are co-authors of the book *Burnout: The Secret to Unlocking the Stress Cycle.* They suggest that stress isn't bad for you but being stuck is. They provide suggestions for what they call completing the response cycle. Among other key ideas, they explain why men and women feel stress and burnout in different ways. They define the **human giver syndrome**, implying that many of us fall into the trap of believing that resting is selfish.[76]

Many of my female clients resonate with the human giver syndrome — trying to be all things to all people, meeting everyone else's needs, being others-centered, and attempting to get everything done. We must use caution to not adopt the lure of OVER responsibility; it's a drain on well-being and mental health. It may be tempting to jump in and do the thing yourself; however, this is not a sustainable strategy.

They recommend readers devote 42 percent of their time to rest and treat it as non-negotiable. Other ideas to assist in completing the stress cycle include deep, slow breathing to down-regulate and build a sense of serenity, laughing, showing physical affection, crying, and expressing yourself creatively, all of which are supported by science.

How will you know when the cycle is finished? If we feel better than when we started, our bodies will tell us.

Key Points:

- We don't give ourselves enough time and space to relax and rejuvenate in our urgent culture.
- Many find it challenging to tap into a rest state. Scheduling downtime can even feel stressful if you aren't used to it.
- However, this is problematic since we don't enable our bodies to adapt to and recover from the stress we put them under.
- Stressing or activating our nervous system doesn't have to be such a bad thing, provided we give ourselves time to recuperate and enable the system to regroup.

Challenge:

Try shifting more intentionally between engaged and recovering states. When you are in a state of exertion, be all in. Then, make a choice to spend time in the rest and recovery phase. All of this requires becoming more aware and attentive to the signals from your mind and body. How can you schedule intentional rest and downtime this week?

OVERWHELM

Stress can manifest in the form of overwhelm. Mental and emotional strain and tension are common reactions to stressful situations. Overwhelm can be described as a state of mind in which you feel unable to cope with your current circumstances. Feelings of being buried, defeated, or overloaded can cause overwhelm.

These feelings are frequently accompanied by volume concerns, i.e. a feeling that there is simply too much to deal with and that there aren't enough hours in the day. Overwhelm is a strong emotional reaction to a plethora of thoughts, events, and perceived demands. When people remark that they are overwhelmed, they may identify with the sentiment of "I'm drowning..." It is that feeling of flailing or striving to keep your head above water.

Do you ever feel as though there isn't enough time to catch your breath? Do you experience constant anxiety that your life could fall apart at any moment? It's like sitting on the edge of a cliff, on the verge of falling off.

A client, Molly, described her current life situation as feeling like a *"house of cards."* She said, "My life is a mess. It's an intricate, delicate, and complex web of factors, and one little nudge or tiny wind could collapse the whole thing."

Many of us can relate. Life and work have moved at a faster speed than we can adapt to in a healthy way. We're facing human limitations — demands that exceed our capabilities. We are losing our mental and physical health as a result of the trade-offs.

We are running around in a perpetual state of worry that we're not doing enough of what we think we're supposed to be doing. It creates a cycle of overwhelm that we are behind where we should be. Many are living in a chronic state of hurried busyness, in the hot pursuit of chasing the next best thing. All the while, we feel strained, inadequate, and perpetually preoccupied.

GUILT

Guilt is yet another modern-day affliction. Many experience a state of dis-ease that they aren't doing what they're meant to be doing, which adds to already elevated levels of stress. Having unnecessarily high expectations of yourself or others will leave you feeling disappointed. My friends and I refer to this common sentiment as being in a **constant state of disappointment**. It can feel like a slow burn.

Common comments from clients:

I SHOULD… get up earlier, get an hour of cardio in, call my grandparents, schedule the kids' dentist appointments, go to bed earlier, drink more water, call my friends, cook healthier, get more done, be more productive, lose weight, volunteer more, get groceries, walk the dog, eat more kale, increase my steps, be further ahead in my career, be making more money, complete more tasks, do more yoga, make more progress, get a promotion, learn a new language, ask for a raise, watch less Netflix, spend more time with the kids…

Feel free to fill in your own version of the **SHOULDS.**

Key Point:

This emotional spinning must be reprogrammed, and if you can relate, you can revise it.

Challenge:

Consider examining your internal expectations to assess if they are realistic. Who says you should be doing more, getting more done, achieving more, and being more productive? What is it based on? And for what purpose?

Closer examination reveals that these are frequently phantom expectations — fake, imaginary, idyllic, and impossible to achieve.

We are being suffocated by them. I can't count the number of coaching conversations that have started something like this.

> **Client:** *Everything is falling apart. I should have done ___ for_____ last week. I was supposed to handle _____ by _____. I didn't do _____. I should be doing _____ this week and I should have done _____ today. I needed to be _____ for _____ and I wasn't. I just can't get it all done.*

What I hear is that my clients experience internal pressure and feel as though they are falling short. As a coach, I want to validate and recognize their experience without necessarily agreeing with it. After empathizing and communicating that I hear them, what I feel inclined to explore is what data and evidence exist to support the external pressures, which may or may not match the internal expectations they are experiencing.

You should be doing _____ according to what? Or who? This general type of inquiry can begin to dismantle the belief that "everything" is falling apart and reduce the intense feeling of despair, overwhelm, exacerbation, inadequacy, frustration, or whatever emotion is present.

Watch out for the intoxication of improving yourself to death and chasing an unrealistic ideal or the underlying sentiment that it is never enough. With this mindset, we never arrive; the desired destination just keeps moving further away. Operating with this paradigm can fuel unnecessary dissatisfaction and discontent.

Key Points:

When you feel overwhelmed, refrain from doing more. Over-efforting may not be the answer. The pressure you experience may be made up or exaggerated.

Challenge:

If feeling overwhelmed, look closely at the expectations you are fueling. Are they real or phantom?

UPGRADE YOUR RELATIONSHIP WITH STRESS

Since stress gets a bad rap as it aligns with negativity, psychologist Kelly McGonigal proposes that you can upgrade your relationship with stress. She suggests it is beneficial to foster the belief that the effects of stress can be positive, constructive, and generative rather than harmful. She indicates that even if you are convinced that stress is bad, you can foster a healthier mindset that will help you thrive.[77]

The <u>story</u> you tell yourself about stress <u>matters</u>. I learned an important lesson about this from my son, Stephen. Stephen is 22 at the time this book is being written. He grew up as an athlete and was involved in competitive sports during all seasons. When he was 12, his baseball team was in a national tournament in Cooperstown, New York.

The Cooperstown tournament is well established. The experience is formal and organized, and the expectations are clear. The lawns are manicured, and the fields are perfectly groomed. I'm pretty sure we weren't allowed to walk on the grass.

Our team was scheduled to play in the first game of the tournament at 8 a.m. The coaches were important mentors to Stephen and had a strong impact on him growing up. They invested in developing him as a player and expected a lot from him. It was a competitive crew and not for the faint of heart in that way. They could be tough.

We all showed up for the 8 a.m. game. The boys were squirrely, and the parents were anxious. The opposing team was from the south, and the players looked like men with beards, especially when standing next to our little guys. They looked like **official** baseball players with fancy uniforms and jerseys tucked in.

We were worried for Stephen and the boys. Some of the players were crying in the dugout at the beginning of the game because of nerves. The parents could hardly stand it in the bleachers. It's not lost on me how silly it sounds feeling **that** anxious at a 12-year-old's baseball game, but we were. The boys had trained for it; most of them played together for a long time, and it meant a lot to them. And we can be a little competitive — at least my husband can be.

Stephen was often the leadoff hitter, but I was secretly hoping he wouldn't be that morning. If I was that nervous, I couldn't imagine how much pressure he must have felt. We were first at bat, and sure enough, Stephen stepped up to the plate. It felt so official, formal, and intimidating. I wished I could protect him from the pressure.

It went quickly because he swung at the first pitch of the tournament (which I don't think you are supposed to do) and hit a home run. They started with momentum, and the pressure eased a bit. To be honest, I don't even remember who won that game.

However, I do vividly remember my conversation with Stephen after the game. I said, "Oh my GOSH, STEPHEN! You Must Have Been SO NERVOUS?!"

Stephen paused, looking perplexed and almost a little serious for a second. He crossed his eyebrows, looking up at me, and said, "Oh... no... I call it **EXCITED.**"

Ah, OF COURSE. My 12-year-old son was giving his psychologist mother a lesson in peak performance principles. I'm sure he had similar physiological signals from his nervous system being activated, yet it hadn't occurred to him to think of that state as being negative. He interpreted it as a good thing—he was ready for the big game. This is certainly not the only insight I've gained from my kids over the years.

Key Point:

What you call stress matters.

STRESS STUDIES

I later learned about research on this exact phrase that Stephen shared with me. Studies done by Ian Robertson support that telling oneself "I am excited" can shift emotional demeanor from a place of threat (stressed and apprehensive) to a mindset of opportunity (ready to go).[78]

According to Robertson, individuals who appraise their arousal as excitement rather than panic perform better. The sensations experienced before a big event are natural and functional, and if we perceive them positively, they are likely to have a positive impact on performance.

Key Points:

- Again, the language you use matters and can impact your perception of circumstances.
- You can craft your thoughts and language to create your experience.
- Referring to anticipation as excitement rather than a threat can be useful when facing daily stressors that aren't placing you in danger.
- To achieve peak performance, experts suggest maintaining and managing an optimal level of arousal.
- By managing your internal state, you can engineer and learn to adjust your internal thermostat as you respond to stressors.

JUST ENOUGH

Not experiencing any stress is not healthy and leads to apathy, atrophy, or deterioration. Yet, an overabundance of stressors can tax the system. Learning how to lean into the sweet spot and adjust and modify your level of arousal and activation to properly meet the demands of your environment is part of building psychological fitness.

Key Points:

In simple terms, moderate stressors can help you develop resiliency and immunity. Severe stressors can do damage, and the absence of stress can result in mental atrophy. If you approach stress and use it for your benefit, it can help enhance physical and mental health.

Challenge:

Consider what Sapolsky identifies as four important components of reducing stress and how you can apply them to your life this week.

Predictive information — Look for signs that the stress is going to increase (deadlines). Knowing gives you a chance to prepare and have agency over your response.

Stress management outlets (exercise, relaxation, and breathing) — Be proactive in learning what methods are most effective for managing your stress.

A positive outlook — Foster the belief that things can get better rather than worse. We will review this in the section on Learned Optimism.

Connection with others — Social support from others is critical to managing and mitigating stress.

PHYSICAL EXERCISE AND STRESS

◇◇

In order for man to succeed in life, God provided him with two means: education and physical activity. Not separately, one for the soul and the other for the body, but for the two together. With these two means, man can attain perfection.
—Plato

◇◇

Finally, a discussion about stress without at least briefly acknowledging the mental health benefits of physical activity would be incomplete. Physical exercise has a significant impact on your well-being and ability to cope with stress. The evidence for the health advantages of exercise is overwhelming. It appears to be as beneficial as certain drugs in treating depression and anxiety.

Exercise, according to John Ratey, the author of *Spark: The revolutionary new science of exercise and the brain,* is a powerful medicine for your health.[79] Research suggests you can beat stress, enhance mood, reduce memory loss, and function more effectively by engaging in physical exercise.

According to Ratey, aerobic exercise upgrades your brain so that it becomes your best defense against depression, addiction, aggression, menopause, ADD, and Alzheimer's.

Physical fitness promotes psychological fitness. Getting exercise benefits mental health. Studies have supported how exercise helps reduce anxiety.[80] In *Move the Body, Heal the Mind,* neuroscientist Jennifer Heisz addresses how physical movement contributes to brain health. According to Heisz, exercise increases neuropeptide Y, which soothes the amygdala, providing a calming effect. She also proposes how working out can decrease depression and dementia and how physical inactivity can exacerbate such conditions.[81]

Many models of depression point to a lack of serotonin as a contributing factor, which can be treated with antidepressant drugs. Not everyone with depression responds well to such treatment. Other studies indicate depression may be connected to inflammation in the body, which could induce an immune response and impact the brain accordingly.[82] The right exercise can reduce inflammation.

The effects of physical activity on depression have been explored in depth. Results indicate that exercise has a significant, large antidepressant effect in individuals with depression. These findings have huge implications as scalable, cost-effective, and low-risk treatment for depression and anxiety.

Researchers proved this by reviewing research data in a robust study of studies known as a meta-meta-analysis. Findings indicate a large amount of quality evidence that physical activity reduces anxiety and depression in non-clinical populations.[83]

You're already aware that exercise is beneficial to your health, but you might be thinking you're too busy and stressed to incorporate it into your daily routine. Wait a minute! There is some positive news about exercise and stress.

Stress can be relieved by almost any type of exercise, from aerobics to yoga. Even if you are not an athlete or you are in poor physical condition, a little exercise can go a long way toward stress relief. Just a bit of movement can improve your well-being.

HOW MUCH IS ENOUGH?

For starters, any increase in activity is progress. There are many schools of thought and endorsements of what type of exercise and how much is ideal. Ask your doctor and research what will be best for you.

A general guideline to enhance physical health is to engage in both cardiovascular and strength exercises three to five times a week. Recent research suggests that even mild leisure exercise is associated with a lower incidence of depression.[84] It may not take much movement to enhance your mental health. If that sounds overwhelming, consider exercise snacking.

Meet Niko. My client Niko was healthy and fit, yet he was falling short of personal fitness goals. As a working parent of three kids, Niko felt pressed for time. It was difficult finding longer periods of time to dedicate to exercise. Since being active for short periods of time throughout the day also provides health benefits, Niko tried "exercise snacking."

This was a system to incorporate short bursts of strength and aerobic activity throughout the day. Between meetings, Niko would do repetitions of sit-ups, squats, or push-ups and save longer cardio workouts for the weekends and one morning per week. My client is a vigilant behavior tracker, so all activities were documented.

Attaching behaviors to existing events and monitoring progress contributed to the success of this self-created program. Over the course of a few weeks, Niko felt back on track and ready to take training to the next level.

Key Point:

Physical activity is crucial for mental health, stress management, and physical fitness.

Challenge:

If you don't have a regular exercise routine, try exercise snacking or incorporating short bursts of activity to get started.

REGULATE YOUR INNER STATE BY GENERATING CALM

Many high achievers are good at becoming stressed. You set your sights high and keep pushing through, moving in fifth gear. However, as we know, this pace burns people out, derails productivity, and leads to exhaustion. When stressed, your perception becomes restricted, and you see the world differently. Stress constricts your attention to sift out the static, but it can prevent you from seeing the bigger picture. When you experience an alert state of calm, your attention is broader, and you can be more creative.

Consider stepping off the hamster wheel and taking a break from the hustle. Philosophy, wisdom literature, neuroscience, and common sense indicate that cultivating a calmer, relaxed state of mind will improve the quality of your energy, focus, attention, and creativity. Regularly engaging in practices that generate a calm mindset will help you handle challenges more effectively.

Meet Raj. My client Raj was working on increasing focus and managing stress. He realized by taking more frequent breaks during the day, he felt more engaged and productive. He was being more consistent about being active after work and unplugging from his computer.

Raj noticed that feeling the tension was giving him tunnel vision and constricting his thinking. By pulling away from his desk for short breaks and making use of leisure time, it helped him feel more creative and expansive in his thinking and produce higher quality work.

Key Points:

By tapping into your ability to calm the nervous system, you'll be more mindful and will create a more intentional space between a stressor and how you respond. You'll be more equipped to navigate through challenges more effectively if you engage in practices that promote a calm mindset on a regular basis.

Challenge:

Try any of these practices to manage your stress and soothe your nervous system. They are simple and take only a few minutes. While some provide guided support, most of the tools below are considered *inside-out* ways to foster calm (vs. outside-in, which is dependent on external stimuli, i.e., food, drink, etc.).

Breathing Exercises — Managing your breath is a powerful and accessible way to manage stress and emotion.

- 4-7-8 Breathing exercises: Breathe in for four counts, hold for seven, and breathe out for eight. Dr. Andrew Weil explains this simply at his site (drweil.com).

- Engaging in a physiological "sigh" brings autonomic arousal levels down — two inhales through the nose followed by an extended exhale.

Mindfulness/Meditation — There are many meditation frameworks. Regardless of the style, the point is to practice bringing the focus back to the center. The benefits of mindfulness are impressive. Start with one to two minutes.

- A few meditation applications to support you: 10 percent Happier, Headspace, Calm, Insight Timer.

Visual/Optic Tools — Neuroscientist Andrew Huberman proposes that you can leverage your visual system to generate calm. When you are focused on a near-term object, it enhances your cognitive focus, providing more of a portrait-mode state. Looking further out at the horizon provides more panoramic vision.[85] Engaging in this "soft gaze" can relax you. A natural application is being in nature, taking in the landscape, such as a sunset or sunrise. It can also allow you to recognize things in your field of vision that would otherwise be overlooked.

You'd be amazed what you can see when you slow down and gaze softly. I experienced this recently in an impactful way. I was in Santa Barbara for a work commitment, and I had one day to experience the area. My visit was during the winter, and, being from Minnesota, it was mission-critical to get to the beach. I walked several beaches and, despite being 70 degrees and sunny, I hardly saw anyone. I passed less than 10 people on my initial walks. I suppose 70 degrees feels differently for someone coming from the tundra.

I was particularly interested in one area with cliffs and hiking trails that looked glorious. I mapped out a plan to access the desired area, which required parking a half mile away from the beach and walking through a trail in the woods. I picked a random parking lot and headed out on the trail.

The area was called Monarch Butterfly Grove. There were pictures of butterflies along the trail, which I thought was strange because I didn't see a single butterfly around. I was hustling along, eager to get to the beach, listening to my podcast on 1.7 speed, which is typical for me.

I happened to notice a few groups of people standing on the edge of the trail, looking into the woods. It caught my eye because they looked enthralled, yet what I could see as their view didn't capture my attention. The trees and bushes are nice, but there didn't seem to be anything special.

I finally got curious enough that I stopped and asked someone what they were looking at and inquired about the butterfly signs. **Are there supposed to be butterflies here or something?**

He looked at me and paused for what felt like a while. He then said,

"Yes, there are butterflies. But. To see them, you have...to...be...Still."

Ahhh... another learning moment for me. I turned off my podcast, removed my headphones, and followed his lead. He told me what to do. Look out at the horizon without focusing on anything and be quiet. If you listen closely, you'll begin to hear rustling. At the tips of the tree branches or above the bushes, you'll see the fluttering of butterflies.

Unbelievable. Thousands of monarch butterflies right there in front of us. It was almost an out-of-body experience when time stood still. Had I not stopped to pause, I would never have noticed them. It was an a-ha sacred insight for me, a massive reminder from the universe to slow down, to not miss the special moments.

Every winter, more than 100,000 monarch butterflies migrate to Goleta, California. What serendipity for me to come across this miracle of nature! We will all interpret these sacred moments differently. For me, it was not luck or coincidence. It was a spiritual experience, which included a powerful (painfully missed) sense of my mom's presence.

Yoga — Any type of yoga can help stress management and regulate your internal state. Yoga classes often end in the relaxation pose called Savasana. Savasana is defined as a meditative posture in which one lies on one's back, typically considered the final resting pose of total relaxation. While it seems easy, this can be one of the most challenging elements of a movement meditation practice, at least for me.

When I began practicing yoga, I didn't understand the importance of Savasana. I was an uninformed student. Initially, I'd arrive late and feel tempted to leave early once the "work" was done until I learned the importance of it.

I'm no yoga expert, but from what I learned, the real settling, integrating, and metabolizing of the mind and body happen in Savasana. It offers time for you to assimilate while you are in a calm, relaxed state and to reap the benefits of the work you've just done. All I know is that words can't quite describe it. You just need to experience it.

Yoga Nidra — This form of guided meditation generates a relaxation response, a state between waking and sleeping, typically practiced lying down. More information can be found here: YogaInternational.com.

iRest — iRest is a modern adaptation of Yoga Nidra, based on similar principles. The iRest protocol was developed by Dr. Richard Miller, a spiritual teacher, author, researcher, and clinical psychologist. In this method, Miller blended traditional yoga practices with psychology and neuroscience. A 10-step protocol is offered as a technique for self-inquiry and finding equilibrium. You can learn more here: iRest.org

Loving-Kindness Meditation — As highlighted by Sharon Salzberg in *Lovingkindness: The Revolutionary Art of Happiness*, loving-kindness meditation, also known as metta meditation, is focused on creating and enhancing feelings of goodwill, kindness, and warmth toward others.[86] While this might sound woo-woo, stay tuned because the results are backed by scientific evidence. In short, being intentional about generating positive thoughts and compassion for yourself and others increases positive emotions and decreases negative emotions.

Researcher Barbara Frederickson and her colleagues found that practicing seven weeks of Loving-Kindness Meditation increased love, joy, interest, gratitude, pride, hope, amusement, contentment, and awe.[87] The practice also contributed to increases in resilience resources such as social support, mindfulness, life satisfaction and purpose, and fewer depressive and illness symptoms.

Mantra examples for self-loving-kindness meditation include: *"May I be safe, peaceful, and free of suffering. May I be happy. May I be healthy."* Mantras to foster compassion for others are similar: "May you be safe, peaceful, and free of suffering. May you be happy. May you be healthy."

Meditation teachers encourage considering loved ones during this practice, as well as people who you experience as neutral, and eventually even individuals you may not have fond feelings toward.

BLENDED INSIDE OUT/OUTSIDE IN SENSORY INTERVENTIONS

Walking, forward movement, warm water exposure, sauna, foam rolling, and massage all have calming benefits. Fidgets can solicit calm, even for adults. Mild movements slow down the monkey mind. Other methods include calming music, pleasurable smells or taste (oils), and activity that gets you out of worry mode and into your body.

REGULATE YOUR INNER STATE BY ACTIVATING THE NERVOUS SYSTEM

These days, many are experiencing malaise, flatness, low energy, and lack of motivation, as residue has built up from the pandemic and global uncertainty. Many external stressors that we can't control can lead to feelings of helplessness. Learned helplessness is the notion of *— **What's the point? Why should I even try?*** It fuels a sense of powerlessness and can contribute to depressive symptoms.

Monitoring your thoughts and emotions, and cognitive reframing, are effective psychological tools to enhance mental health and well-being. Modifying your behaviors and actions are also avenues to improve.

We make the mistake of waiting until we feel like doing the thing we know would be helpful. It could be the project we've been putting off, paying bills, addressing conflict, completing boring tasks, exercising, engaging in complex work, etc. If that time hasn't come yet, it's not coming anytime soon. So, you need to demonstrate agency, take action, and do the thing—whether you feel like it or not.

Key Point:

Action creates traction, and mood can follow the action.

Challenge:

If you struggle with hypoarousal (low),
consider these strategies:

Modifying Your Breath — Engage in super-oxygenated breathing. Emphasize a long, nasal inhale with a quicker exhale. Repeat this technique 20–30 times.

Cold Exposure — While the detailed science behind this technique is beyond this excerpt, studies have shown that exposing oneself to cold temperature has health benefits. Supporters suggest cold therapy activates the nervous system by triggering eustress vs. distress.

Positive hormonal, immunal, and neurotransmitter effects can occur because of cold exposure. Ice baths are an example of a commonly leveraged treatment after physical activity for recovery and muscle soreness. Early studies also show that cold exposure can improve depressive symptoms. I see it as a low-risk intervention. If nothing else, it will wake you up, and at the least, you will experience momentary vitality. It's worth the discomfort. Suggestions: cold water plunge, ice bath, cold shower, cryotherapy.

DO HARD THINGS BUT START WITH A SMALL ACTION

To spark motivation, start small. The law of inertia (per Sir Isaac Newton) tells us that a body at rest tends to stay at rest. A body in motion tends to stay in motion unless stopped by a greater outside force. Take the first tiny step to get the laws of motion in our favor.

By engaging in a first action, you are making the decision to invest in yourself, making an emotional deposit and indicating to your brain that you matter. Picking up the phone to make a doctor's appointment or looking up your gym's membership options is a strong start.

Motivation science also tells us that you need to move the goal post closer. If you can't work out for 30 minutes, start with a walk around the block. Doing this every day consistently will have a compound impact.

Do hard things but expect a struggle because taking action isn't supposed to be easy.

DOPAMINE

There has been a lot of talk about dopamine lately. *Dopamine Nation*[88] and *Dopamine: The Molecule of More*[89] are current best-sellers. We often relate the term "dopamine hits" to experiencing gratification. Thought leaders tell us dopamine is not the pleasure molecule, and rather, it's the molecule of motivation.

According to science, dopamine release is not from achieving goals but occurs during the pursuit of goals. The dopamine experience is about wanting, pursuing, and anticipating and generates energy to initiate behaviors.

Daniel Lieberman and Michael Long clearly describe dopamine's role in *Dopamine: The Molecule of More.* They recognize how dopamine is the chemical of desire that always asks for more and is the source of our urges. It is behind **why** we seek and pursue. They note how it is why we succeed and also why we engage in addictive behaviors.

Too much pleasure without pain is dangerous for humans. If pleasure is too readily accessible, it blunts the positivity of the experience. There aren't any shortcuts. We need to go through the struggle to get to the other side and experience pleasure. You may have heard the Navy SEALs reference "embrace the suck." Or another saying, "If you have to eat the frog, don't stare at the frog for too long."

Key Point:

Pleasure that is too easily accessed will quickly lose its appeal and impact. The more we work for something, the greater the reward.

Challenge:

Do one thing that you have been avoiding and tolerate the distress that comes with it.

CHAPTER 3

BURNOUT

◇◇

Burnout is nature's way of telling you, you've been going through the motions your soul has departed; you're a zombie, a member of the walking dead, a sleepwalker. False optimism is like administrating stimulants to an exhausted nervous system.[90]
—Sam Keen, *Fire in the Belly: On Being a Man*

◇◇

In May 2019, the World Health Organization recognized burnout in the ICD-11 as an occupational phenomenon. It is intense...**nature's way of telling you you've been going through the motions and your soul has departed?** Burnout is no joke. It isn't, "I'm a little stressed out; I have too much to do." Rather, it's a void of physical, emotional, cognitive, and spiritual energy, significantly impacting health and well-being.

Burnout is experienced as emotional exhaustion or depersonalization.[91] Symptoms are often thought to be caused by work-related stressors. Outside of work, caring for a family member without reprieve also contributes to burnout.

The key components of signposting burnout are exhaustion, cynicism, and inefficacy. Individuals who are burned out feel exhausted, jaded, and isolated and often experience a lack of meaning and purpose. Those experiencing burnout described it as complete and utter mental and physical depletion. Their bandwidth becomes significantly more limited, and their attitude toward work is negatively impacted. People experiencing burnout can have difficulty focusing and feel disengaged with their work.

What is less often noted is how burnout is a condition that is created by a maladaptive workplace. Christina Maslach has extensively researched burnout.

She identifies six risk factors in organizations contributing to burnout.[92]

1. A high workload with high employer expectations
2. Lack of autonomy at work
3. The sense that your efforts remain unrecognized
4. A lack of community among work colleagues
5. The perception that your employer is not being fair
6. Difficulties finding meaning in your role

Key Points:

Addressing workplace concerns and risk factors is critical to addressing burnout. People who experience burnout are not flawed; it's often an infrastructure problem. Burnout is a demand-capacity imbalance when more is required than a person can provide.

Challenge:

If you notice signs of burnout in yourself or others, ask for help and support so you can make changes.

Part II:
OBSTACLES

Chapter 4:
What Gets in the Way?

HERE IS A COMMON CONVERSATION STARTER.
"How are you?"
"THINGS are busy."
"Yes, but how are YOU?"
"I'm **busy.**"
"How are you **feeling**?"

This is where people get stumped. In the rush and pursuit of more, it can be challenging to access and identify how we are really feeling and doing. We can be swept up in a frenetic activity without pausing to assess our condition.

Do you ever feel like you are consistently in chase mode, yet you never get there? Or ever feel like you are the one being chased? To achieve psychological fitness, it's important to get a handle on what is hindering your mental health, both internal and external.

Many factors can be barriers to well-being. Obvious obstacles include adversity and trauma. Natural disasters, poverty, war, violence... these all do damage and can get in the way of thriving. Beyond external situations that contribute to emotional distress, the internal barriers we create for ourselves are often overlooked.

Busyness, hurriedness, and distractibility are a few conditions that can get in the way of thriving and flourishing. Pursuing unattainable goals, people pleasing, perfectionism, feelings of overwhelm, and exhaustion are also common barriers to psychological fitness.

Feeling short on time and resources can deplete well-being. The pursuit of immediate gratification can lead to indulgence and damage your mental health. Being afraid of being bored or alone can even halt growth.

Approval seeking and fear of judgment or disapproval can hold us back from living an optimally mentally healthy life. Comparing ourselves to others creates distress and keeps us stuck, as does being in a victim mindset. These internal factors are in our control. We'll explore several such obstacles as well as potential antidotes to reduce the impact.

BUSYNESS

Many have been conditioned to believe that a busy life is a worthwhile life. 'Being busy means you matter.' We can rescue ourselves from this oppressive narrative, the false belief that we can or should do it all.

There is no shortage of things to be doing, balancing, advancing, and achieving. It has contributed to a collective state of overwhelm. We are on the brink of collapse. The pernicious impact of social media doesn't help. Social myths contribute to an internal set of expectations, which for most high achievers is out of human reach.

What if we held the key that could release us from the prison of phantom expectations? What if we challenged the assumptions we internalize based on external and cultural pressures?

The good news is that re-visiting our expectations that lead to unnecessary suffering is in our control. We can relieve the pressure of this type of emotional prison.

Meet Peyton. Peyton grew up as an athlete. He was on a competitive sports team and committed to physical training. Peyton applied the same level of discipline to professional pursuits and experienced corporate success (per corporate measurements of external success). Things were going okay until they weren't. Peyton was burning the candle at both ends, receiving rewards at work in terms of influence, the scope of responsibility, and increases in compensation. Yet, it was coming at a cost. After years of working 70+-hour workweeks, dealing with various physical ailments and strained relationships, Peyton realized it was time to get help.

Insights from Peyton:

Someone asked me what I do for fun. It was really a simple question, yet I drew a blank. Paralyzed. I had no words, and I realized at that moment that I couldn't remember the last time I did something fun. I've been rushing, hustling, pursuing, and running around... and why? I hadn't even stopped to think about what this was all for.

There is a lot of running around, generating unnecessary urgency. I'm guilty of it. When our children were younger, our family of seven needed help. At one time, all five kids were under the age of seven. For two years, we had an au pair from Columbia named Claudia. She had an endearing way of pointing out our cultural nuances, family quirks, and environmental differences.

One of her frequent observations was when we were hurrying around getting kids in and out of the car going to and from activities. I have a propensity for urgency, which Claudia politely noticed. She would gently say, why are we in a hurry again? Usually, I did not have a good answer.

As it turns out, it wasn't important to arrive at the homecoming parade 15 minutes early. Nor was it necessary that we got to the museum just that much faster. We typically did not have real deadlines, yet I found myself hustling the kids along more than necessary, out of habit. My kids were used to the pace; it was a way of life for them. When we had little friends joining, it was apparent they were not accustomed to this energy. I would occasionally hear my kids asking their friends why they were so slow.

It is reinforced in our culture to be in perpetual motion. Without intentional pause and opportunity to reset, this can be destructive to well-being and mental health. Most of us have not practiced having open time and space, being calm, and sitting in stillness and quiet. We live in a world of overstimulation, and as author David Brooks says, he's losing the attention war.

BEING BUSY AND STATUS

According to research, an individual's perceived level of busyness can be linked to their self-worth and how others perceive their status. In some circles, being busy and overscheduled can signal one's social position. Individuals who choose to be busy may feel needed, in demand, and essential, which can boost their self-esteem. It's not uncommon to hustle in the pursuit of feeling relevant.

USING BUSYNESS TO NUMB YOURSELF

Staying busy can be a method to escape or numb difficult sensations and situations, in addition to its link to feelings of self-worth and status. You won't be able to dwell on what's upsetting you if you're preoccupied. Many operate with the fear of slowing down.

PRODUCTIVE VS. BUSY

The terms **busy** and **productive** are often used interchangeably. Busyness doesn't equal productivity. You can be busy without making good use of time. Being productive entails making progress, finishing a task, or accomplishing a goal. You can be productive without being busy.

TIME AND BUSYNESS

The desired state of having more time, feeling less stressed, and reducing our commitments sounds idyllic. The problem that is not discussed as much is the challenge of the chopping process. To create more time, space, and effort, something needs to go.

It is difficult to minimize obligations. It requires acknowledging what we can't do, asking for help, and saying no. The terror of no is often greater than the desire for freedom. Many resist saying no due to the risk of rejection and disappointing others. Most people I interact with on a daily and weekly basis are tired and weary yet find themselves in this perpetual cycle.

A common coaching topic is time management. We often say, *"I don't have enough time."* This is a tricky problem to solve since time is finite, and there is nothing we can do to change the concept of time. We all experience an exactly equal amount of 60 seconds in one minute, 24 hours in one day, 7 days in one week, and 365 days in one year.

Perhaps saying "I don't have enough time" is just another way of suggesting you just don't want to. We don't necessarily have that option with mandatory commitments, yet many obligations are optional.

Key Point:

Beware of living a hurried, busy life. Hustling in the pursuit of feeling relevant will come at a cost and will not provide what you are seeking.

Challenge:

- Prior to committing to negotiable requests, hit pause.
- Reflect on how this will fit in your life.
- What are you willing to subtract to make room for it?
- Communicating a clear yes or no to people is an assertive exercise and is essential for healthy boundary setting.

DISTRACTIBILITY

Do you find yourself becoming easily sidetracked? You are likely experiencing this because you are constantly interrupted by invaders such as texts, slack messages, notifications, reminders, and so on. You are not faulty if this is the case. Reminders are designed to interrupt you, yet they are more disruptive to your attention than beneficial.

The omnipresence of technology, as well as the numerous ways it accesses us, is damaging our attention patterns. The urge to be connected and respond quickly to new inputs is driven by the abundance of information and communication. People are under pressure from both real and self-imposed nonstop demands.

Distractibility is a common current condition. Managing attention and staying focused is challenging for many people these days.

Was it always this way? Have people always been this easily distracted?

In modern times, can we blame digitalization for our attention crisis? Is it all external factors that are causing a lack of focus? It's easy to point the finger at our gadgets, the internet, social media, and innumerable communication channels. Why don't we just go on a digital detox if that's the case? What about just removing ourselves from the invaders by turning off our devices?

Amishi P. Jha researches **attention**. In her recent book, *Peak Mind,* she challenges this idea by reminding us how people have been turning to yoga, meditation, and contemplation practices since ancient times to offer relief.[93]

We can become distracted by external factors or internal disruptors (negative self-talk). Despite external inputs and reminders pinging us, much brain drain is still in our heads: worries, regrets, thoughts, emotions, envy, etc.

Procrastination and distraction are related. The primary reason we procrastinate is to avoid emotional discomfort. Common distractors also release us from emotional distress. If you have ever grabbed your phone without realizing it to check messages, you can relate.

Key Points:

While external inputs can be distracting, what often erodes our attention are internal factors (self-doubt, negative thinking, worries, etc.), creating unnecessary static and noise.

Challenge:

Observe what internal distractions are keeping you from being present and focused at the moment.

MIND-WANDERING VS. DAYDREAMING

Jha distinguishes mind-wandering (having off-task thoughts when engaged in a task) vs. daydreaming (task-free, providing ourselves the chance to have spontaneous thought, conscious reflection, and creativity).

There can be benefits to allowing yourself to daydream on occasion for the mind to explore and not be constricted. Daydreaming allows the brain to go inward and develop its own stream of conscious ideas separate from the external world and reality. In this condition, your attention is unguided and inwardly focused.

Mind-wandering is having thoughts that are unrelated to the task at hand, potentially causing distraction or difficulty focusing. Daydreaming can be intentional, while mind-wandering can be intrusive. Either taken to an extreme can be disruptive.

Key Points:

There is a difference between intentional daydreaming and mind-wandering that reduces our effectiveness. While some daydreaming is enjoyable and healthy, like most things, if you overdo it, it can interfere. Mind-wandering may be experiencing off-topic thoughts that are likely rooted yet not relevant to the task at hand.

MULTITASKING

Distractions in today's world leave us exhausted, pressured, and overwhelmed. Multitasking is enticing because it allows you to get more done in less time. However, multitasking can be draining and often contributes to inefficiency. We must acknowledge our processing systems' limitations: we are serial processors, not parallel processors. Our minds are not operating systems like computers.

For most involved or complex matters, the brain is not designed to simultaneously engage in multiple tasks. Instead, the brain is toggling and shifting back and forth between activities. This process proves to be inefficient. Studies indicate that this shifting results in tasks taking more than twice as long to complete.[94]

Take a moment to consider everything that is currently in front of you. If you're like me, you've got several browser windows open (each with tabs you "need"). In the background, your email inbox is steadily filling up. Instant messages start popping up. And, of course, there's your phone. To put it another way, you're multitasking.

True multitasking — doing more than one job at the same time — is a fallacy, according to various studies. The reality is that people who believe they can divide their attention between many tasks at the same time aren't accomplishing more. They do less, are more stressed out, and do worse than those who only perform one task at a time.

I am guilty of succumbing to the temptation of multitasking. However, for tasks that require cognitive exertion, it doesn't work. We are intended to focus on one thing of significance at a time. While we can likely make dinner and listen to music at the same time, we can't effectively process two sets of inputs simultaneously.

A 2009 Stanford study confirmed the brain is incapable of multitasking.[95] When we try to multitask, our brain works harder by switching between multiple tasks quickly. This context switching is draining and provides enough of an interruption that it can take up to 20 minutes to refocus on the original task. That's a lot of wasted time.

In *Altered Traits*, experts Daniel Goleman and Richard Davidson describe a phenomenon called attentional blinks.[96] This is the reduced level of attention after we identify something we have been focusing on. A simple example is a Where's Waldo exercise. After an individual identifies Waldo, there is a temporary blind spot in one's perception, reducing the ability to intake additional information.

Key Point:

As you focus on one thing, it leaves your attentional resources lacking for the next available cue.

Challenge:

The attentional blink can be lessened through mindfulness training and practice.

- Specifically, vipassana meditation lessens the blink since it cultivates an "open-monitoring" practice of awareness.
- Vipassana meditation is the practice of scanning your body with attention and observing sensations that arise without reacting.

Similarly, don't be lulled into pretending to work. Most people check their emails more than 70 times a day. Pretending to work is when you are attending to something, yet it really isn't resulting in a productive outcome. You are spinning your wheels. Audit your pretend-to-work tendencies.

Sophie Leroy researches the impact of constant task switching on the brain. Her research shows that the brain finds it difficult to switch between tasks, resulting in attention residue. When we shift from Task A to Task B, part of our attention often stays with the prior task (A) instead of fully transferring to the next task (B). According to Leroy, attention residue happens when tasks are left unfinished, and we carry this concern to the next demand at hand.[97]

What this means is that we have fewer cognitive resources available to perform the second, subsequent task, and performance is inclined to suffer.

Key Points:

How you monitor and manage your attention can affect **mental health and well-being**. Shifting too frequently compromises the quality of your attention and thinking. Attention residue clogs your problem-solving systems and harms productivity and performance.

MANAGING YOUR ATTENTION

Thankfully, you can compensate and proactively manage your attention. Richard Davidson and colleagues have researched attention extensively. A groundbreaking study in 2007 provided strong evidence that the brain's attentional systems can be trained.

Maura Nevel Thomas writes about attention management and proposes that to manage your life, you need to control what you pay attention to. A key part of managing stress and being productive, according to Thomas, is strengthening our skills in attention management. [98]

Attention management is the practice of controlling distractions, being present and mindful in the moment, experiencing flow, and maximizing focus. It involves being proactive and intentional rather than reactive in the face of circumstances. It is a reminder that we can focus on activities that we choose based on our life priorities and goals.

According to Thomas, since productivity is about directing your activities to what is important to **you**, managing your attention is how to pursue the life you want.

◇◇

A disciplined mind leads to happiness, and an undisciplined mind leads to suffering.[99]
—Dalai Lama XIV, *The Art of Happiness*

◇◇

Key Points:

- The quality of your attention determines the quality of your life.
- The more your mind wanders, the less happy you'll be.
- When you aren't paying attention, inputs are not integrated, synthesized, and encoded. In other words, you don't learn either.
- Your attention is a valuable commodity.
- We all experience modern external as well as internal distractions. You are, however, not doomed to the impact of distraction.
- You can enhance your ability to concentrate and focus and decrease your tendency to procrastinate through practice.

Challenge:
Attention Management Interventions

- Listen to white noise while concentrating.
- Turn off all notifications, reminders, slack channels, etc. Consider turning your phone off or put it on airplane mode when engaging in work.
- Physical exercise enhances focus for several hours after the activity.
- Increase exposure to sunlight in the a.m.
- Schedule 90-minute increments for deeper work; 20-minute blocks for tactical work.

ATTENTION REGULATION MINDFULNESS PRACTICE

Here is another endorsement of how meditation can help you (more on mindfulness and meditation later). Mindfulness practices foster effective attention management. As Sharon Salzberg has said, "We don't meditate to get better at meditating; we meditate to get better at life." A key benefit of meditation is attention regulation, as the effects are even more pronounced for those who tend to multitask frequently.

In a 2016 experiment, two groups of participants were asked to take a concentration test. Prior to taking the test, one group meditated for 10 minutes, and the other surfed the internet for 10 minutes. The meditators performed better, and the improvement was most notable for the multi-taskers.[100]

A 2013 study supports the long-term impact of meditation: students who learned and practiced meditation for two weeks prior to a graduate school entrance exam improved their scores by up to 30 percent.[101] Teens and parents with teens, you may want to re-read that last sentence.

◇◇◇

I cannot say this frequently enough. The goal is not to clear your mind but to focus your mind—for a few nanoseconds at a time—and whenever you become distracted, just start again. Getting lost and starting over is not failing at meditation, it is succeeding.[102]
—Dan Harris, *Ten Percent Happier*

◇◇◇

17-MINUTE PRACTICE

According to scientist Andrew Huberman, a simple one-time 17-minute practice of closing your eyes, quietly resting, and paying attention to your breath and inner state can produce long-term attention enhancement. This activity can rewire your brain and possibly even offset age-related cognitive and memory decline. It is an accessible intervention that can help with ADHD symptoms.

OPTIMIZING ALERTNESS AND COGNITIVE FOCUS

Our body temperature is at a low point two hours before we wake up. As we rise, the body temperature increases, which triggers cortisol and increases focused cognition. Huberman reminds us that according to this model, our prime cognitive focus time is four to six hours after our temperature is minimum (2–4 hours after we wake up). Try scheduling more complex tasks during this time.

CHAPTER 4

DEEP WORK

Cal Newport, a computer science professor at Georgetown University, created the term "deep work" and expanded on it in *Deep Work: Rules for Focused Success in a Distracted World*.[103] He endorsed the importance of engaging in the lost practice of deep work, which he defined as distraction-free, high-concentration work that improves your skills and creates more value in less time.

Conversely, he described shallow work as non-cognitively demanding tasks with little focus and often done while distracted (checking emails, social media feeds, instant messages). For knowledge workers, the movement away from deep work is coming at a cost in terms of our stress as well as the quality of work output. According to Newport, deep work is difficult, and shallow work is easier, making visible busyness a proxy for productivity.

Deep work is particularly important for current-day knowledge workers, as they are expected to process high volumes of information. Engaging in deep work is valuable because it optimizes the amount of productivity in a certain amount of time.

It is focusing, single tasking, for extended periods of time, without interruption. Doing so, you access a deeper level of brain processing, maximizing creativity and big ideas. The two core skills needed for deep work are the ability to concentrate intensely and the ability to overcome distraction.

Newport's rules are as follows:

1. Create rituals for deep work habits.
2. Embrace boredom. Train the skill of intense concentration without giving way to the discomfort of boredom.
3. Quit social media. The addictive elements of social media are not conducive to deep work and deep thinking. Social media = shallow work.

4. Drain the shallows. Avoid shallow, low-value tasks. *The Shallows* is a book written about the negative effects of the internet on our brains and lives.

While most of us aren't ready to quit social media altogether, we could benefit from applying some of these key principles to engage in more deep work.

SPEED/FASTER

There is also a lot of emphasis on quickness. Carl Honoré, a Canadian journalist, acknowledges we live in a period when we are hooked to speed.[104] Speed dating, text messaging, crash courses, and drive-throughs are all readily available options. Meditations can even be listened to twice as fast (not that I would know).

It can seem as if we are racing against the clock, contributing to feeling rushed and mindless. But one can only go so quickly for so long. It affects your physical and emotional health, as well as how you interact with others.

Hurried people are less likely to be nice and more likely to act impatiently. According to Daniel Kahneman's research, people in interpersonal circumstances are more inclined to make incorrect decisions. Consistently operating at a frenetic pace reduces the quality of judgment, impedes learning, and can lead to emotional dysregulation.

Neuroscience research demonstrates that when individuals are in a relaxed, calm state, the brain is engaged in deeper and more nuanced complex modes of thinking. Psychologists refer to this as slow thinking.[105]

While moving faster may be useful in some situations, we have hit a point of diminishing returns. Faster isn't always better. There is something called the "Slow Movement" that is getting momentum. From Slowmovement.com:

> The Slow Movement aims to address the issue of 'time poverty' by making connections. This website supports a growing cultural shift toward slowing down. On this site, we discuss how we have lost connection to most aspects of our lives and the natural world and rhythms around us, and how we can reconnect—how we can live a connected life.

People are longing to downshift. There is a trend toward minimalism; people who are choosing voluntary simplicity in all aspects of their life.

Key Point:

Faster isn't always better. Being rushed and hurried can cause you to be mean, impatient, and less effective.

Challenge:

Slow down. Practice mindfulness, although a few minutes daily. Consider the benefits of slowing down and downshifting in even small ways to a more connected life.

THE STOP ACTIVITY

According to Dr. Amishi Jha, we are missing out on 50 percent of our life because we are not paying attention.

She distinguishes three sorts of focus:

- The flashlight: a specific, restricted, and focused source of information
- The floodlight: wide, open, and on the periphery
- The juggler: a director, supervisor, and manager

Jha claims that we are all addicted to thinking and doing and that we are less skilled at "being." According to her findings, mindfulness meditation can help us adjust our attention system in a more positive direction.

Jha suggests "anchoring your attention in the present moment and experiencing it without editorializing or making up a tale about what's occurring or will happen." You can improve mental focus, eliminate fog and static, and simplify your mind, helping you live more fully. STOP is an abbreviation for a mindfulness exercise she suggests, like taking a quick brain check.

S: Stop what you're doing.

T: Take a few deep breaths. Re-establish a connection with your breath as a grounding anchor.

O: Observe what's going on within and outside of you.

P: Proceed. Go ahead. Keep doing what you've been doing or don't, based on what you gathered during this brain check. Either way, do it intentionally.[106]

TIME FAMINE

Do you ever feel short on time? Or starved for time? According to U.S. survey results, time stress has a greater negative impact on happiness than being unemployed, which is widely regarded as a common stressor for people. New terms have emerged to capture this sentiment. Researchers Tim Kasser and Kennon Sheldon developed the phrase "time affluence."[107]

They discovered that having an abundant attitude and relationship with time was associated with subjective well-being. Time affluence refers to the feeling that you have sufficient time for nonwork, to pursue activities that are personally meaningful, and to reflect. On the other hand, time poverty is the feeling that one is constantly stressed, rushed, overworked, and behind.

◇◇◇

This situation is so severe it could be described as a 'time famine'—a collective cultural failure to effectively manage our most precious resource, time.[108]
—Tal-Ben-Shahar, *Happier*

◇◇◇

In his book *Happier,* Tal-Ben-Shahar claims that time affluence is at an all-time low. According to a survey of 2.5 million Americans, 80 percent of them do not have enough time to do all their daily tasks. One way to feel wealthy, according to Tal-Ben-Shahar, is to **feel** as though you have an abundance of time for what you need and want to do.

People who feel stressed about time are more likely to be depressed, worried, and unhappy than those who believe they have plenty of spare time.

In a *Harvard Business Review* article, Professor Ashley Whillans describes the term "time confetti" to describe our fractured experience with time. She suggests that while we are striving to increase work and productivity, our sense of time is fragmented due to distractions, leading to increased stress.[109]

TIME VS. MONEY

Beyond meeting basic needs, pursuing time affluence appears to be more beneficial to mental health than the pursuit of more money. Research suggests that people who are willing to give up money in exchange for time are happier than those who spend time trying to make more money.

MAKE TIME COUNT

As people age, they become more aware of how finite time is. According to the socioemotional selectivity theory, as people get older, their focus changes, and they gain more appreciation for their limited time. It can lead to an existential shift: a realignment of priorities, goals, and how to spend time. Age doesn't need to determine this shift in values. You can choose at any time how you view time. You can upgrade the story you tell yourself about how much time you have and how you want to spend it.

Key Point:

Fostering a positive attitude about time promotes well-being and feeling psychologically fit.

Challenge:

Focus on developing time affluence rather than a time-poor mindset.

- Do a time audit; track how you spend your time. Log your activities for a week and note your satisfaction, enjoyment, and effectiveness. Making observations can be an intervention in how you spend your time.
- Find opportunities to decrease or outsource tasks that are low on satisfaction and enjoyment. Increase activities to rank higher in those categories.
- Challenge your assumptions about time, so you are fostering a sense of abundance rather than scarcity.

EXHAUSTION

Once again, we are living in a time of overcommitment and overwhelm. People are feeling exhausted and overdone. Working too hard is detrimental to mental and physical health; it can make you sick. Hard work is not only valued in American culture. In Japan, there is a term to describe death from overwork: karoshi.

Brigid Schulte, founding director of The Good Life Initiative and author of *Overwhelmed: Work, Love, and Play When No One Has the*

Time, reminds us that excess work hours are associated with over 120,000 deaths per year.[110]

The health risks are severe. Cardiovascular diseases, musculo-skeletal disorders, psychological disorders, suicide, cancers, ulcers, and impaired immune function are the top health issues associated with feeling overworked, according to the Centers for Disease Control and Prevention (CDC).

Studies have demonstrated a correlation between the hours that people work in a week and the risk of a heart attack. Individuals working 55 hours a week were 16 percent more likely to develop a risk for heart attack compared to those working 45 hours a week. Those working 65-hour weeks had a 33 percent increased risk.[111]

Once again, according to the American Institute of Stress, feeling overworked can also be destructive to your mental health. Stress is correlated with 75 to 90 percent of medical visits and is estimated to cost the U.S. economy approximately $600 billion annually.

The WHO found that 488 million people were exposed to the risks of working long hours, and more than 745,000 people died that year from overwork, which resulted in a stroke and heart disease.[112]

It's also clear that increasing work hours is not correlated to better outputs. While Japan is known for long workdays, the country has a lower productivity rate than most. On the other hand, Norway has an average workweek of 37.5 hours and has significantly higher productivity rates. These are clear signals that something needs to change, and we can make changes.

Meet Kai. Kai is a high-achieving professional who experienced burnout early in his career. After a period of recovery, internal work, and personal growth, he transitioned to a new industry and organization. He remains proactively and consistently engaged in working on his mental health and well-being.

Insights from Kai:

*Where I'm from, people are taught to turn the fatigue off —
throughout high school, college, and in the workforce. Because
it's seen as a sign of weakness. I learned at a very young age to
ignore the signs of long-term fatigue and ended up on a path of
burnout. My stress would accumulate over time. I had trouble
identifying when I was tired and making sense of the cues my
body was telling me. It has helped to learn techniques, both
having more awareness and developing resilience coping skills.*

*It has been challenging to be able to identify what kind of mental health state I'm in. I've had to practice taking a deep breath,
checking in with myself, and being able to identify my emotions
and how I'm feeling. I've buckled down and made changes to
make longer-term impacts toward living my best life. I'm trying
to live a more intentional life. A key part of that is prioritizing
recovery.*

Key Point:

You can make personal changes to avoid exhaustion.

Challenge:

Take more time for recovery.

THE ERA OF INDULGENCE

◇◇◇

*We humans are unhappy in large part because we are
insatiable; after working hard to get what we want, we
routinely lose interest in the object of our desire. Rather
than feeling satisfied, we feel a bit bored, and in response
to this boredom, we go on to form new,
even grander desires.*[113]
—William B. Irvine, *A Guide to the Good Life:
The Ancient Art of Stoic Joy*

◇◇◇

Humans have also always faced the challenge of INDULGENCE: the pursuit of pleasure and the gratification of desire. The hedonic treadmill is a metaphor for our tendency to persistently pursue one pleasure after another. We feel a momentary sense of bliss, yet we return to baseline quickly. Hedonic happiness defines well-being in terms of the attainment of pleasure and feeling good and avoiding pain.[114]

On the other hand, eudaimonic happiness is achieved through experiences of meaning, purpose, and self-realization. The problem is the insatiability of pleasure; it is impossible to **stay** satisfied.

A common experience is when we reach a lofty goal and have a feeling of emptiness afterward. Michael Phelps speaks to this experience after breaking Olympic records and winning gold medals in swimming competitions. In the HBO documentary *Weight of Gold*, he describes experiencing a sense of sadness, depression, or even despair soon after his victories.

The concept of hedonic adaptation suggests we adjust quickly and return to a set point. For example, individuals who win the lottery return to their original levels of happiness after the novelty wears off. Some even report feeling less happy months after their win. Conversely, people who experience major accidents and experience physical disabilities generally return to their pre-accident happiness levels after they have habituated.

A simple daily example is how our first sip of coffee tastes great in the morning yet loses its effect after a few cups.

The definition of indulgence is to give way to our desires. Those who find themselves in constant pursuit of pleasure will realize the target keeps moving. We never get quite enough, especially of things we don't need.

We live in an era of overabundance, with risks and temptations more accessible than ever. Anna Lembke addresses this in *Dopamine Nation*. She reports that 70 percent of the world's deaths are attributable to modifiable behavioral risk factors like smoking, physical inactivity, and diet.[115]

Engaging in hedonistic behaviors and pursuing pleasure only for pleasure's sake backfire and result in anhedonia. Anhedonia describes a reduced interest in activities a person used to enjoy. It refers to a decreased ability to feel pleasure, which speaks to the paradox of the hedonic cycle.

As mentioned, Daniel Lieberman highlights how dopamine is more interested in the chase and pursuit, not the experience itself. Dopamine is about anticipation and moving toward not the actual experience of pleasure. The presence of dopamine indicates possibility and seeking, not arriving.

Conversely, the H&N's (here and now chemicals) are what provide pleasure from current emotion and sensation. H&N's include oxytocin, endorphins, serotonin, and endocannabinoids. An example of an endocannabinoid is anandamide, coined after a Sanskrit word representing delight, bliss, and joy.

According to Lieberman, dopamine is all about **getting** things, not **having** or experiencing things. If you live in a tent, dopamine makes you want a house. If you live in a cabin on a lake, dopamine makes you want a mansion on the lake. It has no standard for good and seeks no finish line.

According to Lieberman, "The dopamine circuits in the brain can be stimulated only by the possibility of whatever is shiny and new; never mind how perfect things are at the moment. The dopamine motto is 'more.'"[116]

Isn't there a **middle path,** a way to find a happy medium? Just enough pursuit, just enough tension, and just enough pleasure? In his book, *The Sweet Spot*, Paul Bloom proposes that painful experiences are not to be avoided at all costs. He suggests discomfort adds value to life if experienced in the right balance.[117]

He describes how the pain-pleasure paradox can explain why suffering can lead to satisfaction. Why do people pursue experiences that will promote pain and suffering? Training for endurance events, watching disturbing movies, or eating spicy foods?

Life is full of paradoxical reactions. We cry about sad, happy, and funny things, and we cry when we're nervous. The opponent process theory of experience reminds us how our minds seek balance and homeostasis. So, after a period of pain, we can experience more pleasure than we would have without the initial sense of pain.

You can engineer circumstances to enhance future pleasure in this way. Taking an ice bath provides the initial discomfort of cold and can enhance the sense of relief afterward. Similarly, if you step into a hot bath, it can burn for a second, but the calming effect of it can feel worth it.

Bloom describes motivational pluralism, how we are a blend of complicated motivation, drive, and enthusiasm in search of the sweet spot that will maximize our life experience...noted in his subtitle, the "key to a good life."

Key Point:

Doing hard things can be rewarding and worth the suffering.

Challenge:

Consider how you can apply these paradox principles. Can you engineer a healthy balance in your life, aligning your efforts or discomfort to maximize the benefits?

WE ARE FED LIES

What does success look like? We are all raised with some version of what life — the dream — is supposed to be. Here are a few versions of it: get good grades, participate in extracurriculars, build your resume, get into a good college, get a well-paying job, get married, buy a house, have two kids, drive a nice car, get a promotion, etc.

The consumerism version: if you wear this cologne or perfume, you'll attract a future mate; if you drive this car, you'll be admired; if you wear this brand, you'll be desired; if you use this computer, you are cool.

Once you do all that, you'll be happy and successful. Inevitably, at every step along the way, once a milestone is met, we are quick to move on to the next. After a few years of adulthood, people often pause, scratch their heads, thinking, wait a minute… ***IS THIS IT****? **Is this all there is? After all that sacrifice?***

Beneath the surface, there can be an underlying belief: ***I was told if I did all this, then I would be happy. All the chase,***

hustle, accumulation of wealth, achievement, and success...
all for what? A whole lot of stress and responsibility.

Is it worth it? This developmental phase often happens around age 40. As one nears 50, it can become more like, **wait a second, this is crap.** We spend all this time in pursuit of the next thing and worrying about what people think. Now we realize **it doesn't matter what people think, and they were never thinking of us, to begin with.** This insight is gained through life experience, and we can't necessarily hurry along the learning.

Meet my client Jaylen. He is a high-achieving, successful professional who is an amazing, insightful, and self-aware human.

Insights from Jaylen:

I had always self-identified that my life is great, but I'm still depressed. I have a great partner, I'm athletic, and I have a great job. My family is healthy and loves me. I have friends that care about me.

Despite all of this, I've been very much struggling for most of my life. I still feel a ton of pain. I'm still languishing in a lot of ways. Growing up, I had misconceptions about what the path to thriving looks like. I had a childhood filled with Disney films and young adulthood filled with Facebook and Instagram. We're given a repeated message of here's what happily ever after looks like.

If you do XYZ, you never have to worry about anything for the rest of your life. In a lot of ways, you're being sold the Greenwich housewife story. If you have a lot of money, family, and friends and you don't have to worry about anything.... Then your life's just perfect, and that's just kind of what you do for the rest of your life.

I've felt confusion and discomfort with those messages. The first step on the road to recovery for me was to be able to sit and try to understand my pain more.

What I've learned is that you can work on mental health just like any skill set. I never thought about how you can train for better mental health, just like physical health. I've learned that I could practice intervention and generate a higher rating on the mental health continuum at any time.

I also have more awareness now that my state changes. A week ago, I was overwhelmed and having a down moment. This week I have more energy and feel more engaged. I've learned that happiness is a skill you can learn and work on. Learning to set realistic goals has been helpful. Actually, realistic isn't the right word. More like attainable. Thinking about my best attainable self rather than my best self is better.

FEAR OF BOREDOM

Untrained warriors are soon killed on the battlefield, so persons untrained in the art of preserving their inner peace are quickly riddled by the bullets of worry and restlessness in active life.[118]
—Paramahansa Yogananda, *Autobiography of a Yogi*

Restlessness is a pervasive condition. People fear idleness. Results from a University of Virginia 2014 study suggest that most people prefer pain to boredom. According to this research, people would rather **give themselves an electric shock** than sit quietly and think. Wait…what? Yes, you read that right.

◇◇

In 11 studies, we found that participants typically did not enjoy spending 6 to 15 minutes in a room by themselves with nothing to do but think, that they enjoyed doing mundane external activities much more, and that many preferred to administer electric shocks to themselves instead of being left alone with their thoughts. Most people seem to prefer to be doing something rather than nothing, even if that something is negative.[119]
—University of Virginia psychologist
Timothy Wilson et al.

◇◇

Participants who elected to self-zap gave themselves an average of 1.47 shocks in a 15-minute interval. One participant shocked himself 190 times. Scientists strive to make sense of this occurrence. In short, it points to humans fearing idleness. There is a fine line between idleness and boredom. According to writer Colin Wilson, most animals dislike boredom, but humans are tormented by it.[120]

BOREDOM can uncover uncomfortable thoughts and feelings, which are often blurred with activity, busyness, and movement. As Virginia Woolf stated, we are "always giving parties to cover the silence."

Researchers from the shock study propose that one explanation is that the untrained mind does not like to be alone with itself. Is it that the brain prefers to be active, the negativity bias of the brain searches for potential threats, or our typical environments provide excessive stimulation?

There is even something called boredom anxiety. Thaasophobia is described as the fear of sitting still, being idle, and being bored.

Even if fearing boredom doesn't resonate, many are at least uncomfortable with downtime because it has become unfamiliar. We no longer have a natural cadence of downtime when our minds can explore, drift, and daydream.

In *Doing Nothing is Something*, Anna Quindlen writes, "I don't believe you can write poetry, or compose music, or become an actor without downtime — and plenty of it — a hiatus that passes for boredom but is really the quiet moving of the wheels inside that fuel creativity."[121]

Not having regular downtime comes at a cost, and when it does occur, it makes people nervous. There is also a name for leisure anxiety, freizeitstress.

Do you ever feel stressed about how to spend your free time? It could be that you want to fill your free time with as many activities as possible, which can generate anxiety. Or you may feel restless when your calendar is open, not knowing how to best use your time. When your schedule is richly full, and then there is a gap with no plans, it can create low-grade discomfort.

Cultivating some feeling of boredom can cause us to look more deeply within ourselves and tap into insight that is not available on the surface and during the daily hustle of life.

A generation that cannot endure boredom will be a generation of little men, of men unduly divorced from the slow processes of nature, of men in whom every vital impulse slowly withers as though they were cut flowers in a vase.[122]
—Bertrand Russell, *The Conquest of Happiness*

Every summer, we bring groups of our kids' friends to our summer lake cabin, which is a remote location in nature. There is no cable, no landline, or big screen TV's. The kids who have been coming up for years understand and appreciate the atmosphere. For a few, it can take a few days to settle in. You can sense the initial discomfort some have with the reduction in screen stimuli. They all do eventually sink into the rhythm of being at the lake and quickly decompress.

It's an experience of replenishment and nourishment for your soul that can be accessed when you are removed from the daily stressors of life. It's time on the lake, sleeping in, taking walks, enjoying sunsets, campfires, boat rides, floating on the lake, deep conversations, leisurely meals, and board games. I call it my happy place.

Regardless of these potential factors contributing to restlessness, you can engage in practices to train your mind. To increase your tolerance for boredom, consider spending more time sitting still, reflecting, contemplating, being quiet, and seeing what shows up for you.

Key Points:

- You can train your mind by engaging in intentional reflection practices.
- The more you rush, the less you reflect.
- The less you reflect, the less you understand.
- The less you understand your thoughts and feelings, the more you will remain stuck.
- The more stuck you are, the more likely you are to become hostage to your negative emotions and thoughts.

Challenge:

Spend more quiet time contemplating. It will broaden your perspective and enhance your emotional health.

ACCOUNTABILITY VS. VICTIM MINDSET

People who have a victim mindset are perpetually frustrated and disappointed. They feel like bad things happen to them. This attitude fosters a sense of helplessness and thoughts such as:

Why bother trying? It won't work. I've already tried all of that. Nothing works.

People with a victim mindset tend to foster the idea that people are against them or the world is against them. They often feel like things are out of their control.

It can be tempting to blame others and circumstances for misfortune. It can be lulling to sink into this negativity, as it can feel safe and familiar. While it can be tempting to stay there because then you don't need to take accountability, what feels good in the moment isn't necessarily good for you.

Being accountable takes work. Taking responsibility requires exertion, effort, and often doing things you don't want to do or FEEL like doing.

In *The ONE Thing*, Gary Keller says, "Taking complete ownership of your outcomes by holding no one but yourself responsible for them is the most powerful thing you can do to drive your success."[123]

The antidote to feeling helpless or like a victim is to take accountability. You are responsible for your reaction to life circumstances. Believing you are a victim of your situation is sacrificing your personal power.

The previously mentioned author and endurance athlete David Goggins is all about extreme accountability. He states denial is the ultimate comfort zone but will get in our way. He warns of the risk of victim or entitlement thinking. "Don't focus on what you think you deserve. Take aim at what you are willing to earn." He aligns with the path of the warrior — one who shows up consistently, no matter what.

In his works, Fred Kofman uses the terms **victim** and **player** to describe these attitudes of openness or defensiveness you can adopt in challenging situations.[124] Someone with a victim mindset focuses on what they can't control. Being a victim helps one to avoid the blame by focusing on external factors and other people. Conversely, players focus on factors they can influence, which creates personal empowerment.

Key Points:

Being a victim will keep you stuck. Being a player provides constructive agency over your life, which will build your sense of self and self-esteem.

Challenge:

No one is coming to save you. Take responsibility.

It's in responsibility that most people find the meaning that sustains them through life. It's not in happiness. It's not in impulsive pleasure.
—Jordan B. Peterson, author and psychologist

You can find hope and encouragement in fostering your sense of personal agency and ability to make progress. Experiencing agency is feeling in command of your life and taking responsibility for being the author of your story. Passivity is the opposite of agency. Having a victim mindset is also the opposite of personal agency.

A victim mindset is believing that everything happens "to us" and that we are helpless in the face of the circumstances we face, leading to hopelessness and disempowerment.

❮❯

Character—the willingness to accept responsibility
for one's own life—is the source from which
self-respect springs.[125]
—Joan Didion, author

❮❯

Key Point:

Taking accountability for your life is necessary for empowerment and fostering agency. A victim mindset can be tempting, but it leads to helplessness.

Challenge:

Drop what you no longer want to carry, what is getting in the way, and what is holding you back. You can decide to let go of shoulds, resentments, false expectations, and victim thinking, the undercurrents of self-doubt and guilt.

❮❯

Progress is the product of human agency. Things get
better because we make them better.
—Susan Rice, American diplomat and author

❮❯

OBSTACLES AS OPPORTUNITIES

Some see difficulties as significant obstacles and major setbacks. There is an old story about two shoe salesmen sent to a remote area to sell shoes. One salesman wrote to his company, **"I'm not going to be able to sell shoes here. No one wears any."**

The other salesperson wrote, **"Great opportunity to sell shoes here. No one has any."**

Former Navy SEAL commander Jocko Willink is the ultimate accountability guy. He fully embraces the title of his book, *Extreme Ownership*. His response to problems is, "Good! When things are going bad, there is gonna be some good that's gonna come from it. Got beaten? Good. You learned. We have the opportunity to figure out a solution."[126]

Key Point:

You can adapt the stories you tell yourself about problems.

Challenge:

Find the opportunity in the perceived obstacles and setbacks you are experiencing.

ADVERSITY/TRAUMA

To state the obvious, not all pain and suffering are equal. Feeling stressed about being stuck in traffic is not like the trauma involved in crises like abuse, war, disease, etc. Regardless of the level, severity, frequency, and intensity of adversity, life is going to be a struggle. It is **not supposed to be easy**. I mention this because we often feel disappointed and surprised when something bad happens like this isn't supposed to happen "to me."

When you get to the top of a mountain, while you can enjoy and rest for a minute, you'll soon realize there's just another mountain to climb. You don't ever overcome all challenges and get to the place of no problems.

Life is cyclical. When going through tough times, perhaps you can find solace in the notion that this too shall pass. Prior to COVID-19, it was reported in a World Health Organization (WHO) study that 70 percent of people across 24 countries have experienced traumas, with an average of 3.2 traumatic events over the course of a lifetime.[127] The coronavirus pandemic has accelerated the rate of anxiety and risk for post-traumatic stress (PTS). PTS is 83 percent higher now than prior to COVID-19.

Bessel van der Kolk wrote the brilliant book, *The Body Keeps the Score: Brain, Mind, and Body in the Healing of Trauma*. He speaks to the powerful impact of trauma and the mind and body:

> *Traumatized people chronically feel unsafe inside their bodies. The past is alive in the form of gnawing interior discomfort. Their bodies are constantly bombarded by visceral warning signs, and, in an attempt to control these processes, they often become experts at ignoring their gut feelings and numbing awareness of what is played out inside. They learn to hide from their selves.*[128]

Van der Kolk suggests that keeping secrets and suppressing information about trauma create an internal war. He describes the healing power of allowing yourself to know what you know, which takes enormous courage.

He acknowledges how the traditional brain-disease model overlooks four components.

1. Our capacity to destroy one another is matched by our capacity to heal one another. Restoring relationships and community is central to restoring well-being. (This is huge-more on the power of connection and accompaniment later).

2. Language gives us the power to change ourselves and others by communicating our experiences, helping us to define what we know, and finding a common sense of meaning. Naming experiences provide meaning and sense-making.

3. We can regulate our physiology, including some involuntary functions of the body and brain, through breathing, moving, and touching.

4. We can adapt social conditions to create environments in which children and adults can feel safe and thrive.

Some trauma treatments use insight and understanding to manage memories and behavior; however, he proposes that trauma-related problems are not due to deficits in understanding. He describes how the triggers alert a deeper region of the brain driving perception and attention and how insight is not sufficient to address these triggers and alarms.

There are many effective treatment modalities to address trauma. There is hope in knowing people can heal and recover from traumatic experiences.

You may have heard of Madonna Badger, who speaks about resilience. She is a woman who, while living in New York, lost her three daughters and both parents in a fire. She shares how she learned from *The Tibetan Book of Living and Dying*.[129] She challenged herself to see the lighter side of things. Understanding how humor is creating space where she felt there was no space has been key to her healing process.

There was no way she could think her way out of why such a tragedy could occur. She realized she had to act. Experiencing such heavy grief, she just didn't want to move or move on. She describes trying to get through the days. It was all she could do to just get out of bed. Stand up. She would repeatedly tell herself, "You're not crazy. You are sad."

Badger reflects in her talks on how to find peace and how peace isn't an end game. She describes her loss as a God-shaped hole. Her journey has involved finding a spiritual life that makes sense to her. The hole can be filled when people choose to love, feel love, and forgive. Her story of recovery is powerful in terms of how she continues to choose to stand up rather than feel like a victim. Total inspiration.

Healing is supposed to hurt. It is tempting to search for a quick fix and temporary relief from a physical or emotional injury. The bleeding needs to be stopped, yet we need to ensure we have identified the source.

Recovering from trauma requires professional support and recovery plans. When people feel depressed and anxious, often the last thing they need to do is listen more to themselves. They need external support, guidance, and help.

◇◇

Although you may not always be able to avoid difficult situations, you can modify the extent to which you can suffer by how you choose to respond to the situation.[130]
—Dalai Lama XIV, *The Art of Happiness*

◇◇

Philosophical and Buddhist teachings have referenced a psychological equation of suffering, suggesting resisting reality is a pain multiplier. Suffering = Pain x Resistance.

As Kristen Neff writes in *Self-Compassion,* "Our emotional suffering is caused by our desire for things to be other than they are."[131] A small amount of pain, like waiting in long lines, can amplify suffering if we resist it.

Key Points:

- When you are in pain, you don't need to exacerbate the suffering.
- You will face adversity and unexpected obstacles during life.
- What determines your experience is how you view and accept it.
- Remembering that you are not a victim of your circumstances is empowering.
- You can even find joy in the discomfort with practice.
- While what doesn't kill you makes you stronger is an annoying cliché, there is some truth to the idea. We do not become strengthened by pleasant, passive experiences.

You have power over your mind—not outside events.
Realize this, and you will find strength.
—Marcus Aurelius

Much learning and growth come from overcoming difficulties in life. The path of least resistance does not have a great deal to teach us.

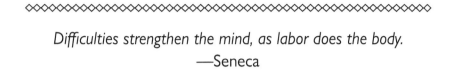

Difficulties strengthen the mind, as labor does the body.
—Seneca

There is hope for recovering from adversity and even using it as a transformational opportunity, and there is now a name for it. The concept of post-traumatic growth (PTG) was developed by Richard Tedeschi, Ph.D., and Lawrence Calhoun, Ph.D., describing positive psychological change experienced as a result of struggling with challenging, stressful circumstances.

It is the psychological transformation that can occur after a stressful situation — a way for people to see purpose in their struggle. According to Tedeschi and Calhoun, people can recover and thrive post-trauma and can even create a deeper appreciation of life.[132]

The theory suggests how transformational change can occur following trauma. People can create new and helpful insights and experience hopeful enlightenment. As they recover, the process can occur through therapeutic intervention or through personal reflection.

PTG can show up as positive responses in five areas: appreciation of life, relationships with others, new possibilities in life, personal strength, and spiritual change.

Key Points:

You can recover from adversity and trauma. You can also use it as a transformational opportunity for growth.

Challenge:

Upgrade your views on adversity. In what areas of your life can you see challenge and adversity as catalysts, learning moments, or opportunities? How can you redefine these experiences as crucible moments?

FORGIVENESS AS HEALING

Forgiveness is important for mental health and psychological fitness. It allows you to move beyond painful memories and upgrade a negative mindset that may be generating distress in your life. By learning to forgive, you empower yourself in new ways.

Forgiveness has been defined as a "***conscious, deliberate decision to release feelings of resentment or vengeance toward a person or group who has harmed you, regardless of whether they actually deserve your forgiveness.***"

Forgiveness does not mean approving of or excusing past offenses. It is simply choosing to let go of anger, bitterness, and resentment. Forgiveness is for you, not others. It is a process of change rather than an event.

FORGIVENESS IN PRACTICE

Forgiveness can be described as a process of decreasing negative resentment-based feelings, motivations, and thoughts. Psychologist Everett Worthington suggests a five-step process in the acronym REACH, often used in a therapeutic context.[133]

R = Recall a painful event. Think about a person who hurt you and feel the ill effect of the hurt. Do not wallow in self-pity. Take deep, slow, and calming breaths as you visualize the event.

E = Empathize from the perpetrator's point of view. When survival is threatened, a perpetrator may hurt innocent people.

A = Altruistic gift of forgiveness. This can be a difficult step. Recall a time when **you** hurt someone, felt guilty, and were forgiven.

C = Commit to a ritual of forgiveness. Write a "certificate of forgiveness," a letter of forgiveness, reflections in a journal, expressions in a work of art, poem, or song, or tell a trusted friend what you have done.

H = Hold onto forgiveness. This can be a difficult step because memories will recur. Forgiveness does not delete the event; rather, it is an adjustment in the narrative, story, and tag lines that a memory carries.

THE FORGIVENESS LETTER

Writing a forgiveness letter can facilitate self-healing and soothing. The letter should be written in physical form with pen and paper. It doesn't need to be structured but consider a few guidelines. Write your thoughts and feelings about the event that occurred. Describe when it happened and how it affected you after the event. Perhaps you can address what led up to the event and the details surrounding it. If it is helpful, you may consider what the other person was experiencing in their life. Consider ways to assert your intention in your words to live in the moment, let go of anger, and move forward.

PEOPLE-PLEASING

◇◇

If we seek social status, we give other people power over us. We have to do things calculated to make them admire us, and we have to refrain from doing things that will trigger their disfavor.[134]
—William B. Irvine, *A Guide to the Good Life: The Ancient Art of Stoic Joy*

◇◇

Many of us are raised to be **others-centered** and **people-pleasing.** We are conditioned to seek acceptance and approval from others. However, this can result in unhealthy concerns about what people think of us. It can become a never-ending pursuit of seeking applause and recognition.

Our definitions of success are often based on societal and cultural standards, commonly oriented toward material wealth and social status. These ideals can create internal suffering for people, as it can result in a never-ending state of chasing validation of worth in external sources.

Part of the antidote is to foster awareness of how this paradigm is not helpful. For optimal mental health and well-being, we need to transition our external locus of control to a stronger internal locus of control.

You will not truly enjoy life if you are enslaved to what others think. A key principle worth reviewing is that you are not responsible for others' behavior, and they are not responsible for your well-being and sense of self. What if you created a life where you were not emotionally dependent upon others' liking, approving of, or appreciating you? No one would have the power to make you happy or miserable. This is emotional freedom.

I'm not proposing not caring at all about what others think since that is not healthy. Having no concern or regard for the feelings of others describes sociopathology.

Key Point:

Unhooking and becoming unconsumed with what others think of you provides emotional freedom.

Challenge:

What would look different in your life without the burden of fearing the judgment of others?

What others think about you is none of your business.
—Jack Canfield

You are also not responsible for others' feelings. If you abandon yourself to relieve or rescue others from their emotional experience, you will find yourself in the danger zone. It is emotionally depleting, frustrating, and is not an effective strategy. It doesn't work.

Key Points:

My feelings are **my** job, and your feelings are **your** job. Maintaining those boundaries is essential to optimal mental health. You can care for others without losing sight of what your own needs are.

We don't need to set ourselves on fire to keep others warm.
—Audre Lorde, author

MARBLE GAME — THE PURSUIT OF VALIDATION

Gaelen Billingsley wrote an intriguing book describing the pursuit of validation from others that captured my attention. According to *The Marble Game, Therapeutic Metaphors for Life,* a common strategy to navigate through life is to avoid the judgment of others at all costs. Many people operate under the frantic need to find someone else to prove that they matter.[135]

Billingsley describes marble solicitation strategies, in which we engage with others looking for feedback and validation of how we matter. Humans fear that they will be exposed as being lazy, boring, or disappointed.

This conscious or unconscious baggage is what weighs us down and can keep us from being our best selves. Billingsley asserts that being alive is not safe and loss is inherent to change. No matter where we are on the trajectory of life, change will find us. It is a certain uncertainty.

Key Points:

Regarding others' approval, you can never get enough of something you don't need to begin with. If I had a magic wand, I wish for you to love and care for people without being controlled by their approval.

Challenge: Reminders for Emotional Freedom and Boundary Setting

- Avoid pleasing others at the cost of taking care of yourself.
- To take control of your life, decide to care a little less about what others think.
- Say "no" more often, even if it could disappoint others.
- Don't consistently compromise yourself to tend to the needs of others.
- Your feelings are your job; others' feelings are their job.
- What people think of you isn't your business.
- Move away from seeing others as a source of your well-being.
- Fear of displeasing others can put you in bondage to them.
- Persistently seeking validation from others will invalidate your self-worth.
- It is disempowering to put someone else in charge of your state of mind.

COMPARISON

<<<<<<<<<<<<<<<<<<<<<<<<<<<<<<<<<<<<<<<<<<<<<<<<<<<<<<<<<>

Comparison is the thief of joy.
—Theodore Roosevelt

<<<<<<<<<<<<<<<<<<<<<<<<<<<<<<<<<<<<<<<<<<<<<<<<<<<<<<<<<>

If you compare, you will despair. It is tempting to look at how others are succeeding or excelling and feel inadequate as a result. My dad always warned against this because there will always be people better looking, smarter, wealthier, more athletic, more productive, etc. You will also always find people who are less wealthy, attractive, athletic, smart, effective, etc. than you are. Either way, making these external comparisons is seldom helpful.

While we will naturally use social cues to help us navigate through the world, measuring and evaluating ourselves against others can be damaging. The key to a healthy life is finding your unique place in the world, understanding where you fit in, and accepting who you are without using the reference points of others.

Status anxiety is rampant with social media messages creeping into our lives, reminding us how insignificant and unimportant we are compared to others' highlight reels. It is an insidious, invisible influence that is eroding people's self-esteem and inserting external ideologies and ideals into their personal space.

People end up feeling subtly judged for not adding up or not being enough compared to the idyllic images they are receiving. Comparing your internal states with the external images of others' results is a faulty process. For years, psychology studies have confirmed that consistently comparing yourself to others can have a negative impact on your health, and it often fosters negative emotions.

Social media channels fuel envy by creating an illusion that others are happier and more fulfilled. A Stanford University study suggests people underestimate the discontent and problems others may be experiencing.

A client said to me recently, why is it always that everyone else is thriving except for me? It is common to *feel* like everyone else is doing awesome and *feel* like you're the only one with troubles.

Decades ago, research studies told us how looking at beauty magazines plummeted females' levels of self-esteem. The studies showed that women's level of self-worth drops significantly after seeing material showing airbrushed models. Making comparisons to others is unavoidable and understanding your social standing can be functional. However, there is a bombardment of too many inputs depicting polished versions of others who people are comparing themselves against.

It requires effort to resist the temptation of comparison. Be on alert for unfair comparisons that leave you feeling less. You can upgrade your thinking and appreciate that it's not a zero-sum game. Others' happiness, status, wealth, success, etc. doesn't need to take away from yours. There is enough awesomeness to go around.

Key Point:

Watch out for the comparison trap. It can lead to despair.

Challenge:

Take caution against comparing others' public announcements with your internal reality. Instead, ask yourself, am I improving? How am I growing? How am I investing in myself?

◇◇

Don't compare yourself with other people; compare yourself with who you were yesterday.
—Jordan Peterson, author and psychologist

◇◇

PERFECTIONISM

Perfectionism can be difficult to define, yet it generally involves the pursuit of unattainable standards and subsequent distress and self-doubt. Perfectionist thinking can keep you trapped and held hostage to what others think of you. It fuels the preoccupation with the judgment of others.

Perfectionism is pervasive among high achievers. Many resist identifying as a perfectionist because they insist they are far from perfect. It isn't about being perfect; it's the never-ending pursuit of excellence, yet the goal post keeps moving. People with maladaptive perfectionism end up in a perpetual cycle of seeking to be enough, yet they fall short, fueling distress and self-criticism, leading to self-destructive thinking and negative internal judgment.

Brené Brown, the author of *The Gifts of Imperfection,* among many other meaningful books, describes it best:

◇◇

Perfectionism is not the same thing as striving to be your best. Perfectionism is the belief that if we live perfect, look perfect, and act perfect, we can minimize or avoid the pain of blame, judgment, and shame. It's a shield.[136]

◇◇

Perfectionism is a trait typically driven by internal pressure to avoid judgment or failure. It involves setting unrealistically high expectations of self/others where good is never good enough. While various factors contribute, fear of disapproval, as well as feelings of insecurity and inadequacy, are common. It involves the unreasonable and self-defeating ambition of getting something absolutely correct.

Perfectionists create an abstract picture of an ideal situation, which is impossible in reality. They fail to budget for the right amount of time, effort, difficulty, and challenge that is required to achieve the desired goal.

Characteristics include unrealistic standards, fueled by fear and judgment, harshly self-critical, difficult to please, low self-esteem, procrastination, or fear of making mistakes. People with maladaptive perfectionism are at risk of developing a range of clinical issues, including depression, anxiety, eating disorders, etc.

In a large 2016 study on perfectionism and burnout, Hill and Curran found that individuals experienced very little or no benefit from having high personal standards compared to people who didn't have them. People with maladaptive perfectionism experienced significantly more burnout.[137]

High Achievers

High achievers often experience an internal force to progress and achieve the external success that can generate discontentment. This relentless pursuit can often result in loneliness and isolation. The internal drive can be experienced as an insatiable need to accomplish more and can be coming from a deficient emotional state.

Receiving external reinforcement for these accolades can amplify the need for more pursuing to prove value and worth. When scaling back is suggested to high achievers, there is often a fear of becoming complacent, content, or less than excellent. This is problematic because it can be driven by a sense of unworthiness, which does damage to the psyche.

It leads to a perpetual comparison of being better than, worse than, above, or below others. A partial antidote is a practice of caring just a little less. Caring too much can fuel distress and disease. Care **minus five** can lessen the emotional burden many high achievers carry.

Meet Bellamy. Bellamy is a professional who works in a high-pressure industry and is prone to internalizing stress. Facing exceptionally high expectations, Bellamy rarely takes a break or goes offline out of concern of disappointing superiors or team members. Bellamy experienced fear of setting boundaries and reported feeling a constant state of hypervigilance. However, as he was about to be a new parent, it was time to set some boundaries.

Insights from Bellamy:

I realized I just couldn't live in a state of being on, always available, and consumed with work. It's like I couldn't escape it. It became such a pattern and habit that I really didn't know another way.

I decided that I needed to scale back just a bit. A few times each day, I would focus on things other than work. It was uncomfortable. I didn't like it, but I did it anyway. I stopped giving an automatic yes to requests. Instead, I would take some time to think through a response and send back an alternative. The majority of the time, it was well received.

So, as I tested this out, it worked. People were okay with me scaling back. In fact, I'm the only one who noticed. The quality of my work didn't suffer; actually, it probably improved. And I feel a lot better.

Key Points:

You can embrace the pursuit of excellence without the toxic level of self-persecution. You can pursue and stretch without damaging and judging.

Challenge 1:

Accept yourself as you are. Know that you are enough. Consider emotional levity and embrace the lightness, so unnecessary pressures don't feel so heavy.

Challenge 2: Your Personal Book of Awesome Exercise

I recommend that you start keeping a journal or notebook to record your awesomeness, including but not limited to wins, achievements, people giving you thanks or gratitude, positive feedback, compliments, recognition, reinforcement, rewards, acknowledgments, expressions of admiration or love, etc.

Try to create a regular practice of writing these experiences, pen to paper. Keep your journal close by so you don't forget. Consider recording regularly on a daily or weekly basis. It's important because we remember the bad stuff; insults and critical feedback can sting deeply. We are much more likely to ignore or overlook the many positive cues we get from those around us.

This exercise will serve several purposes. You will have a written log of wins, stories, and examples to access for future performance reviews or interviews. Also, on a bad day, you can review the positives from previous days as a reminder of how awesome you are.

Lastly, when you look for certain things, you see more of them. If you search for the positive inputs coming at you, you'll see and experience more of them. Just like if I tell you to look for white cars the next time you are out driving, you will notice that there are white cars everywhere.

A common reaction is that after keeping the "book of awesome" for a while, people will often note how they never realized how much positive input they really get.

It's known as the frequency bias, illusion, or the Baader-Meinhof phenomenon. It was named after a situation when a newspaper reader was telling a friend about the West German Baader-Meinhof gang, an uncommon topic, and the next day, the friend reads an article about it in the news.

Similarly, when you read and notice an unusual word, it's likely to keep showing up suddenly. In reality, the frequency hasn't changed; you just notice it more because you're paying attention to it.

Meet my client, Alex. Alex is an incredibly effective and well-liked leader with a great sense of humor and an engaging interpersonal style. Alex is quick to give credit to the team and tends to be self-effacing, even self-deprecating, at times. Even though Alex's funny comments seemed light-hearted, Alex tends to undervalue their own worth. While others would not necessarily recognize it, internally, Alex was also harshly self-critical.

I suggested the personal book of awesome exercises, and Alex laughed it off. It sounded silly. And, how embarrassing if someone were to find it! Who keeps a book of awesome things about themselves?

CHAPTER 4

Alex is not the only client who has pushed back on this exercise, and I get it. I grew up in Minnesota; we are taught to be humble and not to draw attention to ourselves.

Alex and the others who resist the idea typically agree to at least try it. Some will concede and commit, yet they prefer to call the journal by a different name. **My personal book of not terrible. My personal book of not sucking.** Or something entirely different to throw potential finders off. **Quarter one projections. Team accomplishments.**

In the end, those who start their book of awesome are glad they did.

Now, let's look at the path forward.

Part III:
THE PATH FORWARD

Self-Regulation

SELF-REGULATION PLAYS AN IMPORTANT ROLE IN MENTAL HEALTH, WELL-BEING, AND PSYCHOLOGICAL FITNESS. It refers to the process of managing thoughts, feelings, and behaviors, enabling you to meet goals and be effective in your life.

Many skills mentioned in this book relate to effectively regulating oneself in the face of difficulties. You are learning ways to manage your thoughts, emotions, and behaviors to enhance mental health. It isn't about suppressing, ignoring, over-controlling, or resisting.

Rather, it is about identifying patterns in thinking, feeling, and behaving and making modifications that will lead to greater well-being.

Effective self-regulation is about intentionally responding, being aware of the moment, pausing before reacting, and making decisions that align with your values. The concepts of self-control and self-regulation seem similar. To differentiate, self-control may be more localized, inhibiting specific impulses at the moment. Self-regulation is a broader dynamic in which feelings, thoughts, and behaviors are **managed,** not controlled.

Dysregulation in emotions, thoughts, or behaviors can result in negative consequences and impact performance, relationships, effectiveness, etc. Consider how conflicts become exacerbated by people unable to self-regulate. More extreme dysregulation can be a factor in mental illness.

Understanding how to manage yourself is vital to healthy psychological development. If children learn the skills to self-regulate (process intense emotions, modify destructive thinking, and manage behaviors), they stand a better chance of growing up to be adults who can do the same. Providing social-emotional training for kids and adolescents helps prepare them for the pressures of life.

We are in a precarious time with opportunities for education on how we can self-regulate better, grounding in the reminder that we have a choice, and we can train and practice accordingly.

The next section continues to offer practices to build your psychological fitness.

Chapter 5:
Cognitive Training

Everyone that's alive is endowed with a brain that has the capacity to change itself.
—Andrew Huberman

Cognitive training, brain training, and mind training are all terms for a similar concept. Science proposes how we can promote brain health, which is beneficial for mental health. Cognitive training also involves attending to the mind and the quality of our thinking.

There are cognitive exercises designed to help people improve their memory or the ability to concentrate and pay attention. Some experts endorse being proactive in learning new skills to combat dementia or cognitive decline. We are still at the forefront of understanding how to optimize mind and brain health as well as the complexity of mind-body connections.

NEUROPLASTICITY OF THE MIND

As mentioned, neuroplasticity relates to the brain's ability to alter, conform, and improve both the structure and composition through time and in response to stimulus and experience. Your brain can change due to mental activity. This concept is a huge step forward in science.

As a human, you can change your behavior and thinking in ways that CHANGE your brain's physiology. You can adapt your emotional style, thinking processes, and sense of well-being, and your brain can adapt accordingly.

Various research studies analyzing human behavior and the mind suggest brainy activities can encourage new nerve cell connections and promote the synthesis of new brain cells, leading to cognitive "plasticity" and the development of functional reserves that protect from potential cell loss.

Here are a few basic mind exercises that can contribute to psychological fitness.

Mentally Stimulating Activities

Activities like sketching, painting, and other crafts that require motor engagement and mental work can be healthy for the brain. Reading, taking classes, and engaging in "mental contortions" such as word puzzles or mathematical computations can foster brain health.

Online 'brain games' are popular and promote cognitive enhancement. Researchers are still exploring the variables involved. At this time, generalizability of such brain activities is inconclusive. In other words, practicing an online 'brain game' will likely result in an improvement in your effectiveness in playing that game, yet may not generalize to other cognitive tasks.

Learning Something New

Challenging your brain to learn a new skill has proven benefits. There is no limit to what skills can be developed — learning a language, instrument, athletic skill, board games, gardening, or chess strategy.

Nutrition

There is a deluge of scientific studies providing increasingly precise nutritional guidelines to enhance physical and mental health. Details are beyond this section, but the idea is worth exploring. For example, common suggestions include increasing the intake of omega 3, fish, and vegetables, similar to a Mediterranean diet.

Physical Exercise

To reinforce a previous message, engaging in cardiovascular and strength activity contributes to brain health. General activity and movement will enhance healthy brain activity as well as alleviate anxiety and depression.

Seek Interpersonal Connections

When you're stressed, it can be tempting to isolate, yet proactively pursuing interpersonal interaction and being with a community elevates mental functioning. Interacting engages numerous parts of the brain advantageous to your thinking and emotional health.

Meditation

Meditation entails focusing one's concentration in a peaceful, controlled manner. As mentioned throughout this book, practicing meditation has been shown to offer numerous health benefits for the body and brain. Meditation has been found to increase the thickness of the prefrontal cortex. Elevated brain functions, such as greater awareness, focus, and decision-making, are managed by this brain area.

A groundbreaking long-term neuroscientific study was conducted on nuns. It revealed interesting results on the power of neuroplasticity and agency we have over our brain development and potential decline.[138]

The nuns were actively involved in learning and teaching and, therefore, remained engaged cognitively and continued to stretch their thinking. Autopsies of their brains revealed signs of Alzheimer's disease lesions. Despite this, they were able to design workarounds to reduce the impact of the damage on their brains.

This, among other research studies, supports that brain function can be altered through cognitive activity, such as meditation and cognitive-reframing approaches.

Managing Attention

Again, mental activities such as managing attention and directing focus can shape the physiological structure of the brain. Scientists often say that neurons that fire together wire together and, in doing so, create new synaptic linkages.

<><><><><><><><><><><><><><><><><><><><><><><><><><><><><><><><>

One of the key practical lessons of modern neuroscience is that the power to direct our attention has within it the power to shape our brain's firing patterns, as well as the power to shape the architecture of the brain itself.[139]
—Daniel J. Siegel, *Mindsight: The New Science of Personal Transformation*

<><><><><><><><><><><><><><><><><><><><><><><><><><><><><><><><>

Siegel notes how practicing increased attention amplifies neuroplasticity by stimulating neurochemical release. So, any attention management techniques mentioned in this book (i.e., mindfulness, meditation) will upgrade the physiology of your brain.

THINKING PATTERNS

◇◇◇

*The untrained mind keeps up a running commentary,
labeling everything, judging everything. It is best to ignore
that commentary. Don't argue or resist, just ignore.
Deprived of attention and interest, this voice gets quieter
and quieter and eventually just shuts up.*
—Plato

◇◇◇

It can be easy to believe the stories we tell ourselves. Our mental models are our perceptions, deeply ingrained beliefs, and values shaped by our unique way of perceiving the world. They are genuine but incomplete.

◇◇◇

We don't see things as they are. We see things as we are.
—The Talmud

◇◇◇

The idea that we have influence over our state of mind and viewpoint is empowering. We can upgrade our thinking when one method of thinking is no longer helpful. Each of us has our own mental models and ways of interpreting events in the world. These mental patterns are real but not comprehensive.

CHAPTER 5

Mental hygiene is just as important as physical hygiene. We don't stay clean after a shower; we still need to bathe the next day. It's also critical to look after the cleanliness of your thought patterns if you want to be healthy.

◇◇

If you are distressed by anything external, the pain is not due to the thing itself, but your own estimate of it.
—Marcus Aurelius

◇◇

Paying attention to your thinking requires mindfulness and intention. Thoughts are information, not facts. Intrusive thoughts are often irrational but can be diffused. While you can't control what thoughts surface, you can <u>decide</u> which thoughts to introduce next.

◇◇

The happiness of your life depends on the quality of your thoughts.
—Marcus Aurelius

◇◇

Key Points:

Your mind is shaped by your thinking. When you are triggered emotionally, your perceptions and thoughts can become distorted. You can upgrade your thinking patterns so they serve you in a healthier way.

Challenge:

Pay closer attention to your thinking patterns.

RECOGNIZING YOUR MENTAL MODELS

Mental models or internal memes act as a guideline to assist in navigating the world. They can become second nature, operating in the background. These narratives provide a list of heuristic rules to choose from, and we often stick to them because they have previously worked for us.

They can show up in the form of core beliefs or thinking patterns that have developed through conditioning and experiences. Often, you can come to a point in life when something goes awry, and your mental model makes less sense. We think our models predict how the world works, but then something unexpected occurs.

At some point, you might surrender, confront these internal systems, and discover the issue is a symptom of a dysfunctional system, not the actual presenting problem.

Meet Pat. Pat grew up with the underlying belief that if you work hard, you will be rewarded. Pat was a conscientious student and earned A's through high school and college. Transitioning into the working world, Pat assumed the same model applied.

If you work hard, prepare, and do your best, you will be promoted. While this proved to be true for the first few performance cycles, Pat then faced disappointment. The subsequent review was still a high rating of *exceeding expectations*, yet Pat's peer was promoted.

The internal belief is that if you do your part, it will result in external recognition, which sounds reasonable yet is incomplete. Once Pat leaned more into corporate life, it became quickly apparent that performance was only part of the story predicting who would be promoted.

There were other factors that hadn't been considered. They include policies, length of time in the role, specific competencies desired at the next level, the necessity of self-advocacy, relationships, organizational dynamics, potential biases, and how aware the leaders making hiring decisions are of employees' achievements and contributions.

Self-awareness and contemplation are required to recognize your thought processes. We operate with **core beliefs** that influence how we navigate in the world. We can experience situations that challenge those systems and can subsequently assess and upgrade our models of thinking.

Take some time to think about the mental models, beliefs, and assumptions you've formed. How are they working in your life? Are they helping and serving you, or are they in the way?

Example: Holding the belief that self-care is selfish will not serve you in a healthy way. Upgrade: Self-care is my responsibility.

Example: Operating with the belief that crying means you are weak. Upgrade: Expressing emotion in a healthy way is critical for well-being.

Key Point:

When people change their perspective, it changes everything.

Challenge:

Improve your mental strength. Your mental neuroplasticity challenge is to find one mental model or thinking pattern that no longer serves you well and upgrade to a more generative and complete belief system.

COGNITIVE DISTORTIONS

Everyone experiences biases in their thinking. Cognitive distortions are exaggerated, or irrational thought patterns can contribute to psychological damage. Particularly when experiencing intense emotions, perceptions can become out of proportion.

Common examples include overgeneralizing, catastrophizing, and all-or-nothing thinking. We can jump to conclusions based on unhelpful connections that have developed over time. These patterns can become invisible, automatic, and difficult to notice.

When taken to an extreme, thinking errors take a toll on mental health and can contribute to symptoms of depression and anxiety. With practice and increasing awareness of these biases, you can learn to respond with more adaptive thinking.

Key Point:

When you are triggered emotionally, your perceptions and thoughts can become distorted.

Challenge:

Reflect on how your thinking can become tainted. What distortions resonate? Do you over-personalize? Awfulize? Make assumptions? Engage in "should" thinking?

COGNITIVE REFRAMING

Cognitive reframing is a psychological approach to changing how you view and perceive a situation by detecting and breaking unreasonable and maladaptive thinking. Learning to reframe negative events more constructively can lead to positive physiological changes that impact how you feel, react, and comprehend your surroundings.

Since it allows us to see problems from different perspectives, cognitive reframing can be a useful technique for discovering new ways to think about old problems. Broadening viewpoints can facilitate new synaptic pathways and connections to develop.

You can transform the way you view things through this process. There are repercussions to viewing things adversely or in a pessimistic frame that you would not experience if you interpreted them in a more generative way.

Making shifts in your narrative results in changes in your brain's neural pathways, reinforcing a future pattern of response. Thanks to neuroplasticity, by practicing how you interpret and respond, it will become more automatic.

I was hiking in Denver recently and overheard a conversation of some official-looking mountain bikers as they were getting ready to start their trek.

Biker 1 said, "Ohhhh man...I'm just thinking about how hard the next few hours are going to be. It's so hot. I'm hot already."

Biker 2 responded, "Really? I was just thinking about how awesome I'm going to feel when we're done. Try that instead."

We get to decide what interpretation and perspective we are going to focus on.

COGNITIVE RE-FRAMING METHOD

Here is how to apply the **ABCDE Method:**

A = Activating Stressor

B = Belief

C = Consequence

D = Dispute

E = Effective new belief

Example

I failed the test → I'm an idiot → anxiety, distress → I'm a terrible student

In the example above:

I failed the test = **Activating Stressor**, i.e. the event

I am an idiot = **Belief**, i.e. thoughts or interpretation of the event

Anxiety, Distress = **Consequence**, i.e. the resulting feeling, leading to more negative thoughts (I'm a terrible student)

In this scenario, the disputation is that the student would challenge the thought with more discernment, assessing the facts rather than assuming the initial thought of being an idiot. The dispute would be considering another interpretation: perhaps it was a difficult test, many struggled, the student could have studied more, or reached out for help.

Disconnecting from catastrophic thinking leads to a proportionate mindset. After putting the thoughts and assumptions on trial, the student may arrive at a more reasonable, right-sized interpretation of the event.

Effective new belief for the student: "This is a tough subject for me. Since I am conscientious about school, next time, I'll spend more time preparing and asking for help. Studying has obviously worked for me in other classes since I'm getting all A's and B's."

Another example of the ABCDE model:

Overcooking dinner → I'm a terrible cook → disappointment, discouragement, frustration → Everyone hates my cooking

Disputation: What is the evidence that everyone hates his cooking? Making one mistake does not equal being terrible at cooking. All chefs have overcooked a dish at some point.

Climbing down the ladder of assumptions that all people hate his cooking just because of one small incident will reveal the distorted elements of his thinking.

Effective new belief: everyone makes mistakes. One minor mishap is not a failure or does not justify awfulizing the whole experience. Now I know what to do when cooking this meal.

Reminders to Use Healthier Language

- Replace I should. Instead, use I will, I could, I would like to, I can.

- Challenge the "should." Are these real or phantom expectations?

- Identify and disrupt maladaptive thoughts to change how you perceive a situation.

- Try putting your thoughts on trial and challenging your initial assumptions. Do you know those thoughts to be true? Are they opinions, facts, features of an idea, or impressions?

- Reinterpreting negative events in a more positive light contributes to physiological brain changes.

Key Points:

You have the capacity to upgrade your thinking patterns so they serve you in a healthier way. Cognitive reframing is a powerful tool to enhance mental health and potentially decrease symptoms of anxiety and depression.

Challenge:

Apply the ABCDE method to situations that tend to trigger a biased thinking trap in your life.

Cognitive Distortions Worksheet and Cognitive Reframing Tool

Access supportive worksheets for cognitive reframing in your free psychological fitness resource guide here:

Psychfitguide.com/book.

JOURNALING

Modifying thinking patterns can be made through verbal processing, as well as written processing. Reflecting on and articulating thoughts and emotions through writing is helpful. Preferably, you should do it the old-fashioned way with pen and paper. Writing has been shown to provide therapeutic advantages. Journaling about daily events and reactions can be healthy, as can reflecting on difficulties.

Experiments have shown that writing about painful situations reduces sadness and anxiety symptoms. Writing about traumatic, negative, or painful events might not only help individuals find a safe disclosure procedure but also help them create stronger coping strategies, according to James Pennebaker's key work.[140] Pennebaker's writing therapy technique has been assessed in over 200 studies, confirming the overall mental health benefits.[141]

Another narrative psychologist, Laura King, discovered that writing about good events improves health and increases global cognitive focus.[142]

Meet Chen. Chen works for a consulting firm and is a parent of four. Chen is committed to personal development and enhancing mental health, with one of the goals being more aware of triggers. Journaling has been helpful for Chen in improving self-awareness and self-regulation.

Insights from Chen:

I do this thing where I write how I feel about a triggering incident for 15 minutes. I do this several times throughout the course of a week. In doing this, I realized a lot of my feelings of anxiety were coming from my mental traps. I've been able to articulate a more long-term thinking trap that has been getting in my way.

As I redo this exercise a week later, after I have recovered, I'm able to see this more clearly. By doing this, I'm learning to sit with myself and my feelings, and I'm able to recognize that it passes through.

The emotional tone of the event significantly changed after a week. I realize that doing the exact same exercise with two different mindsets helps reveal some of the messages I've been telling myself that aren't healthy. Creating space to see the differences diffuses the impact.

IRONIC PROCESS

As you read this, **try not to think about an ORANGE BALLOON**. The more you try **not** to think about something, the more space it tends to take up in your mind. The science of the ironic process theory suggests that suppressing thoughts takes effort, and the pressure can build.

Trying to **ignore** thoughts that keep surfacing can deplete cognitive energy. It's the psychological process in which deliberately trying to suppress certain ideas or thoughts makes them more likely to surface.

Providing a cognitive release can be freeing. We can release the pressure by providing a valve for thoughts to be expressed. Writing down our ideas forces us to use language and name our thoughts and emotions. Our minds make more sense of it this way.

Do you remember what you weren't supposed to be thinking about? Don't think about an orange balloon.

Key Points:

What you resist in your thinking can persist. Engaging in written reflection is a healthy way to process and sort through complex thoughts and feelings.

Challenge:

Consider spending 15 minutes daily, four days in a row, writing about a difficult life event.

WORRY VS. CONCERN

"My life has been filled with dreadful misfortune, most of which never happened," declared Montaigne, a 17th-century French philosopher.

We endure more tragedy in our thoughts than in reality. Worry is a psychological deception that our minds play on us. We believe that by worrying, we are influencing the outcome. We're not. We were never completely in charge of the outcome. Worrying does not adequately prepare us for future difficulties, yet it can generate anxiety and distress.

Worry and fret are typically focused on the future yet sometimes based on a warped understanding of reality. Often, the fear does not match the danger. For example, a common fear is public speaking. People can experience panic and worry thinking about presenting to a group, yet it is not a right-sized response that makes logical sense. In such an example, the fear feels real, yet the danger is exaggerated.

Concern, on the other hand, is a constructive response to a potential threat. If your child is sick, it makes sense to feel **concerned** and, therefore, do what is appropriate to address the illness: attend to how they feel, take care of them, treat the symptoms, and call a doctor if needed.

Worry is often a needless struggle that can foster a victim mindset since it's often directed at events out of our span of influence. Worry results in needless debilitation and can be driven by insecurity.

In the documentary *The Last Dance*, Michael Jordan's ability to be mindful and present was highlighted. A favorite comment was when journalists asked if he was apprehensive about the upcoming game. He said, "No, why should I be worried about a shot I haven't taken yet?" He made it sound so easy. It seems obvious yet difficult to remember in real time.

Planning and preparation are not the same as obsessing over scenarios that have a low probability of occurring. Much rumination is tied to unlikely events.

I was a frequent mental inventory taker, scanning my consciousness for objects of concern, kind of like pressing a bruise to see if it still hurts.[143]
—Dan Harris, *10% Happier*

Key Points:

Worry is a negative spiral of thinking that unnecessarily depletes cognitive resources without affecting the outcome. The concern is healthy and can provide a constructive response to the stressor.

Challenge:

If you find you have a propensity for worrying, challenge yourself to examine your habit and consider ways to re-direct.

- Ask yourself, does this worrying serve me? What is actual and factual? Am I controlling the outcome?
- Try an experiment. When you feel excessive worrying, stop, write down all the worries (even if irrational), and put them in a jar to relieve your brain.

FEAR — FALSE EVIDENCE APPEARING REAL

When you get rid of your fear of failure, your tensions about succeeding… you can be yourself. Relaxed. You'll no longer be driving with your brakes on.
—Anthony de Mello, Jesuit priest and author

For everyone, failing can be a painful process. Often even worse and more debilitating is the fear that you could fail. As we've discussed, fear tends to infiltrate and exaggerate your thinking patterns. When facing an upcoming event or a high-stakes situation, it is easy to anticipate the worst. Due to the negative bias in the brain, we often focus on the worst possible case scenario.

We can make all sorts of inaccurate assumptions born from insecurity and fear. The FEAR acronym describes it well; we tend to see false evidence appearing as real.

When in uncertain or new situations, this fear response is more apt to dominate our thinking. For example, when transitioning to a new job, it is common for people to experience self-doubt, or the popular phrase, imposter syndrome. Often, they come from a familiar work setting in which they felt mastery and experienced success and strong performance in their role.

Meet Netra. Netra is an accomplished product manager who was in a new role for two months. According to all accounts, Netra quickly integrated into the role and was already having an impact.

Initial feedback from superiors was positive. The value of the work was recognized verbally as well as in writing. Peers were sending emails thanking Netra for contributions to the team. Direct reports were responsive and expressed appreciation for Netra's collaborative leadership style.

Despite these positive inputs, Netra was experiencing a great deal of self-doubt, with an inner voice questioning if enough was being done. It just **seemed** like people were disappointed, which made no sense rationally, considering all the positive feedback from multiple levels.

For a time, Netra resisted the inputs, convinced that the contribution wasn't enough. Upon closer reflection and discernment, Netra was able to unhook a bit from these assumptions after re-considering the facts and continuing to check it out in their environment.

Netra understood that this fear response of questioning one-self is normal and expected in a new work situation where every-thing is unfamiliar, especially when one is on an unsteady learning curve. The underlying questioning and fear did fade with time, and looking back, Netra was able to recognize the distorted pattern.

Key Points:

When faced with failure or a negative experience, interpretations can also be tainted by fear. When experiencing a perceived or real failure, the initial response can be globalized, internalized, or over-generalized.

Meet Morgan. Morgan experienced accelerated professional success, being promoted every 18 months for a decade. When up for a vice president role, the progression slowed, and Morgan didn't get the promotion. Morgan was not only disappointed by the news but also felt like a failure as a person.

Thoughts included, *I'm never going to get promoted, my career is shot, I knew I'd be found out, everyone will hear about this, this is a career killer, I'm worthless.*

It was as though upon hearing this news, the previous ten years of strong performance and success had been deleted. Morgan was consumed with self-persecuting thinking *for a while.* Eventually, the thoughts did diffuse and pass. With reflection, Morgan moved beyond the disappointment, re-framed, and learned more about what needed to happen to get to the next level. After a few weeks, Morgan said, "I guess it's important not to believe everything I think."

You don't get to choose whether terrible things happen in life, but you do have control over how you react to them. Disappointment leads your mind to fool you and lead you to believe falsehoods. Failures will paralyze you, demotivate you, and reduce your chances of success in the future unless you learn to respond to them in psychologically appropriate ways.

Key Points:

Worrying is not planning and preparing. It is often not helpful or constructive and depletes you of emotional and cognitive resources. The most crucial thing to do after a failure, psychologically speaking, is to understand its influence or how it affects your ideas, feelings, and behaviors.

Challenge:

When you notice that you are worrying, pause and ask yourself, is this thought helpful? Is it preparing me in a healthy way?

UNDERSTAND WORRY AND ANXIETY PATTERNS

Asking yourself if worrying is genuinely preparing you is a test. Is it beneficial or distracting to be concerned about a forthcoming event? Is it an attempt at distraction or control that can't be controlled?

Author Judson Brewer proposes a strategy for dealing with worry in his book *Unwinding Anxiety: Train Your Brain to Heal Your Mind.*[144] According to Brewer, worry and anxiety have a simple pattern that looks like this: anxiety is a trigger, then worrying behavior leads to increased anxiety.

His strategy involves making a list of your anxiety triggers as the first step. Recognize three elements: the trigger, the behavior, and the result. Brewer presents a model for breaking the anxiety habit.

Consider this scenario: Feeling distracted at work is a trigger, and the behavior is to check social media. As a result, you get frustrated about losing focus and concerned about upcoming posts, which leads to increased anxiety and worry.

Brewer suggests creating a plan to recognize what you'll do instead when you are triggered. Plan to replace the old behavior with a new one, which requires forethought.

For example, if you start feeling distracted at work, instead of logging into social media, get up and take a walk or get a drink of water to break the cycle. Remove yourself from devices connecting to social media and re-engage in a specific work task. Tune into how you are thinking and feeling during and after the trigger response cycle. Changing behaviors is one method to disrupt the cycle of worry and anxiety.

Key Points:

Worry and anxiety exacerbate each other. Thoughts, emotions, and behaviors are connected. Adapting behavioral responses is an effective way to modify thinking patterns associated with worry and anxiety.

Challenge:

Identify common triggers and your typical responses and create a plan to insert a different behavior.

CAROLINE LEAF'S MODEL

In her work, psychologist Caroline Leaf describes how to clear your mind of congestion. Developing new behaviors requires time; thus, according to her theory, the more you exercise, the stronger you grow in self-regulation. Leaf suggests practicing memory building to strengthen your thought patterns, maintaining emotional hygiene, and empowering your mind to form new neural connections.

The very first step is to heighten awareness and gain a better understanding of what is happening in your life. Then there's taking the time to think about how your emotions are signals telling you something. Leaf suggests writing down such notions to find clarity. She advises extended periods of rest and analysis, as well as more stability in how you recuperate and evaluate the issue.

When you take the opportunity to calm your brain, you will be able to reclaim your control and react with purpose rather than overreacting. She recognizes the need for **effort** since there is no easy fix. To study, synthesize, and respond in novel ways, you need time.

You can look to your thinking patterns as messengers or warning signals. Like other cognitive training models, to manage your mind, Leaf suggests taking the time to explore and understand those signals with intention.

In *Cleaning up your Mental Mess*, Leaf describes a process she calls the neurocycle to manage your mind. She describes the mind as always thinking, feeling, and choosing, which shapes brain structure. The neurocycle is a five-step process to clean up your mental mess and enhance resilience. Leaf suggests spending 15–45 minutes daily for cycles of 63 days to develop healthy habits.[145]

Step 1: Gather awareness of how you are feeling mentally and physically. What are some emotional and physical cues you are experiencing right now?

Step 2: Reflect. Get curious about your emotional experience. If you are feeling exhausted or overwhelmed, inquire with yourself what could be contributing to these feelings. Consider why you may be feeling this way.

Step 3: Write down your reflections so you can organize your thinking and gain clarity on your thoughts and emotional experience.

Step 4: Recheck. Review your writings and make observations. Assess what you are noticing and if there are patterns. Reframe your perspective by challenging yourself to find another way of interpreting the situation.

Step 5: Active Reach. After you have written down and re-conceptualized your thinking, identify a constructive action you can take when those thoughts occur — a positive, affirming statement or a few deep breaths. This is a way to replace destructive thinking with more constructive action.

Key Points:

Regardless of which practice you employ, there are ways to proactively upgrade your thinking patterns. Planning for how you'll respond to triggers builds psychological fitness. You can break and curtail the anxiety habit. Many methods work, involving awareness, reflection, planning, experimenting, and re-doing the process.

Challenge:

Identify common triggers and your typical responses and create a plan to insert a different behavior.

Have you been able to avoid thinking about the image of an orange balloon?

Chapter 6:
Emotional Regulation

W E ARE ABOUT TO TALK ABOUT **FEELINGS** AND **EMOTIONS,** SO I DON'T WANT TO LOSE YOU. BUILDING PSYCHOLOGICAL FITNESS ALSO IN-VOLVES UNDERSTANDING AND EFFECTIVELY REGULATING EMOTIONS. All thoughts and feelings can be explored and under-stood. Accepting and embracing your emotional experience can help you work through them in a healthy manner.

What comes to your mind when you hear about **emotions**? Have you ever wondered why it is necessary to discuss emotions? How you feel can determine the quality of your life. Your emotions can make your life miserable, neutral, or magical. It is essential to understand your emotions. They play a vital role in your life.

Emotions impact perception.

Psychology professor Dennis Proffitt helped develop the idea of embodied cognition: how consciousness is impacted not only by our minds but also by our bodies. In *Perception,* Proffitt and jour-nalist Drake Baer propose that we live in our own perceptual re-ality.[146] Our relative size even influences our perception. A small child will view a hill as being bigger and steeper than a larger adult would.

According to Proffitt and Baer, many factors influence per-ception, including physical ability, age, energy level, strength, con-fidence, and mood for starters. Our interpretation of our surroundings is scaled to body size and our ability to interact with our environment.

The terms **feeling** and **emotion** are often used interchangeably. They are connected and interrelated with some distinction. The debate about the difference between feelings and emotions is somewhat theoretical. Understanding how both play into your mental health is what is important. There are situations when it is sufficient to use the terms interchangeably.

Feelings can be considered subjective perceptions of emotions — how you interpret emotion and give it a name. We could say that emotions are a deeper state produced consciously or unconsciously, and feelings are what we use to make sense of the experience.

Emotions can arise as sensations in the body. Your feelings are influenced by your emotional state yet generated from your thinking. For example, you may notice the feeling of discomfort when someone challenges you with a difficult question in a meeting. You may blush, and your breathing becomes restricted. Your mind may label the feeling as embarrassed or awkward. Feelings can be interpretations of situations and experiences and will vary from person to person.

WHY IS IT RELEVANT?

Developing awareness of your feelings, as well as your emotional experience, is important to have agency over your mental health and well-being. Have you noticed how when you feel bad, things seem harder than usual? It's difficult to face the world when you're unhappy or depressed, as those who have experienced it know. Emotions alter sensory perceptions. For instance, people listening to sad music perceive a slope steeper than those hearing cheerful music.

EMOTIONAL HEALTH

It's healthy to experience a full range of emotions. The point is not to be void of negative feelings. Emotionally healthy people typically have control over their ideas, emotions, and actions. Emotional health contributes to resilience in dealing with life's challenges.

According to emotional expert Susan David (*Emotional Agility: Get Unstuck, Embrace Change, and Thrive in Work and Life*), how you navigate your inner world — your everyday thoughts, emotions, and self-stories — is **the** most important determinant of your life success.[147]

David recognizes emotionally agile people know how to gain critical insight into situations and interactions from their feelings and use it to adapt, align their values and actions, and make changes to respond in a healthy way.

She describes **emotional agility** as a process that allows you to navigate life's challenges with self-acceptance, as well as with a clear and open mind. The process is learning how to hold your emotions and thoughts loosely, facing them courageously and compassionately, and then moving beyond them to create constructive life change.

Dr. David shares four key concepts:

- **Showing Up** — Face (rather than ignore) your thoughts and emotions with curiosity and kindness

- **Healthy Detachment** — Unhook from and observe your thoughts and emotions to see them for what they are — just thoughts, just emotions — so you don't over-identify with any thought or feeling.

- **Walking Your Why** — Identify your key values to provide the direction needed to keep you on your path.

- **Moving On** — Make small and deliberate adjustments to your mindset, motivation, and habits in ways that are aligned with your values. Find the balance between challenge and competence so that you're neither complacent nor overwhelmed.

Why Is Emotional Agility Important?

Emotional agility is about having a range of feelings and emotions in response to varied situations that one encounters daily. It helps to be adaptable and flexible so that you can change or shape yourself as per the situation. Understanding that feelings are temporary and will pass is important to avoid getting stuck in emotional rigidity. It's common to get stuck in painful emotions and exacerbate them through resisting or not processing them in a healthy way.

THE CONNECTION BETWEEN EMOTIONAL AND MENTAL HEALTH

In the book *How Emotions Are Made: The Secret Life of the Brain*, Lisa Feldman Barrett challenges traditional models of emotion and provides alternative views about the emotional experience. She suggests not everyone responds in the same way to the same emotions. The experiences people have with their emotional and physical reactions vary.

Barrett endorses a theory of constructed emotions, suggesting emotions develop spontaneously, concurrently, and simultaneously in different brain regions.[148]

According to this theory, **each emotion is influenced by one's experiences**. Sensory inputs pre-dictate responses, which the brain either reinforces or adapts based on prior experience. According to Barrett, emotional responses are also created in this way. Emotions can elicit varying responses depending on the context.

Barrett suggests emotions aren't fixed or innate, yet they are constructed depending on one's experience, culture, and environment, and variations in emotional expression are attributed to socialization and language differences.

The source of emotions is in each person's individual experiences. We learn to link emotions with behaviors, which can reinforce the response cycle. By learning to better distinguish between emotions, we can learn how to regulate our emotional experiences more effectively.

Key Point:

Practicing feeling your emotions will help you become better at identifying and differentiating them.

Challenge:

Create a little distance between you and your emotion. I'm depressed vs. I am feeling depressed. I am having some feelings of depression. Enhance your emotional literacy and build out your vocabulary so you can describe your feelings with more precision.

EMOTIONAL REGULATION

Emotions and feelings are valuable. They help you navigate through the world. They have a purpose and will tell you something about what you are experiencing. However, again, while they are signals, emotions aren't facts, so appreciating how to effectively interpret and moderate your emotions is essential for well-being.

While it is unrealistic to think you can resist feelings or urges before they show up, you can influence the feelings, how you make sense of them, and how they affect you. Emotional regulation is a process of influencing and moderating how you experience the feeling. You can manage your emotions by learning about their message and how you can enhance or reduce intensity. Professor James Gross is a subject matter expert on emotions. He states:

Emotion regulation refers to the processes by which individuals influence which emotions they have, when they have them, and how they experience and express these emotions.[149]

Key Points:

Your mood can be a stable state, yet feelings and emotions represent an immediate experience and response. You can train yourself to adjust the emotional intensity, which can help you modulate your overall mood.

BENEFITS OF EMOTIONAL REGULATION

Regulating your emotional experience will allow you to respond to situations from a centered place and is associated with stronger mental health. Healthy emotional regulation is associated with resilience, coping, well-being, and improved interpersonal interactions.

People who practice emotional regulation are more resilient and can more effectively manage stressful life events. Negative emotions can be particularly tricky to handle. Practicing your response and relationship with negative emotions can decrease the impact they can have.

When dealing with negative emotions, it can be a useful reminder that feelings are temporary and transient and always pass. Having healthy ways to process and work through painful emotions is critical to mental well-being.

Therefore, accepting negative feelings is also part of emotional regulation. The goal is to improve your distress threshold and experience negative feelings in the now rather than fleeing, internalizing, numbing, or escaping them.

The concept of psychological mastery is referenced in the popular book by Timothy Gallwey, *The Inner Game of Tennis*. Understanding how to effectively manage intense emotions is described as the ultimate competitive advantage. By effectively managing emotional experience, performance will be better. If not managed, negative feelings can be a distraction and can impair performance.[150]

Key Points:

Whether it is regulating your thoughts or emotions, seek awareness first. Then understand how to best decondition if you start mental spinning.

◇◇

*When I see an anxious person, I ask myself, what do they
want? For, if a person is wanting something outside of
their control, why would they be stricken by anxiety?*
—Epictetus

◇◇

Here is a thought-provoking idea: it has been said that anxiety
and stress come from too much expectation and ambition. Do
we foster disappointment and negative feelings simply by how we
establish expectations?

Again, remember that thoughts and feelings aren't facts. They
are real, yet they are simply <u>signals</u> and <u>messages</u> to be noticed. To
manage anxiety, find a way to resist exacerbating negative feelings
and thoughts until they are overwhelming. You can foster awareness without becoming overtaken by strong feelings.

Key Points:

Emotions are fluid and dynamic. Developing a healthy
relationship with feelings is important for mental health.
Regulating your emotions will not be fully mastered, yet
you can optimize your emotional experience to help you
navigate and respond to life constructively.

Challenge: Reminders to Improve Emotional Regulation

- Psychologist Susan David provides practical suggestions in her HBR article, *Three Ways to Better Understand Your Emotions*. She suggests naming your emotion. Labeling is an important first step in effectively handling emotions.[151]

- Develop your emotional vocabulary. Having more descriptive, accurate words to describe your feelings is helpful. Move beyond the obvious, accessible, and familiar feelings.

- As you label your emotions, rate them on a scale of 1–10. How often do you experience this emotion? How intensely are you experiencing it?

- David also reinforces James Pennebaker's findings on the links between writing and emotional processing. Try a writing exercise to reflect on a difficult experience, a life transition, or a situation you are having trouble reconciling.

- If experiencing intense, severe emotions, try distracting yourself, change your environment, move your body, or engage in a self-soothing behavior (bath, stretching, walking, music).

- Monitor boundaries with others' emotions. Emotional contagion is picking up the emotions of those around you. It's an indirect phenomenon that emotional states can be impacted by others who are in their vicinity or near their physical space, even without direct contact. Positive and negative emotions can be contagious through subtle actions such as non-verbal cues.

- Similarly, fostering positive emotion to counter excessive negativity is useful when in balance.

ATLAS OF EMOTIONS

The Dalai Lama started a program to assist people in becoming more aware of emotions. His goal was to build an emotional map to help people achieve a tranquil mindset, which he accomplished with the *Atlas of Emotions*.

Dr. Paul Ekman created a map as an interactive tool for expanding emotional knowledge and illuminating the emotional journey. It offers a framework and descriptive language to describe the emotional experience.

The online tool (Atlasofemotions.org) can assist you in gaining more command over your emotional responses. The process is similar to other models: understand and express what you're experiencing and become more aware of what stimulates your mood and how you react. The interactive website features a chronology with a trigger that causes an emotional reaction and behavior. The goal is to come up with constructive and useful responses.

BRENÉ BROWN

In her recent book, *Atlas of the Heart,* Brené Brown reinforces the importance of increasing emotional literacy. She provides this guide to help you understand and regulate your emotions. Engaging in a deeper reflection of your strong emotions so you can understand what you are feeling and where it is coming from is critical to well-being. According to Brown, enhancing your emotional vocabulary will enhance your relationship with yourself and others.[152]

Key Points:

Gaining awareness and command over your emotional responses will help you foster mental health and psychological fitness. Understanding and expressing what you're experiencing and becoming more aware of your triggers will help you generate useful responses.

Challenge:

Spend some time studying the nature of emotions, use language to describe your feelings, and practice methods to effectively process your emotional experience.

Mindfulness
The Ultimate Self-Regulation Tool

As suggested throughout this book, mindfulness is a practice of present-centered awareness that fosters the healthy detachment of emotions and thoughts, which are recognized, accepted, and allowed to pass without over-internalizing the negativity or stress.

As the title states, in *Mindfulness in Plain English,* Bhante Gunaratana provides a clear, simple overview of mindfulness and meditation. He asserts the practice of meditation makes the promise of mental cultivation that can bring the mind to a state of tranquility, awareness, concentration, and insight. He sees the purpose of meditation as being personal transformation.

As your mind becomes still and calm, tensions, fears, and worries subside.[153]

Two overlapping practices are prayer and contemplation. He identifies prayer as addressing a spiritual entity and contemplation as a prolonged reflection on a certain topic. Both are concentration exercises that can produce deep calm and a sense of peace and contentment.

He offers suggestions to foster attitudes conducive to meditation, including don't expect anything in particular, don't strain or rush, don't cling, let go, accept what arises, be gentle and curious with yourself, view problems as challenges, and don't contrast or compare.

The mind is described as analogous to a cup of muddy water. The longer it settles and is allowed to be still, the muck falls to the bottom, and the water becomes clearer. Mindfulness is described as nonjudgmental observation, impartial watchfulness, nonconceptual awareness, bare attention, non-egoistic alertness, or participatory alertness.

Being mindful is being in a state of readiness without being burdened by past pains or future worries. Meditation is the training ground to instill these mental habits. There are many styles of meditation, and all require practice to experience the mental health benefits.

◇◇

Mindfulness helps us get better at seeing the difference between what's happening and the stories we tell ourselves about what's happening, stories that get in the way of direct experience. Often such stories treat a fleeting state of mind as if it were our entire and permanent self.[154]
—Sharon Salzburg, *Real Happiness: The Power of Meditation*

◇◇

You can start practicing mindfulness by following these steps:

Be attentive and focused. Find ways to calm down and observe more details in your environment. Use all your senses to perceive your surroundings (smell, vision, taste). For example, intentionally notice the taste of a good meal or the temperature outside.

Enjoy the moment. For just a few minutes at a time, pay attention to what you are doing with a curious, open mindset. Look for simple pleasures to enjoy.

Temporarily suspend judgment. Treat yourself with self-compassion as you learn to be more mindful. Approach the challenge from a state of inquiry, not evaluation.

EMOTIONAL HEALTH AND HAPPINESS

What is happiness for you? What comes to mind when you hear the word *happiness*? There are countless definitions. The term *happy* can refer to a range of pleasant, positive, or good emotions ranging from contentment to sheer delight.

Common constructs of happiness have been connected to your subjective emotional state, fulfillment, gratitude, moments of joy, experiences of pleasure, optimal engagement, interpersonal belonging, how you grow and make progress, and many more components. Philosophical teachings often refer to happiness as living the "good life."

For most people, the exact definition may not matter. You probably know the feeling, you like it, and you want more of it.

Ed Diener's pioneering work combined several facets of happiness underneath the umbrella of *subjective well-being*, including the evaluation of emotional states as well as overall life satisfaction. If people report feeling good about their well-being and feeling satisfied with life, perhaps that is the defining factor.

Diener offers common thinking errors we make in predicting future happiness, as outlined here:

- Narrowly focusing on a single factor or period in time, rather than considering the big picture.
- Overestimating the long-term impact of our choices.
- Forgetting that happiness is an ongoing journey rather than a destination.
- Paying too much attention to external information, overlooking personal preferences and experiences.

We'll cover more later, but here are a few reminders about happiness. People report positive states of fulfillment and happiness when they are engaged in worthwhile activities. While drinking margaritas on the beach can feel pleasant, this isn't when people report feeling their best.

Moderate your expectations. You aren't supposed to feel happy all the time; it is fleeting, and no one experiences consistent elation.

RICK HANSON — HARDWIRING HAPPINESS

Rick Hanson, a well-known clinical psychologist, addresses the previously mentioned negativity bias, or the brain's natural pessimism. His construct of "hardwiring happiness" sets forth a simple strategy for building new brain structures full of joy, compassion, courage, and calm through the underlying power of daily experiences.

This concept affirms you can develop, enhance, and reinforce practices and habits to develop psychological fitness, which results in physiological changes in the brain.

Hanson endorses cultivating the resources you need, including safety, connection, and satisfaction.

To build resilience, he proposes intentionally enriching positive experiences in your life through a **HEAL model:**

- **H**ave a beneficial experience
- **E**nrich it
- **A**bsorb it
- **L**ink it to life

Engaging in a consistent practice as the HEAL model allows for reinforcement and internalization of positive inputs and experiences, leading to brain changes.[155]

What Factors Determine Your Level of Happiness?

Sonja Lyubomirsky studies happiness, and her research has produced impactful results. She describes happiness as:

><><><><><><><><><><><><><><><><><><><><><><><><><><><><><><><><>

the experience of joy, contentment, or positive well-being, combined with a sense that one's life is good, meaningful, and worthwhile.[156]

><><><><><><><><><><><><><><><><><><><><><><><><><><><><><><><><>

Lyubomirsky and colleagues' research supports predictions from a model of well-being. The intention to increase happiness under optimal conditions can be effective. According to these studies, happiness level is influenced by three components: a genetically determined set point, happiness-relevant situational factors, and happiness-relevant activities and practices.

The activity category provides the best opportunities for enhancing sustainable happiness.[157] This research shows one can improve well-being by making the right changes in life. Suggested practices and activities include regularly counting your blessings, pursuing meaningful personal goals, or engaging in random acts of kindness.[158]

In her book, *The How of Happiness,* she highlights key findings that happiness is roughly determined by:

- 50 percent genetics
- 40 percent daily activities/internal factors
- 10 percent life circumstances

Life circumstances or external factors may include marital and socioeconomic status and other societal influences.[159] The great news is you have 40 percent agency and control over your happiness.

As a review, here are some suggestions for how to promote happiness:

- Enhance social connections, increase intimacy, and have meaningful interactions with others.
- Let go of the "pursuit" of happiness. Trying too hard can feel like trying to catch steam. Let go of the will or expectation to capture happiness.
- Count your blessings. Mentioned throughout this book is the power of practicing gratitude consistently. Well-known studies by Michael McCullough, Robert Emmons, Lyubomirsky, and others have reinforced the mental health benefits of giving thanks. More on this later…
- Experiment. Understand yourself and figure out what will give you the most impactful boosts.

Key Point:

You have agency over your sense of happiness.

Challenge:

Reflect on what happiness means to you. How can you orchestrate increased levels of happiness?

◇◇◇

Happiness is not the belief that we don't need to change;
it's the realization that we can.[160]
—Shawn Achor, *The Happiness Advantage*

◇◇◇

Chapter 7:
Psychological Fitness Practices

THROUGHOUT THIS BOOK, WE HAVE COVERED CORE COMPONENTS OF MENTAL HEALTH, STRESS AND BURNOUT, COMMON OBSTACLES FACED, AND OPTIONS TO BUILD PSYCHOLOGICAL FITNESS. This chapter offers additional evidence-based practices to enhance mental health and fitness. By doing the internal work, you'll move toward positive mental health.

Meet Riley. Riley is a leader in a fast-growing technology company who experienced early career success. After months of investing in personal development work and implementing some of these practices, Riley experienced profound changes.

Riley's reflections:

Last year it felt like I was climbing mountains. After doing some inner work, I feel like I now have equilibrium. I still have the knowledge of things that are opportunities for me, but it's better because I have a toolset now. I know doing the practices helps my mental health. The things I don't have tools for, I understand how to find resources that can help. I struggled with personal anxieties for a long time. Waking up now and being like, wow, everything's okay. I feel okay, and it will be okay — this is unfamiliar to me.

What has helped? Using anchors. Ensuring that my values and the things that matter to me continue to be at the forefront when challenges and obstacles come through. If I'm struggling to sleep, I understand the anchor is exercise, good eating, and not drinking too much alcohol.

I've worked on raising my mental health baseline. I focus on what gets me into the green zone. I haven't been in a better place in as long as I can remember. It's about building toward health rather than focusing on concerns.

Meet Hayden. Hayden is an executive and parent of two who, despite having a busy and demanding life, has consistently and incrementally integrated well-being practices into daily life.

Hayden's reflections:

It's no small commitment but building out these habits really works. I have so much more energy. By focusing on my everyday well-being, I feel what's possible. By doing these practices, I'm enriching my life. It's helping in how I show up in all areas of my life. I used to be easily irritated, and I feel so much less edgy now. I'm a better spouse and parent. I'm more effective at work. I'm easier to be around.

POSITIVE PSYCHOLOGY INTERVENTIONS

To advance collective mental health, we need to simultaneously pursue the alleviation of distress and the cultivation of thriving and flourishing. In psychology, a traditional therapeutic process can be oriented toward processing, healing, and recovery, which is applicable and appropriate for many.

Another approach to therapy or coaching can be considered more present- and future-oriented. Practices suggested by positive psychology thought leaders, researchers, and practitioners are reinforced in this chapter. Interventions can be practiced with a coach, professional, group, or on your own.

Positive psychological interventions (PPIs) are directions, actions, and suggestions that are conceptually founded and empirically proven to increase overall health.[161] PPIs are a series of scientific practices focused on increasing happiness, well-being, and positive thinking and emotions.[162]

Research supports the effectiveness of PPIs, including increased scores on optimism and appreciation and improved mental health and happiness. Fostering character strengths of hope, gratitude, optimism, and forgiveness is shown to enhance mental health, self-esteem, and life satisfaction.[163] Mental health can also prosper from being and doing good, rather than merely feeling good.

PPIs have been described as psychological interventions that increase positive thoughts, feelings, and behaviors. Researchers Sin and Lyubomirsky recognize two essential components of PPIs: improving happiness through positive emotions and thoughts and sustaining the change in the longer term.[164]

Subjective well-being and happiness can be improved through methods involving communication, gratitude, cognitive reframing, and increasing sensory awareness. These practices have been combined under the umbrella of PPIs.[165]

Leading well-being researchers Parks and Biswas-Diener define PPIs as practices supported by scientific research which are evidence-based, address at least one component of positive psychology, and offer long-term benefits.[166]

Positive psychology practices aren't a cure-all and won't be ideal for everyone in all circumstances. Many improve directly and quickly, whereas others advance in a slower, non-linear fashion. While it's difficult to break long-standing behavioral patterns, you need to start someplace, continue the work, and try again.

THE PERMA MODEL

The PERMA Model was created by Martin Seligman, psychologist and educator. Seligman recognizes how fundamental it is to seek out what makes you feel good and happy.[167] He selected these components that individuals pursue because they are inherently motivating and enhance well-being. Unique to this well-being theory, the five categories include eudaimonic and hedonic factors.

These five components of happiness and well-being are represented by the PERMA Model:

P = Positive Emotion

E = Engagement

R = Relationships

M = Meaning

A = Accomplishments

POSITIVE EMOTION

Experiencing positive emotion is naturally related to well-being. As mentioned previously, fostering positive emotion can drown out burdensome, draining, negative emotions. The practice of promoting positive feelings extends to accepting the past, no matter how challenging, and looking forward to the future with optimism. Therefore, practicing positive thinking is one route to fostering happiness. Have you ever noticed that whenever you feel positive and good about something, it feels lighter?

ENGAGEMENT

Being proactively engaged in life is beneficial to mental health. Experiencing engagement allows one to feel a personal sense of agency and effectiveness. The nature of the activity is less important; one could be engaged in work, hobbies, cooking, or interacting with friends.

If you consider the times in your life that you feel the best or most fulfilled, you will likely notice that during these experiences, you are not passively at rest; rather, you have been actively involved in something. It's not time spent in front of television or screens that is amplifying happiness.

RELATIONSHIPS

We have a natural desire to be connected to people and to belong to a group, community, system, or circle. We were born with the need (not just desire) for love, compassion, connection, and interaction. It is reinforced throughout this book how important it is to develop and maintain connections with colleagues, friends, and family. When faced with difficulty, we can help each other.

MEANING

I was part of a conversation recently where people were discussing how perplexed they were about why so many celebrities who live extravagant lives die from suicide. Someone said they should be stress-free; they didn't have to worry about financial stability.

While people can experience luxuries and conveniences in life and appear to have it "easy," clearly, wealth and materialistic items alone don't guarantee well-being or happiness. In fact, extreme fame or fortune can fuel an insatiable desire for more and a loss of perspective on what truly brings meaning and fulfillment.

I was recently on a trip to a resort area and was inspired to experience as much as I could during my limited time. The most amazing part was the natural beauty of the beaches, hiking trails, and cliffs along the water. I also had dinner at a well-known fancy resort (with rooms up to $10,000/night).

While it was gorgeous, the food was amazing, and the service was top-notch, my favorite part was the long conversation with the valet drivers. They asked why I was in town. I told them I'm a psychologist and was filming a course on improving mental health in the workplace.

One of them said, "Man, we need your help here."

Young men told me how they could use such services due to the challenges they faced with some guests. While certainly, they were not referring to all the resort guests, they were continually surprised at how rude, crabby, and mean some people can be on their vacations.

My new valet friends went on to say how this made no sense to them. Guests pull up in $100,000+ cars, they experience wealth and comfort, and they're at an incredible resort with beautiful scenery and world-class amenities. They are on a luxury vacation, yet they are miserable and unhappy.

They mentioned the staff would benefit from learning how to handle such behavior and how not to absorb the negativity they can experience at work. Of course, know this is not to say all people with wealth are bad, crabby, or lack manners. It was simply a healthy perspective reminder about what is important in life. It was inspiring, hearing the insights and the life lessons these young men were learning and willing to share.

Some of their comments: *Maybe they just have gotten so used to luxury that they don't appreciate it much anymore. It's sad they may not have enough meaning in their lives that they need to be so worried about how their calamari is served. Makes me appreciate what I have 'cause I don't want to feel like that in life. Makes me think more about how I treat people. That negativity can wreck your day if you let it.*

This is a good check to remind us that life is about so much more than wealth and materialistic things. Finding meaning motivates people to live and fully engage in life. While it depends person to person what feels meaningful, commonly, the most meaning is found in serving, loving, and making a difference for others and is less often found in isolation or in the pursuit of pleasure.

ACCOMPLISHMENTS

It's natural to feel proud of what you've done or achieved. Accomplishments can boost your sense of self and assure you that you are valuable. When people achieve, they feel happy about themselves and typically want to do and accomplish more and thus grow. Experiencing a sense of accomplishment contributes to well-being and psychological fitness, provided it's kept in check. Over-valuing our worth based on external factors can erode mental health.

IMPACT OF PERMA

Many studies support the impact of intentionally focusing on enhancing each of the PERMA components. It not only enhances well-being but can also decrease reports of psychological distress.[168] Elevated PERMA characteristics have also been associated with physical health, life satisfaction, and professional thriving.[169]

Perhaps the most exciting component of this information is how individuals enhance their well-being in sync with others and provide the opportunity for compound and scalable impact on communities, organizations, groups, and governments.

Promoting thriving and flourishing together needs to be the path forward.

Key Points:

According to the PERMA model, to self-actualize and enhance well-being, you can engage in activities to elevate each of the five components: positive emotion, engagement, relationships, meaning, and accomplishments.

Challenge:

Commit to small actions you can take to foster each of the PERMA areas.

RICHARD DAVIDSON — HEALTHY MINDS MODEL

Richard Davidson is a thought leader at the University of Wisconsin, leads the Center for Healthy Minds, and has been at the forefront of well-being research. Davidson recognizes four pillars of well-being: awareness, connection, insight, and purpose.[170] This model is also grounded in the idea that you can cultivate, nourish, and enhance these components of well-being with continual practice.

Building a sense of awareness involves being mindful of knowing what you are seeing, feeling, and experiencing at the moment.

Fostering healthy connections with people requires incorporating healthy kindness, appreciation, empathy, and compassion in social relationships.

Developing insight is about gaining a deeper understanding of the narratives you tell yourself as well as core self-beliefs.

Upgrading and improving the expectations you have of yourself increases well-being.

Finally, understanding the purpose for <u>what and why you do what you</u> do promotes well-being as well. It is useful to understand what your true north is and how your actions help others and the greater good.

Key Point:

Richard Davidson's model of well-being includes four pillars: awareness, connection, insight, and purpose.

Challenge:

What can you do today to foster awareness and grounding in your current experience?

- How can you cultivate more compassion and appreciation in your interpersonal relationships?
- Take time to engage in deeper reflection about your beliefs and expectations about yourself.
- In what area can you upgrade the narrative you have about yourself into a healthier version?
- Review your sense of life purpose; what are you doing to help and lift others?

POSITIVE PSYCHOTHERAPY

Positive psychotherapy (PPT) is a therapeutic method mostly focused on positive psychology theories. According to PPT, individuals, groups, and institutions thrive under certain influences. Constructive behaviors have been found to promote well-being, including recognizing and utilizing one's abilities and doing selfless acts.

The PPT approach is designed to amplify individuals' strengths and help them understand how to frame problems and challenges in a constructive context. There are multiple resources available, yet Tayyab Rashid and Martin P. Seligman offer both a comprehensive Clinician's Guide as well as a workbook on the application of the practices.[171]

The authors provide thorough resources intended to help clinicians and clients work together to reflect on and apply the suggested practices. I'm offering here some highlights of exercises found in PPT, yet this is not a prescriptive or comprehensive treatment suggestion.

The PPT exercises can help you assess your abilities from various angles, grounded in your strengths, and through reflection, help you generate practical wisdom. There are suggested phases in which to engage in this growth process. The following offers general guidelines of the path with brief descriptions of each suggestion.

Positive Introduction

The person writes a constructive introductory one-page story of their personal tale with a start, halfway, and happy ending in specific terms that encourage the individual to report their best self. The story can include crucible moments of their life that have contributed to who they are today.

Gratitude Journal

Gratitude, again. This practice involves recording three positive events (large or small) at the end of every day and the circumstances that led to these events.

Signature and Character Strengths

The individual gathers data from a variety of sources, such as an online strengths test (viacharacter.org), as well as input from friends and family to create a distinctive strengths profile. The PERMA model endorses fostering and leaning into core strengths, values, and attributes. Grounding in signature and prominent strengths can offer an opportunity to leverage these characteristics in daily life.

Practical Wisdom

This ongoing process involves understanding how to apply and leverage strengths and learning practically.

A Better Version of Me

This is a reflection exercise in which one can envision and consider what a better version of themselves looks like. The language is appealing because considering the best version of yourself can feel overwhelming, unrealistic, and unattainable.

This process entails:

- Setting goals that are observable
- Focusing on behaviors, actions, and habits
- Making changes applicable to your current situation
- Establishing favorable external conditions and social support

- Recognizing specific changes you want to see, i.e. you want to feel more energy, be more connected, be healthier, more productive, more content, etc.

In the exercise, reflect on how the better version of you will be happier or more satisfied, why it will be good for you, and the person you want to become. Lastly, individuals reflect and journal on how they want to be regarded by others. How do you want others to view you?

Open and Closed Memories

The next proposed phase aims at developing positive feelings and coping with unpleasant memories, events, and sensations with the help of others. While the detailed process is beyond the scope here, I'll provide a synopsis.

Typically conducted in a therapeutic session, a person would recall, record, and process emotions associated with unpleasant or painful experiences in a contained and time-compressed way. After practicing meditation, the client writes down unpleasant memories and considers adaptive coping methods.

Maximizing vs. Satisficing

The ideas of maximizing (creating the greatest decision possible) and satisficing (making a "great enough" decision) are introduced. The reflection typically involves an assessment of how to manage expectations intentionally of how one responds to situations. It is healthy to decide when it makes sense to introduce a "good enough" response.

Key Points:

Positive psychology therapeutic practices provide education and enhance the practice of focusing on the positive elements of self and life. In doing so, you can build your psychological reservoir and resources to help handle tenacious or challenging situations.

Challenge:

Consider taking a strengths-based assessment, writing a one-page introductory story of your life, fostering a daily gratitude practice, or reflecting on what a better version of yourself could look like.

ARE POSITIVE PSYCHOLOGY PRACTICES APPROPRIATE FOR ALL?

You may be thinking positive psychology practices are only relevant if you don't have big problems. Or they only apply to people experiencing privilege. What about people in poverty or those experiencing trauma and grief?

Again, these practices are not intended to be a solution for mental illness, trauma, or poverty, as these issues can require deeper, more intensive levels of support. Nonetheless, they can be helpful for most, regardless of immediate challenges, even if only a moment of relief is experienced.

While doing research for this book, I had insightful discussions with Susanne Hoeppner, Assistant Professor of Psychiatry from Harvard University. She is engaged in research exploring positive psychological interventions via a technology application to address challenges such as smoking cessation and obsessive-compulsive disorder.

Hoeppner shared that she was intentional about promoting good and positive psychology to individuals who had limited resources because a lot of times, we pertain positive psychology to individuals who aren't struggling but wish they were happy and satisfied. She said it well:

If you're just so desperately unhappy down in the PTSD or psychological, psychiatric disorder domain, you just concentrate on getting back to not struggling. There's no life that couldn't be a little bit happier, a little bit more mindful, a little bit more enjoyable amidst the big struggles.

They help people create tiny islands of contentment that they can concentrate on and draw strength from. According to Hoeppner, it is recognized that we all have a mixed bag of things that we are dealing with. We can focus on the worst parts or, to get well, we can focus on more good ones — or at least notice the good ones that are also in the bag.

Even getting to a point where one can recognize that not everything in life is rotten, there is that moment … that special connection I have with my dog, or with my daughter, or that I can appreciate a cup of hot chocolate or a walk around the block. Creating these micro experiences is helpful and can cultivate progress toward mental health.

Hoeppner's work is important because there are many little things that we forget are reachable that can have a strong impact. It helps people understand they can train themselves to see and rejoice in that, take strength from it, and hopefully make it grow. These things seem to be important for me and good for me, so I will do more of them.

Key Point:

You can train yourself to create more micro experiences of goodness, regardless of your life circumstances.

WHAT WILL TRULY MAKE US HAPPY?

Many psychologists describe happiness as a positive mental and emotional state. The pursuit of happiness is common in the western world. The problem is that happiness is not static or staying; it comes and goes. So, the pursuit of it is elusive.

As a Yale University Professor, Laurie Santos noticed elevated anxiousness in her students and perceived a mental health crisis, which expanded beyond Yale. It inspired her to create a course on well-being, which is available on Coursera.[172] She recognized that many don't have a good grasp of what will truly bring happiness.

She noticed students felt high levels of stress and seemed overly focused on getting a good job rather than creating a meaningful life. Santos thought exposing and educating students on evidence-based psychological insights regarding happiness and well-being could help.

Students (and people) in the U.S. report unprecedented unhappiness. Santos notes contributors could include fierce competition among high achievers, social media, news anxiety, uncertainty, and too little free time.

A few highlights from Santos' course include understanding that happiness is within your control and requires practice and effort. Money is not as important as you think, yet ***interpersonal connections*** are. ***Living in the moment, helping others, express-***

ing gratitude, and getting good sleep are all endorsed. Santos recommends increasing compassion for yourself and others, focusing on your strengths, and developing healthy routines and habits.

Key Point:

Learning about well-being practices can help enhance well-being.

DO MONEY AND WEALTH BRING HAPPINESS?

According to research, once fundamental necessities are addressed, and there is no longer struggle associated with poverty, increased income does not boost happiness. Some propose there can even be an opposing link between wealth and happiness - the more wealth a person has, the less pleased they may be.

Despite what consumerism sells, pursuing materialistic goals can have an inverse impact on happiness. Simply pursuing stuff can generate low levels of discontent or dissatisfaction, moving you away from psychological fitness.

HAPPINESS AND RELATIVE REFERENCE POINTS

Subjective well-being and happiness also depend on the people you are around. Your perceived level of happiness is relative to whom you are exposed. The *Ebbinghaus illusion* explains this psychological phenomenon. For example, silver medal winners are commonly less happy than bronze medal winners. A silver medalist can see through the lens of being just short of first place, and a bronze medal winner may focus on being close to not getting a medal at all.

The problem is these references can be random and insidious. Wherever we are, and whomever we are around, tends to be what we compare ourselves against. In this way, it can mess us up. Social media provides a vast unrelenting source of random comparisons and arbitrary reference points that are available to us at any moment.

Key Point:

Who you are around and your relative reference point matter for determining your perceived experience of well-being and mental health. Watch for the insidious effects of being exposed to random reference points through social media that may be causing damage.

THE SCIENCE OF HAPPY SPENDING

You can increase your happiness by spending time and money on others rather than yourself. When given $5 or $10, the people who share it with others or donate it to charity experience an increase in happiness and well-being, in contrast with those who spend the money on themselves.

Key Point:

You can increase your happiness by spending time and money on others.

Challenge:

Donate money, buy stuff for others, and volunteer your time.

WHAT ARE THE BENEFITS OF HAPPINESS?

Literature reviews indicate that happiness impacts not only individuals but also families, communities, and society at large.[173] A few happiness benefits include higher income, improved work outcomes (productivity, work quality), social rewards (healthier marriages and relationships), more activity and energy, better physical health, and even longevity.

Lyubomirsky and colleagues' studies also indicate that people who experience happiness are more charitable and self-confident, have better self-control, and show greater self-regulatory and coping abilities.

Additional Methods of Building Psychological Fitness

THE CASE FOR NATURE

<<<<<<<<<<<<<<<<<<<<<<<<<<<<<<<<<<<<<<<<<<<<<<<<<<<<<<

We need the tonic of wilderness...We can never have enough of nature.[174]
—Henry D. Thoreau, *Walden*

<<<<<<<<<<<<<<<<<<<<<<<<<<<<<<<<<<<<<<<<<<<<<<<<<<<<<<

We feel better when we are in nature. It is good for the soul, and research is showing us that it enhances physical and mental health, even in small doses. Increased exposure to nature improves psychological fitness. Individuals more connected to nature are happier and experience more well-being. Being in nature cultivates positive emotion, calmness, a broader sense of connection, and enhanced mental health.

In Japan, the term for being in nature for therapeutic and restorative effects is **forest bathing** or **shinrin-yoku**. Spending time in nature, even if it is walking through a park with greenery, provides a beneficial mental reset. It contributes to the enhanced nervous system and heart functioning and a decrease in bowel disorders.[175] This is a particularly important finding, considering the increased time we spend indoors connected to technology.

A recent study of thousands of people in Tokyo, Japan, found that people who spent time outdoors had more positive mental health outcomes, including higher self-esteem, happiness, and life satisfaction, than participants with less access to the outdoors.

Individuals exposed to nature also had reduced anxiety, depression, and loneliness. It was found that even individuals who looked at green spaces from a window experienced similar benefits.[176] You don't need to live in the wilderness to reap the mental health rewards of nature. Even spending more time looking out your window at nature can boost your psychological fitness.

Lisa Nisbet, Ph.D., is a psychologist at Trent University in Ontario, Canada, and studies connectedness to nature. She endorses the physical and psychological benefits and suggests that you can boost your mood and sense of connection just by walking in nature, even in a city park.[177]

A 2019 research review in *Science Advances* supports the outcomes of nature's ability to positively impact mental health, including increasing happiness, effectiveness in managing life tasks, fostering a sense of purpose in life, and decreasing emotional distress. Results also suggest that being outdoors can lead to better sleep and less stress.[178]

Also relevant to mental health, recent studies support that being outdoors reduces stress by lowering the stress hormone cortisol.[179]

People suffering from mild to major depressive disorders experienced elevated moods as well as increased motivation to recover when exposed to nature.[180]

A research review by Gregory Bratman, Ph.D. at the University of Washington, and colleagues confirmed evidence that contact with nature is associated with increases in happiness, subjective well-being, positive affect, positive social interactions, and a sense of meaning and purpose in life, as well as decreases in mental distress.[181]

According to a study in the scientific journal *Nature,* spending at least 120 minutes a week in nature is associated with good health and well-being. How the nature contact was achieved did not seem to matter. Spending two hours on the weekend outdoors or shorter visits throughout the week all resulted in positive health outcomes.[182]

Exposure to nature can mitigate the negative effects of social isolation and loneliness. While interpersonal isolation can be associated with lower well-being, research has shown when people with low social connectedness had high levels of nature nearby, they had higher levels of well-being.[183] So, even though they may not feel connected to others, feeling connected to nature can boost their mental health.

If you are concerned that you don't have time to get outdoors, there is hopeful news about the positive effects of nature. You don't need much to experience the benefits.

According to Erin Largo-Wight, a University of North Florida professor, "We've explored this question in many studies, and our findings suggest that nature appears to have a positive impact on self-reported and physiological stress in as little as seven to ten minutes."[184]

Not surprisingly, it has been found that spending more time outdoors and less time with electronic devices and screens increases problem-solving and creative abilities.[185] Being in nature upgrades mental cognition. Walking and engaging in nature activities enhance attention and focus.[186] Evidence also supports connections to increased performance, concentration, and lower risk of developing attention deficit disorder (ADD).[187]

The hypothesis of how being in nature fosters mental health includes the promotion of mindfulness, slowing down, reduction of external stimuli and screens, as well as the substance phytoncide emitted by trees. Exposure to essential oils may provide antimicrobial properties that influence immunity. Inhaling forest air can also increase natural killer (NK) cells in the body, used to attack infections and other internal invaders contributing to illness. Being outdoors provides vitamin D, sunlight for our vision, fresh air, and opportunities to be physically active.

The notion that exposure to nature enhances focus and attention was endorsed by the Attention Restoration Theory (ART) by Rachel and Stephen Kaplan, which explains how being in nature can replenish and decrease fatigue.[188] They propose that exposure to your natural environment, such as seeing a sunrise, being at the beach, viewing the mountains, or any natural landscape, will capture your attention effortlessly, making you more mindful and attentive.

The Kaplans recognize two kinds of attention: voluntary and involuntary. Naturally, intentionally paying attention to something is voluntary and unknowingly attending is involuntary. Attention Restoration Theory indicates that exposure to nature improves our ability to manage attention, and it offers a reprieve from daily stressors. The perceptual features of nature offer the mind a break from top-down, focused attention and allow for what is referred to as **soft fascination**, which can have a restorative, soothing impact.

Environmental psychology is an area of psychology endorsing how nature plays a role in human development. It involves studying the connection of well-being to your environment.[189] The psychology of environment affirms that we are biologically adaptive to natural environments, exposure to natural light is therapeutic and healthy, and physical environments impact our social identities.[190] The term **biophilia** has been used to describe the natural connection and draw humans toward nature.

Erich Fromm described it as "love for everything that is alive."

This research is applicable to everyone. Even having plants in your home is beneficial for your mental health by enhancing sensory awareness and again improving cognition and focus.[191] You can build your psychological fitness by having plants in your vicinity.

The effects of nature on well-being have also been assessed in prisons. Biologist Nalini Nadkarni has been sharing the medicine of nature with individuals who are incarcerated. According to Nadkarni, exposing violent offenders to nature images for one hour daily reduces their anxiety and stress as well as violent tendencies. Showing images of landscapes, forests, and waterfalls can defuse anger and reduce tension for prisoners who are deprived of access to nature.[192]

Researchers observed inmates in solitary confinement in an Oregon prison for one year. Those who viewed nature videos several times a week committed 26 percent fewer violent infractions than their peers.[193]

Even the sounds of nature can rejuvenate and be restorative. People who listened to nature sounds such as crickets chirping and waves crashing performed better on cognitive tasks than people hearing urban sounds.[194]

Spending time in nature can act as a salve for the mind, providing cognitive benefits. University of Chicago psychologist Marc Berman, Ph.D., and his student Kathryn Schertz evaluated this topic in a 2019 review. Findings indicate that green spaces near schools promote cognitive development in children, and green views near children's homes promote self-regulation behaviors. Adults living in public housing units in neighborhoods with more green space demonstrated better attentional functioning than those with less access to nature.

Overall, experiments suggest that being exposed to nature improves cognitive flexibility, working memory, and attentional control, while more exposure to urban environments is linked to attention deficits.[195]

There has been a focus on green areas in nature studies, but blue spaces (ocean, water, lakes, and rivers) are also shown to have a beneficial impact.[196]

Key Points:

Nature can help you be happier and smarter. Research has demonstrated that being in nature has a positive impact on your mental and physical health and, therefore, enhances psychological fitness. It has been shown to improve well-being, mood, attention, focus, problem-solving, and cognition. It helps reduce feelings of stress and increases a sense of connection.

Challenge:

If you don't live in the woods, find more ways to connect with everyday nature that is accessible to you. Get more plants, garden, walk in your neighborhood, spend time in a park, watch the sunset, sit by a lake, etc.

SAVORING

Savoring can help combat the hedonic adaptation phenomenon (how you adapt to pleasurable experiences that are likely to enhance happiness as they initially did). Savoring is pausing and appreciating the moment and what you are experiencing. It can intensify, deepen, and lengthen positive emotions that come with meaningful experiences in your life or engaging in something you love.

Intentional reflection every day to appreciate what is great right now cultivates well-being.

Fred Bryant is a pioneer in savoring. In *Savoring: A New Model of Positive Experience*, Bryant and Veroff define savoring as:

◇◇

The capacity to attend to, appreciate, and enhance the positive experiences in your life. It's the counterpart to coping, which involves dealing with life's negative experiences.[197]

◇◇

If it helps to have a more prescriptive approach, four types of savoring are described in their work: basking, thanksgiving, marveling, and luxuriating.

Basking — Taking great pleasure or satisfaction in one's accomplishments, good fortune, and blessings. Receiving praise with grace

Thanksgiving — Giving thanks; expressing gratitude

Marveling — Being full of wonder or astonishment through beauty or exercising virtue. Losing yourself in awe.

Luxuriating — Taking great pleasure (and showing no restraint) in enjoying physical comforts and sensations. Indulging in your senses, enjoying rich food or drink, feeling the sun on your skin.

Key Point:

Savoring your experiences can diffuse the hedonic treadmill phenomenon.

Challenge:

Try some of these suggested techniques to savor something special every day for a week. Share the experience with someone else, reflect on how lucky or blessed you are to enjoy such an amazing moment, keep a souvenir or photo of the activity, make a list of enjoyable experiences, and take the time to review regularly.

AGAIN — EXPRESSING GRATITUDE

Robert Emmons is a gratitude researcher who focuses on the psychology of living a meaningful life. Through his studies of thousands of people, research indicates that people who practice gratitude consistently experience physical benefits such as stronger immune systems, lower blood pressure, fewer aches and pains, and better sleep.

Psychological benefits include higher levels of positive emotions, more alertness, joy, optimism, pleasure, and happiness. The social benefits of gratitude include people being more helpful, forgiving, compassionate, and outgoing, as well as less isolated and lonely.[198]

Plenty of research shows that being more grateful can lead to increased well-being.[199] Additionally, cultivating gratitude can decrease anxiety and depression.[200]

Seligman and colleagues endorse writing a letter of thanks. Their study asked participants to write and deliver a letter of thanks to someone who has done something special for them. Results indicated that the letter writers reported increased happiness, even one month after the intervention.[201]

The interpersonal benefits are important; it has been described by researchers as "a social emotion that signals our recognition of the things others have done for us,"[202] as we can consider it to be a social feeling. It promotes supporting, connecting, and appreciating people, which in turn enhances relationships.

Key Points:

Contemplating what you are grateful for, sharing it with others, and expressing gratitude toward others all build psychological fitness. If you are fostering appreciation and gratitude, it leaves less room for negative and toxic thinking. Developing gratitude is like strengthening a muscle. Keeping a weekly gratitude journal is recommended for optimal impact.

Establishing a daily practice of appreciation is one approach to combat negativity bias. Gratitude improves well-being.

Challenge: Consider trying a gratitude practice.

- Compose and send a note of gratitude to someone who has positively influenced your life.
- On a daily or weekly basis, record three positive things that happened that day/week. Try to write one sentence describing each blessing.
- Possible prompts for journaling:

Today I experienced something awesome. It was...
Today I did something that I excelled at. It was...
Here is how I was nice to someone today...
Here is how someone was kind to me...
I heard great news today. It was...
I came upon something inspiring today. It was...

BROADEN-AND-BUILD THEORY

Problems command attention. As mentioned, due to the negativity bias, your brain is on alert for potential nearby threats. In the field of psychology, negative emotions have been studied, and links are often drawn between negative emotions and less favorable outcomes.

Researcher and author Barbara Fredrickson recognized the lack of focus on studying positive feelings and dynamics. She and colleagues have shown us that positive emotions can play a role in buffering against stressors.

Traditionally, negative emotions have been linked to action tendencies more than positive emotions. Action tendency refers to the urge or the need to act in a certain way. For example, fear can trigger us to fight or flight (flee).

Fredrickson proposes that positive emotions may not lead to action tendencies yet can provide more freedom to engage in a wider range of behaviors. Research indicates that positive emotions relate to a "free activation" that welcomes openness, expansiveness, experimentation, and willingness to pursue options.[203]

This notion developed into Fredrickson's Broaden-and-Build Theory of Positive Emotions, indicating that positive emotions broaden our repertoire of potential thoughts and actions in response to stimuli.[204]

Positive emotions foster feelings of creativity, curiosity, and playfulness and expand the options and actions we are able to access. Engaging positive emotion can increase one's receptiveness to subsequent positive events, leading to an upward spiral.

Experiencing more positive emotions allows you to learn, play, and engage with others more effectively. Your thought-action options are broadened through positive feelings, which allow you to access more personal resources to respond in the face of circumstances.

Experiencing positive emotions and maintaining a positive outlook during stressful experiences promotes well-being and resilience.[205]

Key Point:

Fostering positive emotions can build resilience and psychological fitness.

POWER OF PURPOSE

◇◇

Life is never made unbearable by circumstances, but only by lack of meaning and purpose.
—Viktor Frankl

◇◇

Having a sense of purpose is fundamental to a fulfilling life and enriches your psychological fitness. It helps to have a compelling reason to get up in the morning. Harvard professor Ellen Langer has contributed for decades to research on aging and well-being. A study was done in the 1970s by Langer and Judith Rudin assessing how nursing home residents would respond to instructions for taking care of a plant.[206]

The nursing home context prior to the study did not offer much autonomy or decision-making for the residents. In the study, residents in the experimental group were told that they had control over and responsibility for a plant in their room. In the control group, residents were informed that staff would be caring for their plants.

Residents, given the responsibility to care for their plants, experienced positive outcomes, including greater feelings of self-worth. Simply taking care of their plant contributed to positive health outcomes.

Since this famous study, many research efforts have supported the power of people having a sense of purpose and control over their environment. Having such agency and autonomy enhances well-being.

Richard Leider has written and spoken about the purpose for years. His works are practical and inspiring. He offers multiple options for reflection and processing on his website (richardleider.com).

As an admirer of his material, several years ago, I reached out to connect with him and received a prompt reply. We set up a time for a phone call and quickly discovered that he lived one block from my office.

I appreciate his generosity, and his advice has been useful to many. When in doubt or when you aren't sure what your "purpose" is, start with thinking about how you can grow and give. Learn and share with others; much of the meaning and purpose can be found in these two ways. Moving your attention to others will generally foster purpose and meaning.

Studies from the Harvard School of Public Health indicate people who feel a greater sense of meaning and purpose in their lives are more likely to maintain health as they age.[207] A study conducted by Eric Kim linked a sense of purpose to a lower risk of disability, stroke, cardiovascular disease, sleep disturbance, and other medical conditions.[208]

Caring for animals can also provide a sense of purpose. Pets can provide companionship and accountability. Research has shown that Animal Assisted Therapy (AAT) programs within the prison system result in mental health benefits for inmates, life-enhancing and coping skills, as well as decreased negative behaviors.

MAN'S SEARCH FOR MEANING

Even in the face of adversity, the well-known historic psychiatrist Viktor Frankl urges us to seek meaning in life. Regardless of external circumstances, it's up to you to establish purpose and meaning. As a holocaust survivor, Frankl left empowering writings and works about the power we have over our emotional experiences. He challenges us to find meaning in any life situation.

Key Point:

Regardless of the circumstances, you can foster a deeper sense of purpose and meaning in your experience.

FLOW STATE

Have you ever experienced a time when you have become so immersed in something that you lose track of time? Felt like you were really "in the zone" engaging in an activity or task? This is a FLOW experience and as it turns out, engaging in FLOW is beneficial for our mental health.

What Is Flow?

Being in flow is becoming so focused and engaged that you lose track of time and your environment. Flow is a state of consciousness that allows for complete immersion in a task, bringing a deep sense of satisfaction and fulfillment.

When in flow, people report becoming so involved in the on-going activity that they are unaware of other concerns, feel happy, "in a groove," and in control. They experience an intense feeling of concentration, active participation in the activity, and feelings of mastery and success.

The late Mihaly Csikszentmihalyi was the positive psychologist who founded the concept of flow. He developed flow theory in the 1970s as he was studying people who did things for pure joy, even if they weren't rewarded with fame or wealth. He wanted to understand what makes people perform at their best.

He discovered that when people work with intention at their activity or craft and are at the intersection of talent and challenge, their ability increases the most. He describes flow as:

◇◇

...being completely involved in an activity for its own sake. The ego falls away. Time flies. Every action, movement, and thought follows inevitably from the previous one... your whole being is involved, and you're using your skills to the utmost... the holistic sensation that people feel when they act with total involvement.[209]

◇◇

According to Research, Flow:

- Enhances well-being. It is deeply satisfying to work in a state of flow.

- Increases resilience.

- Strengthens endurance.

- Is associated with improved task performance and work longevity.

- Acts as a buffer against stress. Flow experiences protect us from the negative impacts of stress.

- Unlocks creativity. Flow experiences are strongly tied to feeling creative at work.

- Boosts productivity. Studies demonstrate executives in a state of flow are five times more productive than their counterparts. By increasing time in flow by 15 to 20 percent, one can double productivity.

Key Point:

There are well-being, happiness, and mental health benefits to experiencing flow. By facilitating a flow state, you can enhance your psychological fitness and resilience.

Therapeutic Effects of Flow

Recent studies have supported the therapeutic impact of engaging in flow. For example, research suggests the rhythm and mechanics of surfing serve as respite and a generative path toward mental health healing and recovery.

Nick Caddick is a psychologist at Loughborough University in the United Kingdom who dedicated 18 months to researching the impacts of surfing on British soldiers and discovered its powerful impact. Caddick reported how surfing played a role in interrupting the PTSD cycle of symptoms.[210]

It makes sense that as people are in flow, they are fully rooted in the present moment and experience passion and agency over their environment. It provides a **temporary reprieve from daily worries** as well as past traumas.

Furthermore, according to research conducted with veterans in California, surfing helps build resilience and alleviates the distressing symptoms associated with PTSD and depression.

The Neuroscience of Flow

Being in a state of flow requires complete task engagement as well as low rates of self-referential thought, contributing to the well-being and optimal human functioning. The neurocognitive dynamics are still being understood. Flow states appear to be associated with particular brain functions.

Neurotransmitters are the chemical communicators of the brain that the nervous system uses to message between neurons and muscles. Thanks to modern neuroscience, there seems to be a pattern in the brain indicating how a flow state is created. Scientists suggest how the association between neurotransmitters in the brain can produce flow states.

Neurotransmitters include:

Dopamine — It can flood your brain when first in flow. Active in the pursuit phase of activity, it can enhance skills.

Norepinephrine — Activation in your body, including increased pulse and breathing, is a result of norepinephrine, contributing to an increase in arousal and energy.

Endorphins — Endorphins relieve pain and enhance pleasure, producing the sensation often described as "runner's high."

Anandamide — Workouts can also generate anandamide, producing a euphoric effect, which can enhance mood and decrease pain.

Serotonin — Toward the end of a flow state, serotonin is released in the brain, creating an after-glow effect.

You can see how the neurochemical interactions could have a powerful impact, creating an appealing state that people pursue. During flow, you feel power and control over your circumstances, a sense of oneness with the experience, and awareness that your level of skill meets the challenge of the task. Experiencing a feedback loop providing reinforcement that you are effective at engaging in the task is important.

What Does Flow Look like in Your Life?

- Finding the sweet spot between your own skill set and a challenging assignment.
- Being fully "in the zone."
- Tackling a challenge that stretches your mind but doesn't break it.
- Losing yourself in an endeavor.

How Do You Maximize It?

- Prepare. Meditation, exercise, and adequate sleep contribute to the likelihood of flow.
- Challenge yourself. You can't reach flow doing work that is boring and unfulfilling.
- Manage overwhelm... the enemy of flow. A busy and distracted mind gets in the way of the flow.

Key Points:

Optimal experience is something that we can make happen. FLOW builds resilience. Again, there are well-being, happiness, and mental health benefits to experiencing flow. By facilitating a flow state, you can enhance your psychological fitness and resilience.

Challenge:

- Bring more flow into your life. Reflect on flow experiences in your life currently.
- What activity is bringing you flow?
- What could you incorporate to tap into a flow experience?
- Think of what you liked to do as a kid... (must be an active engagement, not passively watching TV). Examples: playing a musical instrument, cooking, gardening, tennis, golf, problem-solving...

ENERGY MANAGEMENT

I believe work-life balance is a myth and generates unnecessary distress, adding one more elusive, unrealistic ideal that we SHOULD be striving toward. Balance is a verb, not a static state, and how we exert energy and attention is going to vary. The idea of time management is also tricky. We only have 24 hours in a day. Time is finite and not negotiable; therefore, it is not really to be "managed."

One of my favorite paradigm shifts is toward effective management of our energy rather than time. According to performance experts Tony Schwartz and Jim Loehr, **energy — *not time* — *is the core currency of high performance*.** A key to living as your best self is to optimize your energy. The concept is summarized nicely here:

◇◇◇

Performance, health, and happiness are grounded in the skillful management of energy. The number of hours in a day is fixed, but the quantity and quality of energy available to us is not. It is our most precious resource. The more we take responsibility for the energy we bring to the world, the more empowered and productive we become.[211]
—Jim Loehr and Tony Schwartz,
The Power of Full Engagement

◇◇◇

Many of us have mastered the art of giving our energy away. Do more, push through, grind, get a side hustle, optimize, work better, and work harder. It can feel like we are trying to improve ourselves to death. Can you relate to any of these? Spend more time with your kids/spouse/friends/co-workers, exercise more, meditate more, be outdoors more, drink more water, eat better, be more productive, walk more, do more 30-day challenges, read more, listen to more podcasts...

The math doesn't add up. It is impossible to do more of everything when we only have 24 hours in a day. Eventually, we will run out of time. If we continue to do more of all of it and sacrifice our rest, this is also problematic.

Do you want to know what will not help you be a high performer and will damage your well-being? Being exhausted. We are human beings, not human doings. We are not supercomputers with infinite capacity. We need to acknowledge and accept our human limitations.

According to this model, we have four dimensions of energy:

MIND

BODY

EMOTIONAL

SPIRITUAL

Once you run out of an energy source, you need to replenish and refuel. If you engage in complex problem solving for a while, your brain needs a rest and reset. After an emotionally exhausting day, you will feel fatigued and need to regroup. People who are spiritually depleted can feel restless or empty. Spiritual energy can be described as faith, belief in a higher power, transcendence, oneness with nature, etc.

We need to upgrade how we optimize our energy in these categories. We were not intended to operate in fifth gear all the time, moving from action to action.

We need to be more intentional about oscillating activity, and energy expenditure needs to be followed by renewal (REST). Elite athletes understand. They treat rest and recovery as just as important as the most intense workouts. They know it's critical for optimal performance and health.

Key Point:

We have limited resources in all energy sources, and once we run out, we need to refuel.

Challenge:

Here are a few reminders (woven throughout this book) to manage your energy and, therefore, build your psychological fitness:

- Incorporate rest, recovery, and ways to de-escalate your stress levels. Create space to reflect, recover, and heal.
- Schedule bursts of activity, working for 90 minutes, then schedule a 5–10 minutes break.
- Be IN or OUT. Strategically and mindfully ENGAGE in what you are doing or purposefully DISENGAGE. We spend too much time in the abyss, half listening in a meeting, half checking emails, and periodically looking at our phones. This creates a "meh" state of energy.
- **Physical** — Be active and exercise but sleep more and schedule more downtime to recover.
- **Mind** — Your mind allows you to focus. To improve the quality of your attention, do not multitask when engaging in complex issues. Silence notifications and minimize channel checking and doom scrolling.
- **Spirit** — Regularly tap into your sense of purpose and create more experiences of awe in your life. It could be your faith, prayer, meditation, nature, or savoring a sunset.

- **Emotion** — Cultivate emotional health by understanding and regulating your emotion. You can use up great energy bandwidth by indulging in negative thinking and feeling, generating unnecessary distress. Journaling and finding ways to cultivate positive emotions can help.
- Incorporate more of what brings you **positive energy.**
- **Decrease energy drainers** (toxic people, unhealthy behaviors, some social media engagement).

◇◇

To be fully engaged, we must be physically energized, emotionally connected, mentally focused, and spiritually aligned with a purpose beyond our immediate self-interest.[212]
—Jim Loehr, author

◇◇

MORE REST

Religious traditions have endorsed a day of rest in the week for thousands of years. Judaism, Christianity, and Islam have a tradition of a day for rest, prayer, or worship. It is a key lesson from the story of Creation in the Bible. God rested from creating the universe on the seventh day of the first week.

This is confusing. In many ways, this tradition feels counter in western culture to hustling and busyness. Social media pushes us to do more, be more, excel more, and fit it all in. It feels incongruent to take a break for rest.

The core belief that resting is selfish or self-indulgent is getting in the way of many high achievers. For optimal health, experts agree that people need sufficient sleep and rest. Without it, our bodies will push back, and our immune systems will become compromised.

Well-rested people remember 80 percent of positive words. Fatigued individuals remember 80 percent of negative words. Since we already have the negativity bias in the brain, when we are exhausted, we are at even more of a disadvantage.

Elite achievers are good at resting. People who perform at a high level tend to have a cyclical way of operating. They can't be at peak performance all the time, so when they work, they really work. Then, they disengage to find renewal.

Key Points:

Our culture trains us to feel shame for rest. One secret to getting more work done and being more effective is to balance intense exertion with genuine recovery.

Challenge:

Oscillate energy exertion with recovery. Rest more.

MORE FUN

In a time of over-optimization and hunger for next-level productivity, it's easy to forget to have fun. Life responsibilities lead us to believe there is no time for play.

Laurie Santos, the previously mentioned Yale University Professor, suggests making a conscious decision to bring more joy into your life by having fun. What we really need is to have more fun through connection. Santos endorses "funterventions" to help recover from and prevent burnout and improve mental health.[213]

Catherine Price's book, *The Power of Fun: How to Feel Alive Again*, addresses what fun is, why it's essential, and how to bring more fun into your life. She suggests conducting a "fun audit," which involves making non-judgmental observations about what you have found to be fun in the past and what elements are involved.[214]

In making these observations, you can reverse-engineer and find ways to recreate such moments of vitality and lightness in your life. Incorporating more fun and playfulness can foster mental health, yet it doesn't imply pursuing pleasure and avoiding responsibility.

Key Point:

There are psychological benefits from incorporating more play and fun into your life.

Challenge:

Consider what moments have sparked fun and joy in your life. Be intentional about re-creating such experiences without an agenda or specified outcome. Is it an activity? Does it involve certain people? A social event? Try not to take yourself too seriously.

LEARNED OPTIMISM

Optimism is considered an attitude of hope and seeing the glass as being half-full. It is derived from the Latin word, **optimum**, meaning "the best." Another definition of optimism is the belief that one can achieve one's objective.[215]

Learned optimism entails cultivating the capacity to interpret events in a positive light. Learned helplessness is commonly contrasted with it and involves a mindset of giving up or why bother trying. By cultivating optimism, we are also compensating for the brain's negativity bias. It is not blind optimism; rather, intentional optimism, so our interpretations are right-sized and not negatively filtered.

Russell Wilson, an NFL football player, gave a Ted Talk in which he claimed that negativity works 100 percent of the time. Although positivity may not always work, negativity leads to feeling stuck.[216]

◇◇

Positive thinking is the notion that if you think good thoughts, things will work out well. Optimism is the feeling of thinking things will be well and be hopeful.
—Martin Seligman, psychologist and author

◇◇

PROSPECTION: THE POWER OF FUTURE THINKING

The process of prospection is thinking about and preparing for your possible future. It involves proactively discovering and generating future options and possibilities so you can adapt forward. It allows you to envision and prepare for upcoming circumstances.

Prospection may involve coming up with an action plan as well as a coping plan and how you will respond to the upcoming possibilities if they aren't as you hoped.

Positive future thinking (PFT) is a way to foster learned optimism. Envisioning a positive future is beneficial to mental health. Not being able to imagine a positive future can fuel negative emotions and mental health challenges.

Future thinking is different than fantasizing, wishing, or hoping because it allows you to make a plan, exert effort, and consider how to work around potential setbacks and obstacles. To employ PFT, you expect to reach an objective and engage in mental visualization.

Athletes and performers have been using tools of visualization for a long time to help them succeed and reach goals. By envisioning a specific outcome, it feels more real and possible. It can also equip you to deal with upcoming stressors as you plan for how you will respond and recover.

Key Points:

You can use the power of imagination and prospection to foster mental health, psychological fitness, and well-being. Consider it to be like future mindfulness. You can choose an outlook of learned optimism to inform your prospection.

✕✕

*We are made wise not by the recollection of our past but
by the responsibility for our future.*
—Bertrand Russell, philosopher

✕✕

Challenge:

Create a personal vision statement. It can help you make decisions and can provide clarity to how you live. It can provide you with a sense of direction, purpose, and a feeling of contentment. There isn't an exact framework but consider these suggestions on how you can create a guide for yourself.

Start a written document to help you feel more balanced and in control over your life and less likely to be reactive. Describe your strengths, interests, key motivators, values, skills, abilities, and goals. Describe what a life well-lived means to you. You can also map your personal vision statement with needs in the world or the job market.

By engaging in such reflection, you can discover your **ikigai**. Ikigai is a Japanese construct describing your reason for being. In Japanese, **iki** means "life" and **gai** describes "worth or value." Ikigai is what brings you joy, bliss, and inspiration.

Consider a Venn diagram of the components above (strengths, interests, motivations, skills, abilities, etc.) and note the overlapping areas to indicate your ikigai, so you can find a way to blend doing what you love, what you're good at and passionate about, with what the world/market needs, and what could generate income.

SERVING OTHERS

I saved my favorite intervention to build your psychological fitness for now. Being of service to others is an impactful way to enhance well-being and relationships and foster a sense of purpose. Paying it forward is a win-win all the way around. Doing good for others will fill your emotional bank account as well as someone else's. This is also referred to as prosocial behavior: any behavior that is intended to benefit another person or persons.[217]

It could involve volunteering, donating money, or random acts of kindness. To engage in altruistic behavior, typically, one would not expect a benefit or reward in return.

While helping others is not sufficient treatment for mental illness, it brings joy, happiness, improved health and longevity, and reduced symptoms of depression and anxiety.

Research demonstrates that volunteering, donating money, engaging in extra acts of kindness, and expressing gratitude to others serve as well-being boosters and mitigators against stressors. Multiple studies suggest that volunteers feel less isolated and report better mental health.

Even small gestures of doing good promote positive emotions and neurochemicals. There is something helpful about getting outside yourself, especially if you feel stuck in negative thinking traps or moods. Focusing on a person outside of **you** can offer relief from your emotional suffering and is linked to decreased stress.

In a large-scale study, researchers surveyed participants about their volunteering habits and mental health every two years from 1996 to 2014. Individuals who volunteered in the past year were more satisfied with their lives and experienced better overall health, and those who volunteered more often reported better mental health.[218]

Quantitative, qualitative, and anecdotal research tells us that volunteerism is associated with increased longevity, resilience, healthier lifestyle habits, strong social support, and decreased emotional distress. Happy people tend to volunteer more often.[219] Additionally, studies suggest that people who start out with a lower sense of well-being may even experience a bigger boost in well-being.[220]

I believe that the most meaningful way to succeed is to help other people succeed.
—Adam Grant, author

Key Point:

The quickest way to enhance well-being is giving WITHIN your limits, as long as you aren't over-compromising yourself.

Challenge:

Pay it forward beyond what you normally would. An extra smile to a stranger at the grocery store can have a positive impact even if they are blocking the aisle while texting on their phone.

Tools for Reflection

Clients tend to appreciate having frameworks, resources, worksheets, and tools to help with reflection and implementing practices for psychological fitness. Several can be found in the psychological fitness guide. Use this tool as a quick resource to reflect and assess key areas of psychological fitness, including your strengths, mission, values, energy drainers, energy boosters, and current mental health status.

Access tools for reflection in your free psychological fitness guide here: Psychfitguide.com/book.

Wheel of Life

Use the wheel of life tool to audit your satisfaction in key areas, so you can decide where to place intention and effort.

Psychological Fitness Planning Guide

Use this document to write your near-term goals and objectives in each category of your life.

Values Exercise

Having clear values can help serve as a framework for prioritizing and decision-making in your life. Use this guide to reflect on what is most important to you. How is your life currently aligned with this list? What do you need to adjust in your daily choices? Or do you need to adapt your list?

Part IV:
MENTAL HEALTH
IS A JOURNEY,
NOT A DESTINATION

Chapter 8:
Suffering, Acceptance, and Accompaniment

UPON THE INITIATION OF A COACHING RELA-
TIONSHIP, I OFTEN FIELD QUESTIONS FROM CLI-
ENTS, WONDERING WHAT THE ROAD MAP IS FOR
COACHING. I wish I had an equation, algorithm, instructions, or
guidelines that would provide the guarantees they may be looking
for in their journey of self discovery.

I understand how this question would arise. I wonder the same
thing. There are days I would prefer someone give me a road map.
However, the answers are in the process, whether it's self-improvement, coaching, or living life.

Mental health is a journey, and your path is unique. You can
decide on a general direction to head; however, you don't know
what you'll face along the way. Since you don't know what life has
in store, you must be on the journey, ready to change directions
at any time.

There are some aspects of life we all share, regardless of time
or place. Recognizing and understanding some of these universal
truths is important for mental health. Despite religious, cultural,
and geographical differences, we are all in this together, and there
are many similarities, or common life truths, that affect everyone
in some way.

There can be relief found in naming and understanding some
common and unavoidable life experiences. Sorrow, loss, pain, and
grief are inevitable.

CHAPTER 8

Continuing to deepen your self-awareness and do the inner work to build your psychological fitness will help you navigate through these dynamics. You are learning how to best respond in the face of circumstances.

I was going to call this chapter "universal truths of being human." Realizing it could lead down a winding philosophical, existential, never-ending road of possible dispute, I refrained.

What follows is what I find to be common on the mental health journey. While not an exhaustive list, here are a few common aspects of human experience and factors that influence our psychology that I believe are useful to mention.

IF ONLY

Life can feel dissatisfying, and common themes of living are suffering, jealousy, discontent, and stress. It's easy to get stuck in the "if only" syndrome. If only I had a little more money, if only I could get a promotion, if only I could lose weight, if only my partner was nicer to me, if only people would appreciate me, if only I were taller, in better shape, etc., then I would be happy.

To counter the struggle, we grasp, seek, hope, long for, and strive to fix it. If you could just get A-B-C, life would be better, and yearning would subside. You make progress, then dissatisfaction re-surfaces, and the feeling of progress fades. The perpetual sentiment of - **this isn't enough, not good enough, has to be better** - finds us again.

It seems there isn't an escape from this cycle; it comes and goes. Maybe the acceptance of the certainty that contentment won't last can ease the intensity. One thing we know is that life changes, including our thoughts and mood, affect behavior, experience, attitude, feelings, etc.

EARLY INFLUENCE

Parents and caregivers influence the development of children. The way your parents or caregivers treat you has a long-term impact on you. Your attachment style in adult relationships can be influenced by how consistently your needs were met as a child.

Attachment can be classified into three types: secure, anxious-ambivalent, and anxious-avoidant. You are more likely to have a secure attachment if your caregivers are consistently attentive to your needs.

Understanding how these early relationships affect your outlook and how you interact with people throughout your life can be healing and enlightening. If you faced challenges with bonding in early years, there is hope for your healing and recovery through therapeutic interventions.

Early life experiences will impact you, yet they don't need to determine and define your whole life.

STRESS

As previously addressed, stress is an unavoidable part of life. There is no workaround since your response to stress is a survival mechanism. It affects everyone. Consider suggestions in this book to identify major stressors in your life and develop strategies for addressing them more effectively.

LOSS

Everyone will experience loss in their lifetime. Facing the death of a loved one and living through grief is a human experience that can't be avoided. Learning to navigate grief in a healthy way can lessen the emotional burden. Religion, culture, and traditions have offered people ways to honor and ritualize the experience of human loss.

What they all have in common is honoring the person who has passed and providing space for individuals to process and grieve.

DESIRE TO BE LOVED AND ACCEPTED

Everyone has a desire to be loved, accepted, and valued regardless of who or where they are. Everyone wants to feel important and relevant. Consider how you are conveying to people how they are loved and valued by you. If you want to feel more loved, show more love to others.

HAPPINESS IS A CYCLICAL SENSATION

As previously mentioned, there are misconceptions that happiness is a permanent state that can be attained and lasts. In reality, happiness is a transient experience. It appears, we recognize it, and then it vanishes. Expecting anything else is apt to cause one to feel unhappy. Be reasonable about your expectations regarding happiness in life so you are not perpetually disappointed.

WE EXPERIENCE INTRUSIVE THOUGHTS

If you find that you worry, ruminate, or engage in excessively negative thinking, you are not flawed. Intrusive thoughts invade at any time, and you don't have control over when they show up. Take solace in knowing we all have our versions of intrusive thinking. In fact, it's perfectly normal. As covered, the work is in regulating the thoughts, redirecting intrusive thoughts, and moving along with your day.

WE ARE OUR PERCEPTIONS

We give meaning to our experiences based on our personal mental filters. Perceptions are impacted by attitudes, conditioning, and previous experiences. It is imperative for mental health to remember that how you perceive a situation is not the full picture. It is your perception of the event, not the complete reality of the event itself.

◇◇

Life is what our thoughts make it.
—Marcus Aurelius

◇◇

CONGRUENCE AND INTERNAL ALIGNMENT CONTRIBUTE TO CONTENTMENT AND PEACE OF MIND

When the external persona (image presented to others) and your actual self (vulnerable you) match, it promotes mental health. Aligning actions with your authentic values and beliefs creates congruence, and life feels better. You will be closer to feeling contentment and peace of mind when both your ideal and actual selves are connected.

Pretending to be someone other than who you are to meet the needs of others is draining and depleting.

The more self-aware you are, the more likely you can develop into your best authentic self, and the better you will feel about yourself. Reflecting on core values can help you reside in clarity on what is most important to you. Adapting your personality or interests to please others or seek approval will leave you feeling dissatisfied and dissonant.

◇◇

A man (person) should look for what is and not for what he thinks should be.
—Albert Einstein

◇◇

FEELING ALONE

I've learned that many people frequently feel like they are the only ones dealing with problems and adversity. Also, I hear about how people are suffering, yet they feel guilty about it because others have it worse. Both sentiments can keep people silent and afraid to share problems and vulnerabilities with others. Talking about troubles can help people feel more connected, less alone, and not so isolated in their struggles.

Key Point:

Appreciating the universal nature of factors that impact your psychology can be therapeutic and helpful in generating deeper self-awareness.

Challenge:

Consider how these dynamics affect your psychology, either helping you or getting in your way.

SELF-DEFEATING BEHAVIOR

Have you ever cheated on a diet? Or binge-watched a tv series the night before a deadline instead of working on your project? Or rearranged the furniture instead of returning an uncomfortable phone call? There are multitudes of ways to self-sabotage, including but not limited to procrastination, drugs or alcohol, overeating, and unhealthy interpersonal conflict. We all do it. We avoid doing what's good for us, continue to do what's not good for us, or find a way out of taking healthy actions. It simply doesn't make any sense.

WHY DO WE SABOTAGE OURSELVES?

I don't have a sufficient answer to this question, yet I think about it often because I field the question from others frequently. How I resolved it is this. The best we can do is make progress and harm ourselves less often and less intensely because we all tend to slip back into self-defeating behaviors.

Hans Eising describes the neurotic paradox, reinforcing we all have tendencies to **get in our own way**. It doesn't make sense to our rational mind, yet it's a common human challenge. Any action that gets in the way of your intention could be considered self-sabotage. I used to wonder why I often cleaned out my refrigerator rather than study during finals week. Here are a few potential factors that can contribute to self-defeating behaviors.

SELF-WORTH

A lack of self-esteem resulting in negative thoughts and feelings can feed self-sabotaging behaviors. Even if you don't consciously think so, deep down, you could believe you are unworthy and not deserving of success or happiness.

The concept of cognitive dissonance can illuminate the answer. People prefer consistency when actions are consistent with their beliefs and values. When they aren't, we often make efforts to re-align them, even if it is at a somewhat subconscious level. If we begin to accumulate victories and accomplishments while still viewing ourselves as flawed, worthless, incapable, or deficient, oddly, we can pull the plug to eliminate the cognitive dissonance. It's a paradox, yet for some, if failing hurts, succeeding can hurt more.

CONTROL

Some people self-sabotage to feel in control of the situation. It can feel better to be in control of your failure than to face the possibility of it blindsiding you and catching you off-guard. Then, at least you can prepare yourself for the guaranteed disappointment.

FEAR OF BEING FOUND OUT

As the bar continues to rise, being promoted to a new position or earning more education, the stakes are higher. Rising expectations can generate increased fear and concern about failing. The pressure to succeed and perform can become distracting and increase feelings of self-doubt. It is not uncommon for people to experience what is referred to as imposter syndrome and irrational fear of being exposed as a phony or failure. They convince themselves that they have fooled others into thinking they are worthy of success.

AVOIDING RESPONSIBILITY

If issues aren't resolved in a way that is acceptable to us, it can be tempting to blame others or circumstances rather than take accountability. This victim mindset is tempting because it can seem easier than doing the work of owning responsibility.

HABIT

People drift to familiarity and consistency. Patterns of behavior can become automatic and habitual. Self-defeating patterns are no different. People get used to self-sabotaging because it is familiar and, in this way, strangely comfortable. What is known is often preferable to uncertainty and the unfamiliar, even if it's unhealthy.

BOREDOM

Occasionally, people become bored, and life feels stale. Then, they sabotage by pushing buttons to solicit some sort of response, even if it is negative. So, how do you get yourself to stop sawing off the tree limb you're sitting on? Consider the proverbial root. Regardless of how your self-sabotage manifests, the source of the problem is fear.

Key Point:

You can decrease self-defeating behaviors by considering how you get in your own way and kill your own dreams.

Challenge:

What can you do about it? Recognize when you are slipping or reverting, challenge it, and have a plan to get back on course. If you find yourself in self-defeating behaviors, watch out for the spin evaluating why you did it because it usually won't make sense.

EXCESSIVE SEEKING

We create trouble for ourselves by wanting to do two things at once and be at several places and by wanting more than what we need. As soon as we get what we want, we want the next thing, which creates a sense of insatiability.

It is yet another paradox of life. We are yearning, seeking, striving, and thinking we will grasp it as soon as we get to the bottom of the list and achieve a certain objective. It will be just around the corner, and then no more distress. As soon as we get there, then life will be better. We continue to tell ourselves versions of this story.

We long for self-mastery, self-improvement, being a better person, etc. If you are reading this book, you likely want to improve. You have the best intentions to apply what you learn and be better. The reality is that despite our intentions, efforts, commitment, and practices, we will continue to disappoint ourselves and each other.

Literary figures have been teaching us this lesson for a long time — the answers are within. St. Francis says you are what you are seeking. It's easy to fall prey to thinking the world has the answers. Someone must have an instruction manual. Don't forget the power of looking inward — you hold the answers.

SUFFERING AND ACCEPTANCE

<><><><><><><><><><><><><><><><><><><><><><><><><><><><><><><><><>

Enlightenment is: Absolute cooperation with the inevitable.
—Anthony de Mello, author

<><><><><><><><><><><><><><><><><><><><><><><><><><><><><><><><><>

We are all subjected to suffering. Much suffering stems from attempting to control the uncontrollable and from an internal feeling that we can't handle the challenge we are facing.

Part of the difficulty is also that people think they shouldn't have any problems. We were never guaranteed a life without suffering or difficulty. Yet, many find themselves repeatedly disappointed and frustrated when negative or painful circumstances arise. The sooner we can let go of what we don't have control over, the easier life will feel.

The serenity prayer provides key reminders.

◇◇◇

God, grant me the serenity to accept the things I cannot change, the courage to change the things I can, and the wisdom to know the difference.

◇◇◇

Even if the religious element of this prayer does not resonate, it highlights key principles of psychological health. Acceptance of what is, surrendering, and managing our expectations are simple and straightforward suggestions yet challenging to put into practice consistently, especially if it involves accepting something we find to be unacceptable.

UNNECESSARY SUFFERING

Bruce Tift acknowledges in his book **Already Free** that while western psychotherapy and eastern spirituality take different approaches, both are concerned with achieving freedom from unnecessary suffering.[221] These approaches highlight the human condition's paradox. A Western approach emphasizes striving and growth, whereas an Eastern approach focuses on the acceptance of what is.

Tift argues that, while these approaches are philosophically opposed, people can benefit from both. Each set of principles provides keys to improving our mental health and well-being, allowing us to thrive and flourish.

PERSONAL RESPONSIBILITY

Tift proposes personal responsibility as an antidote to unnecessary suffering, reminding us how to break free from attaching our mental state to external circumstances. Tift proposes this path to emotional freedom is open to all of us. Accepting dualities as part of the inner work allows one to experience striving as a part of being alive, feelings of calm, clarity, and tranquility. It's not a zero-sum game.

Key Points:

Taking responsibility to unattach your emotional state from external situations offers emotional freedom. Accept internal dualities — you can challenge yourself and be successful without self-flagellation or abuse.

Challenge:

Create a mental shift, making room for both reaching for excellence and self-acceptance.

WE WANT TO KNOW WHY

The question "why?" is a common one that people bring to coaching. Why am I so easily distracted? Why can't I concentrate? Why am I afraid to speak up? Why do I judge myself? Why can't I work out on a regular basis? Why haven't I gotten a raise? Why do I keep doing this thing I don't like?

These are often not helpful questions, in my opinion, because the answers are usually insufficient. Why didn't you go to the gym this morning? I'm not sure. You were probably exhausted. It didn't feel right. Working out is difficult. How does that help?

Digging around to figure out why we fall short can become a pointless and discouraging endeavor. I am all for raising awareness, confronting issues head-on, accepting responsibility, and asking difficult questions. However, there are times when it is best to stop punching the bruise and agitating yourself; instead, forge a path forward.

<><><><><><><><><><><><><><><><><><><><><><><><><><><><><><><>

There is no reason to constantly attempt to figure everything out.[222]
—Michael A. Singer, author

<><><><><><><><><><><><><><><><><><><><><><><><><><><><><><><>

For centuries, thought leaders have suggested minimizing desires to alleviate suffering. Be in the present moment rather than worrying about the future or ruminating about the past. Unhappiness can stem from desire; anxiety can be fueled by unfulfilled expectations and ambitions.

Key Point:

Desiring what you have can increase life satisfaction.

Challenge:

Perhaps it is as simple as this — to be happy, want less.

Most of us want to enjoy the present and not entertain our-selves with excessive fears. We want to feel content with what we have. Even though it would provide emotional freedom, it's just so difficult to maintain this state. Seng-tsan, a Zen master from the seventh century, taught that true freedom is being "without anxi-ety about imperfection."

Anthony de Mello's work has deeply resonated with me. He was a Jesuit priest and psychologist who offered clear and insight-ful reminders about our human condition. His writings promote enhancing self-awareness, healthy detachment, and not becoming too committed to certain outcomes.

He cautions us to avoid overidentifying with external factors such as the opinions of others. According to de Mello, attachment and desire are what promote unhappiness. Even if we get what we want, the fear of losing what we have still exists.

✦✦

*The tragedy of an attachment is that if its object is not
attained, it causes unhappiness. But if it is attained,
it does not cause happiness—it merely causes a flash
of pleasure followed by weariness, and it is always
accompanied, of course, by the anxiety that you may lose
the object of your attachment.*
—Anthony de Mello, author

✦✦

Tara Brach, a meditation teacher and author, uses the term radical acceptance. She speaks to our human tendency to exacerbate the pain, leading to unnecessary and additional suffering for ourselves. This reinforces the equation noted previously: Suffering = Pain x Resistance.

She emphasizes the importance of letting go to reduce the conflict between what IS and what we WANT. Brach suggests that we should be gentle with ourselves as we work through the acceptance process.[223]

✦✦

*The boundary to what we can accept is the boundary to
our freedom.*
—Tara Brach, author

✦✦

Brach offers the mindfulness practice of **RAIN**.

R = Recognize the feeling

A = Allow it to be present

I = Investigate and get curious about why it's showing up

N = Nurture yourself without judgment

Key Point:

Suffering is defined as pain multiplied by resistance. Let go of what you have no control over.

Challenge:

Experience more inner peace and contentment by releasing the grip. Lessen the clinging to your burdens.

MEMENTO MORI

Let us prepare our minds as if we'd come to the very end of life. Let us postpone nothing. Let us balance life's books each day. ... The one who puts the finishing touches on their life each day is never short of time.
—Seneca

Momento mori is a Latin term that reminds us that we are all going to die. The maxim originated during the Roman period. Roman war heroes who were celebrating would be reminded of the dark reality that they could die tomorrow as a practice to keep them grounded. For centuries, the skull symbol has been used in art as a reminder of our mortality. We will all die; while it may seem a dark and gloomy message, it can provide inspiration.

Stoics accepted the timeless idea of reminding ourselves of this reality. They appreciated the implied urgency to live life to the fullest right now, without wasting time or postponing anything.

"You could leave life right now," Marcus Aurelius wrote in Meditations. "Allow that to influence what you do, say, and think."

I recently discovered increased meaning in contemplating the transience of life. It motivates me to take risks and prioritize what is most important. Epictetus advised his students to remind themselves of death to avoid excessive desire. In life, there are no guarantees.

Key Points:

Reflecting on the frailty of life can serve as a catalyst for cultivating purpose, perspective, and immediacy to effect desired changes. Fostering this awareness can serve as a generator for living the life you truly desire, at least more often than not. It can help you become the person you truly want to be.

Challenge:

You can let this scare you or use it to motivate you to live a good life right now — starting today. You make the call.

✕✕✕

By contemplating the impermanence of everything in the world, we are forced to recognize that every time we do something could be the last time we do it, and this recognition can invest the things we do with a significance and intensity that would otherwise be absent.[224]
—William B. Irvine, *A Guide to the Good Life: The Ancient Art of Stoic Joy*

✕✕✕

REGRET

Experiencing regret can be a useful learning tool or a method of obsessive self-torture. In *The Power of Regret,* Dan Pink offers insights into how regret can be helpful. He identifies two categories of regret that people experience: regret of action (bullying or hurting others) and regret of inaction (not taking risks or spending more time with family).[225]

His research indicates how common and powerful regrets related to connection are. People regret not reaching out or cultivating relationships over the years. Older people are also more likely to experience regrets due to inaction.

Challenge:

Think about what you will regret **not** doing. What advice would your older, future self offer to you, looking back to where you are now?

Bronnie Ware, the author of *The Top Five Regrets of the Dying*, about her time in palliative care, has done extensive research to understand the dying process. Her data collection involved learning from people facing death.[226]

Among other questions, she inquired about their life regrets. As you can imagine, **I wish I had worked more** did not make the list. Wondering what was on the top of the list? The top regret was, "I wish I had the courage to live a life true to myself, not the life others expected of me."

In the long run, we shape our lives, and we shape ourselves. The process never ends until we die, and the choices we make are ultimately our own responsibility.
—Eleanor Roosevelt

Key Point:

Reflecting on the reality of death and the fragility of life can be a useful tool for improving psychological fitness. To inspire, motivate, and clarify what you want in life, it can be beneficial to reflect on its finality.

Challenge:

Take time to reflect on what a life well-lived means to you. Get serious about assessing how your daily and weekly actions align with your definition of a good life.

CHAPTER 8

SPIRITUALITY, RELIGION, AND MENTAL HEALTH

Enhancing spiritual awareness through practice is a powerful and accessible way to build psychological fitness. Some, many, or most people long for spiritual connection - a belief in a power higher than themselves. How's that for a safe entry into this section?

I'd like to provide a few disclaimers on the above text. I'm not suggesting that people can't or don't experience good mental health without spirituality. People who don't identify as being religious or spiritual in their beliefs or practices can and do experience mental health. To experience mental health, one does not need to be religious or spiritual, and my intention is not to endorse a particular belief system.

Also, spirituality can be challenging to measure and address in the scientific community. Some view results as inconclusive in the scientific journals.

All that said, if utilized and applied in a healthy way, both religion and spirituality **can** positively impact mental health. The healthy elements are potentially due to the promotion of feelings of peace, compassion, forgiveness, and community.

Spirituality is a sense of connecting to something greater than oneself. Descriptions of spirituality may include alteration of consciousness, acknowledging the interconnectedness of things, integration of mind, body, and spirit, and/or relationship with a higher power.

The Latin root of the word spirituality is **spiritus**, meaning "breath" — the breath of life. It refers to the reverence and sacredness of life, often found in the ordinary, often overlooked elements of life.

In the 1980s, Jeff Levin's research indicated that religious people live longer than non-religious people. At the time, his book *God, Faith, and Health* was met with resistance in the medical community.[227] Fast forward to now, the benefits of spirituality are beginning to be more acknowledged in mainstream mental health.

Studies suggest that it is worth considering how spirituality and religion enhance mental health and psychological fitness. There is an opportunity to understand and leverage findings more deeply to foster well-being. Many believe spirituality to be foundational to happiness.

Psychologist and Professor Davis Elkins describes the quest for spirituality as a growing need for passion and depth in one's life. According to Elkins, spirituality is essential to happiness and mental health. He describes the benefits of caring for and feeding the soul.

Plenty of scientific research studies suggest that religious people are healthier physically and mentally. Higher levels of religious involvement have been positively associated with indicators of psychological well-being, including life satisfaction, happiness, positive affect, and higher morale, as well as with less depression, suicidal thoughts and behavior, and drug/alcohol abuse.[228]

While research does not indicate direct causation, there are hypotheses regarding what benefits religion can offer. Religious rituals can provide a healthy way to cope with challenges, especially when it comes to grief and loss. Religion offers consistency and predictability, which can be soothing when facing uncertainty in the world, including time for rest and celebration. Teachings, guidelines, and life lessons are pillars of religion that can support living a healthy life.

Religion provides structure and a community of people with similar beliefs and promotes intimate connections with other members. It creates a sense of belonging and offers a moral framework. These are all important factors in promoting well-being and psychological fitness.

Similarly, mental health benefits related to spirituality include self-reflection, compassion, promotion of meaningful life philosophy, and expression. Spirituality enhances unity with others and the universe overall.

Lisa Miller, a professor in the Clinical Psychology Program at Teachers College, Columbia University, researches the effects of spirituality on the brain. Miller is the founder and director of the Spirituality Mind Body Institute, the first Ivy League graduate program and research institute in spirituality and psychology.

She highlights insights connecting science and spirituality in *The Awakened Brain: The New Science of Spirituality and Our Quest for an Inspired Life*.[229] Miller defines spirituality as both a transcendent relationship with something bigger than oneself (a specific faith tradition or a humanist view of the oneness of life) and an understanding that this connection runs through each of us.

According to Miller, we all have an internal capacity for spirituality built into us. The more you engage in it, the better your brain is suited to handle mental anguish. Miller's studies support that spirituality leads to changes in the brain that can be protective in people who have a risk of depression.

Key Points:

People have looked to spirituality for healing, cures, and meaning for thousands of years. We are drawn to experiencing the sacred, a sense of awe and transcendence. Mindfulness meditation, prayer, and reading spiritual text can accelerate your spiritual journey.

Challenge:

Creating moments that inspire and spark spiritual connection promotes well-being and mental health. How can you apply this to your life?

Dr. Kenneth Kendler at the Virginia Commonwealth University has investigated the relationship between spirituality and mental health. His research indicated that someone could be spiritual yet not religious, and vice versa.

Spirituality could protect against alcoholism, depression, and negative stressful events. The degree to which one person is spiritual is 29 percent determined by genes and 71 percent by the environment.[230] Both Miller's and Kendler's research supports the idea that people have an innate capacity for spirituality.

Brain imaging techniques have been used to assess the impact of spirituality. Results indicate that spiritual people have a thicker cortex, and those who are depressed have thinner regions of the same area.

Miller's research demonstrates that spirituality protects against depression, addiction, and mental illness. She highlights how spiritual experiences can activate your "awakened mind" and deactivate your "achieving mind," leading to mental health benefits.

Key Points:

The achieving mind can be limited, tense, and controlling, and the awakened mind uses areas of the brain that contribute to openness and the ability to see meaning, unity, and connectedness. Research supports that fostering spirituality can have a positive effect on the brain. You can cultivate your spiritual capacity by engaging in meditation, prayer, attending religious services, or spending time in nature.

Challenge 1:

Reflect on what moves you deeply and sparks a sense of awe and transcendental connection (think music, worship, yoga, prayer, hiking, sermons, sunsets, etc.). Design a regular program to incorporate these awe-inspiring moments and activities into your life in small, frequent doses.

Challenge 2:

Try Lisa Miller's suggested "three doors" exercise to build awakened attention. Draw a road on a sheet of paper to represent your life. Think of a hurdle, loss, or challenge you experienced and draw it as a closed door. Next, think about what happened because of that event. What new insight, path, or connection emerged? Draw this as an open door leading to a new path. You might also think of a messenger or guide who helped you at that time. Now repeat the process, identifying two more doors that were closed and how they led to two new ones opening.

COMMUNITY WORSHIP

Here is what I see as a very important part. What seems most clear is that religious people who regularly attend church services and worship in the community experience the greatest benefits, which is another endorsement of the power of community, connection, and being part of something larger than ourselves, together. Being involved in the journey with others enhances the journey. We can only get so far on our own through introspection and private prayer.

Key Point:

Attending regular religious services in the community with others seems to provide the most benefits to enhancing mental health.

Challenge:

How can you tap into small or large group community practice to foster your spiritual or religious beliefs and experience?

MEDITATION AS A SPIRITUAL PRACTICE

We addressed the benefits of meditation for regulating the nervous system, increasing mindfulness, and cultivating calm. Meditation to enhance your spiritual practice also generates mental health benefits. A world-renowned medical expert and author of *The Relaxation Response*, Dr. Herbert Benson, has demonstrated that while chronic stress is harmful to the body, a daily spiritual practice of meditation can reduce stress and promote overall mental health.[231]

The practice of meditation encourages us to observe, notice, and contemplate without becoming hooked by our thinking and responses. Meditation practice can help you deal with emotional stressors as well as physical pain. It offers a channel for enhanced spiritual connection as well.

There was a significant study of intense meditators looking at the psychological benefits of meditation at Shambhala Mountain Center in Colorado. Results indicated that participants experienced improved perception and self-worth. Notably, it has been demonstrated that continued meditation practices and meditation retreats have improved cognition and attention.[232]

Research has also explored the connection of meditation to spirituality, transcendence, and mystical experiences. Meditators often describe having transcendental experiences and spiritual enlightenment when meditating.[233]

Meditating in a group and being in sync with others during practice has compound impact and benefit. Original studies assessing the science of human connection through meditation started with Jacobo Grinberg at the University of Mexico.[234]

Participants meditated together for 20 minutes and then were separated and monitored by EEG. In their separate areas, one of the duo was presented with a ray of light to elicit a shock response. Both participants showed a similar shock response on the EEG readings. The response was perfectly timed with the partner who was given the light variable 25 percent of the time. The control group who had not meditated showed no correlation.

Variations of this study were conducted with similarly intriguing results. Scientists hypothesize that the brain waves being in sync could represent a matched level of consciousness.

Key Points:

Meditation is multi-purpose. It not only increases your mindfulness, helps you manage stress, regulates your nervous system, and cultivates calm, but it is also beneficial when used as a spiritual practice. Doing it in sync and in unity with others multiplies the positive impact. It is yet another endorsement for engaging in practices that boost well-being and build psychological fitness in a community with others!

Challenge:

If you practice meditation, try it with others to amplify the spiritual experience.

CHAPTER 8

IGNATIAN SPIRITUALITY

There are many spiritual paths you can take; some through religious communities. A path in the Catholic tradition is Ignatian Spirituality, established by Saint Ignatius of Loyola, who founded the Jesuits. Attending Santa Clara University had a significant impact on my life. The Jesuit priests were relatable and dedicated to prayer, education, and service, which also resonated with me.

What continue to be pillars of my mental health and spiritual development practices, I learned from the late SCU President, Father Paul Locatelli. I was grateful to get to know Father Locatelli through my volunteer work. I recall him sharing his morning rituals, including exercise, prayer, and meditation (quiet and stillness), and fostering intimate connections with his community of fellow Jesuit priests.

The core principles of Ignatian Spirituality are to live a life of reflection, self-awareness, and discernment, balanced with action while fostering gratitude and serving others. The spiritual exercises proposed are aligned with the promotion of psychological health and fitness: to review and **renew every day, live simply, be a better friend, self-regulate**, and strive to **be a better tomorrow**.

What is referred to as Spiritual Exercises is a combination of meditations, prayers, and contemplative practices developed by St. Ignatius of Loyola, which traditionally involved spending thirty days in solitude and silence. The modern-day practices have been revised so they are more accessible to people who don't have a feasible option of spending 30 days in spiritual reflection alone.

TO WALK IN THE COMPANY OF OTHERS

◇◇◇

To accompany someone is to go somewhere with him or her, to break bread together, to be present on a journey with a beginning and an end... There's an element of mystery and openness.... I'll share your fate for a while, and by 'a while,' I don't mean 'a little while.' Accompaniment is much more often about sticking with a task until it's deemed completed by the person being accompanied, rather than by the accompagnateur.
—Paul Farmer, Harvard University Professor
Kennedy School

◇◇◇

I love the term **ACCOMPANIMENT**. Companionship plays a key role in well-being and mental health. By promoting the practice of accompaniment, we can enhance our psychological fitness and thrive together.

The idea of accompaniment suggests a support role, walking alongside, not intervening or fixing, but rather being a companion during the journey. Being an accompanist requires attentiveness, intention, commitment, openness, and willingness to be engaged in mutual connection. It provides a framework of empowerment and partnership.

It overlaps with the Spanish words ***companero/companera*** (friend) and has a Latin root ***ad cum panis*** (to break bread). Psychologist Mary Watkins uses the term mutual accompaniment to describe someone being in the presence of or journeying with another.[235]

She applied it to a psychosocial domain, suggesting a move away from "expertism" to horizontal relatedness. She suggested the power of walking alongside someone rather than advising or coming from a place of expertise.

Accompaniment is about listening, connecting, understanding, and responding with intention. It augments connections, removes layers of authority or privilege, suggests inclusivity, partnership, not preaching or telling, and learning together rather than "treating" or "advising."

People long for connecting and being included, welcomed, seen, valued, and heard. We are all the kind of person who wants to be relevant. We want to matter. People are designed to be with each other, interact, and work together. A healthy balance is to oscillate between autonomy, togetherness, and collaboration.

Again, personal development requires a blend of solitude and community. Solitude is different than loneliness; it is the **choice** to spend time alone. Loneliness is the feeling of isolation, even if others are physically near.

The negative impact that loneliness has on mental health is disturbing for many reasons; most importantly, this is preventable. The silver lining is that this is something every one of us can take action on.

We have the capacity to reach out more. Even though the number of modalities and channels to communicate with people is more than ever, people are also lonelier than ever. The technological connection has become an insufficient proxy for interpersonal closeness.

In sum, you can overcome suffering through acceptance. Your mental health and well-being are also enhanced through the power of community. By accompanying each other on the journey, you will accelerate your psychological fitness. Learn more about the power of connection in the next chapter.

Chapter 9:

Connection

Shared joy is double joy. Shared sorrow is half sorrow.
—Swedish proverb

MUCH RESEARCH ON RESILIENCE AND MENTAL HEALTH HAS BEEN FOCUSED ON STUDYING PERSONAL QUALITIES, CHARACTERISTICS, AND HABITS. A high premium has been placed on factors related to the individual. The important role that social circumstances, connection, and community play in mental health and the ability to recover from adversity is often overlooked.

Increasing connections and building relationships is an impactful way to enhance well-being and psychological fitness. Increasing social connections, even with strangers, can improve your mood. Engaging in simple connections, smiling, and chatting with people at the store can improve your quality of life. Social connection multiplies well-being and health.

We depend on each other to learn, grow, heal, and be mentally healthy. We are all connected and need each other to thrive.

Ubuntu is an African proverb indicating, ***I am a person through other people; my humanity is tied to yours***. Archbishop Desmond Tutu describes Ubuntu as being the essence of being human, particularly how you can't exist as a human being in isolation. It names our interconnectedness and how the whole is greater than the sum of its parts. The power of community, connection, and relatedness is found broadly across cultures, religions, and belief systems.

What is referred to as the Roseto effect is how a caring community of people with close relationships and connections can have immune benefits. It was demonstrated how the good health of an Italian community (in Roseto, Pennsylvania), including lower rates of heart disease in the 1950s, was attributed to being an active, connected community.[236]

Key Point:

Your social support and quality of relationships have a powerful impact on your mental and physical health.

LONELINESS EPIDEMIC

We are living in an era of loneliness and increased isolation. It is a modern affliction and source of suffering that has multiplied and intensified in recent years.

Technology, social media, and our devices are acting as a proxy for real interpersonal connection and are a false substitute. Interaction with these channels can detract from true personal interaction. The collective loneliness is contributing to mental health challenges as well. Sherry Turkle describes this phenomenon as "alone together."[237]

Being in solitude does not indicate loneliness, and similarly, being surrounded by people does not protect from feelings of loneliness. As the Belgian–American poet and novelist May Sarton describes, "Loneliness is the poverty of self; solitude is the richness of self."

CONNECTION

Language ... has created the word 'loneliness' to express
the pain of being alone. And it has created the word
'solitude' to express the glory of being alone.
—Paul Tillich, philosopher

The pandemic has accelerated awareness of the negative physical and emotional consequences of loneliness and isolation.

It seems men struggle with loneliness more than women do. Thomas Joiner touches on this concern in his book *Lonely at the Top*, suggesting how men can trade external success for a sense of disconnection and emptiness.[238] In youth, boys and girls develop similar close friendships, but as they age, men can lose that level of closeness. As people move into adulthood, it can be challenging to maintain relationships through the seasons of life.

Connecting with people and engaging in the community will help you live longer and be happier. Harvard University conducted a well-known longitudinal study of adult development, following a group of men for eight decades.[239] The men were surveyed throughout their lives, and results indicated that those with social support were happier, more fulfilled in their marriages, and physically healthier.

The study director, Robert Waldinger, summarizes how happy people are in their relationships has a powerful impact on health and longevity. According to Waldinger, taking care of your physical health is important, and attending to your relationships is a critical part of self-care.[240]

Loneliness not only feels unpleasant; it can cause significant damage to people's lives. Feeling lonely can be insidious. It can creep up when you least expect it. It contributes to social anxiousness and impacts confidence.

When you feel lonely, the temptation is to be alone. Isolating can feel like the easier option. However, this is exactly when you need to be proactive and connect to people, even if it feels uncomfortable. Consider loneliness a signal that your needs for connection aren't being met. Instead of fueling the cycle of negative feelings, consider re-directing them toward reaching out.

Key Points:

You can reduce loneliness by enhancing connections and social support. In the spirit of building psychological fitness, you can develop your social fitness. It requires being intentional and effortful in reaching out to find ways to talk with, connect with, and see people.

Challenge:

Do an extra something nice for someone every day. Engaging in prosocial behaviors enhances well-being as well as reduces loneliness. Establish rituals and regimens to foster your interpersonal fitness. How are you nurturing your relationships? What deposits are you putting into your personal and professional connections? Plan social events into your weekly or monthly calendar.

By engaging in a random act of kindness, you decrease your loneliness as well as the recipient. This reciprocal energy is contagious. People receiving prosocial behavior are at least 250 percent as likely to engage in such actions themselves. Consider the possibility of the ripple effect.

You can put intentional practices in place to increase your well-being and enhance happiness through individual practices. Doing so in a community with others will bring elevated results.

Positive social relationships promote resilience, physical health, and emotional well-being. Connections with people help us feel less stressed when we are struggling. Social support reduces emotional suffering. The availability of social support is a key factor in how people face challenges and recover from setbacks.

A NEED TO BELONG

Being part of a community and having a sense of <u>belonging</u> is an important human need. The absence of it can have seriously negative effects. Empirical evidence shows us that people have a strong need to develop and maintain positive and meaningful relationships. This need can serve as a significant driver of motivation and behavior.

The lack of relationships can correlate with depression, anxiety, and even suicide.[241] More recent studies have indicated that experiencing a sense of belonging can improve cognitive abilities, and the lack of belonging can impair such functions in the short- and long-term.[242]

Key Points:

It's all about us, not me. Doing it together is better. Life is better together. We are more inclined to overcome challenges, thrive, and foster well-being when we are on the journey with others.

HEALTH RISKS OF LONELINESS

Close relationships are essential to thriving and flourishing. Extensive scientific research supports this; people who are socially integrated and experience healthy connections with others have better mental health and well-being and lower rates of mortality and morbidity.

There are health risks to not connecting with people. Experiencing loneliness has been compared to having similar negative health effects of smoking two packs of cigarettes a day. A meta-analysis indicated that being interpersonally integrated within meaningful relationships predicts mortality more than health-risk lifestyle behaviors (low activity, smoking).[243] To further support, the American Psychological Association recognizes in its resilience report (apa.org):

◇◇

Many studies show that the primary factor in resilience is having caring and supportive relationships within and outside the family. Relationships that create love and trust, provide role models, and offer encouragement and reassurance help bolster a person's resilience.

◇◇

Professor John T. Cacioppo was a pioneer and founder of the field of social neuroscience and spent 21 years studying loneliness. Cacioppo studied the wear and tear that loneliness has on mental and physical health.

In a 2017 interview with *The Atlantic*, Cacioppo said, "The purpose of loneliness is like the purpose of hunger. Hunger takes care of your physical body. Loneliness takes care of your social body, which you also need to survive and prosper. We're a social species."[244]

Just like hunger gives your body a signal that it needs nutrients, loneliness provides messages that we need interpersonal connection. Cacioppo emphasizes people do best when they both give and receive affection.

In addressing the use of technology and its impact on loneliness, Cacioppo proposed that if digital communication is used as a channel to make plans to connect in person, it is associated with lower levels of loneliness. If used as a **destination**, technology can do more damage to social well-being. Engaging in technology in this way contributes to social withdrawal and promotes non-authentic acceptance, but it doesn't make them feel less lonely.

Cacioppo developed the acronym **EASE** to help people ease their way back into interpersonal connections.

E stands for "**extend** yourself," but extend yourself safely, just a bit at a time.

A is to "have an **action** plan," recognizing that it may be difficult for people who are isolated to reach out. He encourages asking people about themselves and getting others talking about their interests as part of the plan.

S stands for "**seek** collectives." Look for people with similar interests, values, and lifestyles so you can find synergy.

E is for "**expect** the best," don't assume the worst.

Being with people makes things feel easier. Interpersonal presence impacts your perception of difficult situations. Studies show that holding hands during a challenging event decreases feelings of pain. In one study, a romantic partner holding hands with a partner in pain leads to brain waves syncing and pain lessening.[245] This adds to the growing research on the power of the human touch.

Interpersonal connections are protective when facing nearly any challenge. Dealing with adversity together eases the burden. When people anticipate carrying a heavy load **with** someone, it feels lighter. Connecting has a positive impact, even when people are asked to think about a relationship.

THE GEOGRAPHICAL SLOPE

Several studies have explored how social support can influence the visual perception of slants. In one experiment, people were asked to judge the geographical slant of a large-scale outdoor hill. Individuals who were with a friend estimated the hill to be 10–20 percent less steep than when they were alone. Even thinking about a friend, individuals found the hill to appear less steep. Researchers indicated the relationship quality impacted visual perception.[246]

Such studies support the "buffering hypothesis," indicating that social support strengthens our immune system and can be a protective factor against conditions like heart disease, the common cold, and even cancer.

As reports from the World Bank report suggest, social safety nets increase the resilience of citizens. Social support networks are critical to resiliency, especially for the poor and vulnerable. In areas where there is great inequality, people suffer more ill health effects, to begin with.

⋄⋄

Keep in mind that part of growing up is dealing with difficult issues, and the benefits can be great if you have the courage to ask for help. Human beings are not designed to go through life alone. No one has to bear the burden of tough times all by themselves.
—Jack Canfield, author

⋄⋄

Despite the perpetual connection via smartphones, people are lonely. According to a recent study, more than three in five people in the U.S. report being lonely.[247] Estimates of loneliness span from 55–75 percent of people currently feel isolated and lonely. Humans are social beings who need to connect and feel a sense of belonging.

What is required for a quality connection? Authenticity, feeling heard, being seen, and knowing you matter are a good start. Healthy interpersonal connection involves exchanging positive energy, sharing, and building trust. The 2021 World Happiness Report found that people with increased connectedness with others during the pandemic had greater life satisfaction, better mental health, and more resilience.[248]

Key Points:

Experiencing a strong support system will help you overcome challenges more easily and maintain mental and emotional well-being. It decreases health risks and improves physical well-being and longevity. Having strong social connections will enhance your immune system, lengthen your longevity by 50 percent, and act as a cushion against stressors. Having healthy relationships in your life is a shock absorber.

Challenge:

Identify one thing you can do this week to foster a connection with someone who matters to you.

POWER OF BEING PRESENT

The most impactful gift we can give is mindful, intentional attention. Consider the last time someone was 100 percent focused on you and your conversation without outside distraction, invaders, notifications, technology, or people checking their phones. How long did it last? Similarly, when was the last time you were 100 percent focused on someone without distraction? How many minutes did it last?

I see you! I am here!

This is how African Bushmen have been known to greet each other. It is a simple yet profound proclamation of affirming and validating someone's presence. Knowing that you are seen with enthusiasm and even with rejoicing is powerful.

Maya Angelou said one of the most powerful quotations I've heard about the power of interconnection.

◇◇

People won't necessarily remember what you said or what you talked about, but they'll remember how they felt when they were around you.
—Maya Angelou, author

◇◇

SOCIAL SUPPORT TO PROMOTE HABIT FORMATION

Habit Guru Charles Duhigg (*Power of Habit*) highlights the importance of soliciting social support for habit formation. Experiencing emotional connection, gentle accountability partnership, a venue for feedback, and social support is a catalyst for helping change feel easier.[249]

LEARNING IN COMMUNITY

Social interaction can also enhance your learning. According to the 50–50 rule, learning is most effective when you spend half the time studying and doing information intake and the other half interacting with it. It helps to be proactively engaged with the content.

Spending time explaining and teaching information accelerates the learning process. Rather than re-reading information, practice explaining the learned information in your own words. Even better, assemble a live audience who can engage and interact with you around the said content. Partner with someone to re-organize the information, put it into different words, and re-explain it.

ZONE OF PROXIMAL DEVELOPMENT

The zone of proximal development (ZPD) was developed by psychologist Lev Vygotsky. It refers to the range of abilities an individual can perform with skilled or expert guidance but aren't able to perform on their own. The zone of proximal development (ZPD) has been defined as:

◇◇

The space between what a learner can do without assistance and what a learner can do with adult guidance or in collaboration with more capable peers.
—Lev Vygotsky, psychologist

◇◇

The term proximal refers to skills that an individual is "close" to mastering. Others have since expanded on some of these learning theory key concepts.

This learning process consists of the following components:

- The presence of someone with the knowledge and skills to guide the learner
- Providing supportive activities, tools, resources, and instructions, known as scaffolding, provided by the expert that help guide the learner
- Social interactions allow the learner to work on their skills and abilities

MORE KNOWLEDGEABLE OTHER

The term more knowledgeable other (MKO) is clear, referring to someone who has a better understanding or a stronger ability than the learner regarding a particular task, process, or idea. The MKO can be a teacher or an older adult, yet not necessarily. You can learn from anyone who has an advanced skill set that you don't possess.

Key Points:

- Accompaniment enhances psychological fitness... the simple power of walking alongside another during life's journey, sharing vulnerabilities, and being open with people when they are suffering is powerful.
- Offering your presence with others through difficulties can create sacred moments.
- The idea that no one has to be alone can be easily forgotten during times of suffering.
- Remember that the power of connection can bring light to the darkness of those who are struggling.
- The act of sharing and being vulnerable is the glue that binds people together. It puts a deposit of trust into a relationship.
- Companionship eases the suffering and provides a buffer to the struggle. It provides relief, so the hard things aren't as hard.

Challenge:

Identify someone you can accompany on the journey. Search for common ground with others. If you look for it, you'll find it.

POWER OF COMMUNITY

Social support is what often keeps people going during tough times. Both formal and informal networks provide security, allyship, community, and belonging. Other benefits of a social support network include improvement in coping with stressful situations, alleviating emotional distress, and enhanced self-esteem.

David Spiegel's work at Stanford University has shown the positive impact of social support and how it can reduce the negative effects of stress and enhance immune function. According to Spiegel, friends can keep you alive and interpersonal connection has enabled us to survive. He is well known for his research on support groups for cancer patients. Results from many studies indicate how involvement in these support groups improves patients' quality of life and mood and decreases levels of distress and pain.[250]

Maintaining adequate social support is an important buffer against the negative impacts of bad stress as well, including poor immune function and inflammation.

I realize I'm repeating myself yet it is worth reinforcing again how strongly science supports the connection between the biological effects of stress, anxiety, and depression with our interpersonal relationships and social support network.

Therapists report that one of the most common complaints heard is that people feel like they don't belong. My experience with coaching clients is the same, which reinforces the power of a group model. I have facilitated many coaching groups with different topics, types of professionals, and objectives.

Regardless of the content or model, when asked what was beneficial about the experience, almost everyone will say, "I'm so glad that I'm not the only one." There is solace, peace, and comfort, knowing others also struggle.

As mentioned previously, it is easy to get lulled into social media personas and make assumptions about how great everyone else's life is, which exacerbates the feeling they don't belong. An interesting paradox about this is that experiencing feelings of not fitting in is universal. Isolation and loneliness are part of the human experience.

Plenty of studies demonstrate the negative effects of social isolation and loneliness on mood and psychological health. Feeling alone and disconnected are also risk factors for clinical disorders, depression, anxiety, and suicide.

A recent NIH study indicated that the physical and mental health of older people has been significantly impacted due to social isolation.[251] Most have experienced increased anxiety, depression, decreased activity, and a decline in physical health in a multitude of areas.

The psychological effect of extended quarantine has resulted in post-traumatic stress symptoms, anger, confusion, depression, hopelessness, and anxiety across populations and demographics. The impact is ongoing and likely to have long-lasting effects for some.

THE CONNECTION PRESCRIPTION

Interpersonal connection is core to lifestyle medicine, health, and wellbeing. Conversely, isolation has a significantly negative impact on health, even mortality. Having quality connections with people and interaction with a community is important to maintaining healthy life habits as well.

The idea of a connection prescription was proposed by Martino and colleagues.[252] They suggest that prescribing social interactions and friendships has the potential to have a healing effect on patients. A previous Exercise is Medicine campaign helped promote the benefits of physical activity. Similarly, the social connection can be just as impactful. Martino suggests that the time is right for a Connection is Medicine campaign in which healthcare professionals can incorporate this into their equation of care.

We could go so far as suggesting that we need "human connection moment" doses like we take multivitamins. David Siegel says when it comes to development, humans need attention like plants need sunlight.

A recent study conducted by Dr. Yavin Shaham's lab of the NIDA Intramural Research Program affirms the importance of social interactions. In this study, when given a choice between highly addictive drugs or spending time with other rats, the animals almost always prefer social interaction to drugs.[253]

This research highlights the importance of connection and lays the groundwork for how social rewards can be used to prevent and treat addiction. Many evidence-based therapies used to prevent addiction already incorporate these interpersonal factors, and it offers hope for such models to treat other mental health challenges.

In the realm of psychology, seeking social support and connection as a response to a stressor has even been added as an alternative to the fight or flight reaction in the stress cycle.

Shelley Taylor developed the tend-and-befriend theory. According to Taylor's research, when faced with a potential threat, females will lean into caring for their young and seeking connection and support from others.[254] Her work noted that, especially for females, people often affiliate rather than attack each other when stressed or threatened. Females are often inclined to nurture and protect offspring, which Taylor suggests results from increased levels of oxytocin when there is a perceived threat to a relationship.[255]

Key Points:

Again, YOU ARE NOT THE ONLY ONE. Everyone struggles. Everyone experiences loneliness and isolation. Fostering interpersonal connections is critical to maintaining health and wellness.

Challenges:

Enhance your social bonds. What existing social bonds can you enrich? Where in your life can you encourage a new connection?

Try an exercise suggested by Stanford researcher Jane Dutton to promote high-quality interactions with people. Pair up with one person. You each have one minute to build a connection and trust with each other. This exercise often challenges people to search for uncommon commonalities and promotes quick self-disclosure and vulnerability. The shared commitment to having a high-quality interaction can help.

THE EXPERIMENTAL GENERATION OF INTERPERSONAL CLOSENESS

Social psychology researcher Arthur Aron identified a list of 36 questions that generate closeness and intimacy. Instructions are to take 45 minutes to discuss the following questions with someone you want to connect with.[256]

It could be someone new in your life or a current relationship (friend, partner, spouse, colleague, family member). Each person takes a turn answering each question, spending 15 minutes on each set. If 15 minutes pass and you haven't gotten through set I, move on to set II. Each set is designed to be slightly more probing in nature.

Here is a sampling of the proposed questions.

Set I

- What would constitute a "perfect" day for you?
- For what in your life do you feel most grateful?
- If you could change anything about the way you were raised, what would it be?
- Take four minutes and tell your partner your life story in as much detail as possible.
- If you could wake up tomorrow having gained any one quality or ability, what would it be?

Set II

- Is there something that you've dreamed of doing for a long time? Why haven't you done it?
- What do you value most in a friendship?
- What is your most treasured memory?
- What is your most terrible memory?
- If you knew that in one year you would die suddenly, would you change anything about the way you are now living? Why?

Set III

- Make three true "we" statements each. For instance, "We are both in this room feeling…."

- Complete this sentence: "I wish I had someone with whom I could share…."

- If you were going to become a close friend with your partner, please share what would be important for them to know.

- Tell your partner what you like about them; be very honest this time, saying things that you might not say to someone you've just met.

- Share with your partner an embarrassing moment in your life.

SOCIAL PAIN

Emotional suffering can come from perceived exclusion, rejection, or being left out. Such social pain can cause as much or even more damage than physical pain.

Research studies have highlighted similarities between social pain and physical pain.[257] Social pain is referred to as the negative emotions associated with rejection, being excluded, or being left out. Individuals often use descriptions associated with physical pain words such as "my feelings are hurt" or "my heart is broken."

The painful feelings of social disconnection appear to utilize similar neurobiological systems associated with physical pain. The substrates of social and physical pain both rely on opioid processes. Neuroimaging research has shown social exclusion experiences activate the dorsal anterior cingulate cortex (dACC) and anterior insula (AI), both of which have a role in experiencing physical pain.

This shared neural circuitry indicates that altering social or physical pain can influence the other. Social support diffuses the impact of social pain and can reduce the experience of physical pain. It has even been shown that Tylenol (paracetamol; Johnson and Johnson), typically used to treat physical pain, can also alleviate social pain.

Our sense of well-being depends, to some extent, on others regarding us as a You; our yearning for connection is a primal human need, minimally for a cushion for survival. Today, the neural echo of that need heightens our sensitivity to the difference between It and You—and makes us feel social rejection as deeply as physical pain.
—Daniel Goleman, author

HUGGING

Experiencing human touch is important for mental health. It makes sense that interpersonal affection is good for us. It can contribute to well-being, mental health, and therefore psychological fitness.

Hugging can be relaxing and calming. It's another way the neurochemicals, including the "love" hormone oxytocin, are released. The increase of oxytocin can slow the heart rate as well as reduce anxiety.

Oxytocin is a hormone that acts as a neurotransmitter and is considered to play a role in behavior associated with emotional bonding, prosocial behaviors, and trust building. It has been considered to reinforce pair bonding, early attachment between mothers and infants, and romantic partners. Endorphins are also released through hugging, supporting the immediate feelings of pleasure.

Experiencing the human touch can be important to maintaining social bonds and fostering healthy relationships. Research has demonstrated that cuddling can even protect you from getting a cold.[258] Researchers monitored the hugging frequency of adults after they were exposed to a common cold virus. Results indicated that those in the hugging group were less likely to get a cold and had less severe symptoms.

JUST 20 SECONDS

In a study assessing the stress-reducing effects of hugging, individuals were assigned a task of public speaking. The half that received a hug from their partner showed lower stress levels. Having a supportive partner hug them for 20 seconds actually decreased stress.[259]

INTERACTIVE RECIPROCITY

The release of oxytocin plays a role in romantic relationships. The more couples share positive interactions, including affectionate touches, cuddling, and expressing positive emotions, the higher their oxytocin levels. This process can lead to a feedback cycle that reinforces more positive interactions and, therefore, increased oxytocin for both. It matches common sense. By giving love, you'll receive love, which helps you want to love more.

Key Points:

Hugging is good for you. It increases oxytocin levels and decreases stress hormones (cortisol). The benefits seem to come from a twenty-second hug.

Challenge:

Hug more people for 20 seconds. January 21st is National Hugging Day. I can be skeptical of random holidays I've never heard of. Who names them? It is often consumerism driving us to go spend money. I'm not sure who was behind hugging day, but it seems we could all benefit from hugging more. Why not do it every day?

THE POWER OF 12-STEP TREATMENT MODELS

There is much to be learned from the success of the 12-step treatment models of recovery. Alcoholics Anonymous (AA) is an informal society for recovering alcoholics in which individuals join active mutual support groups. As part of this community, they engage in fellowship and support each other in the recovery from addiction. The purpose of AA is to help people stay sober and help each other stay sober through difficult times. Participants work the suggested twelve steps together, sharing their experiences, strength, and hope.

Since AA was founded in the 1930s, it has been effective for millions. Key principles include focusing on a power higher than themselves, finding comfort in knowing they aren't alone, and leveraging a robust sponsor/mentor system to pay it forward and help others recover.

The program involves acknowledging there is a problem with substance abuse or behavior, surrendering, deepening self-awareness, making amends, taking daily inventory, and accepting responsibility for decisions.

The psychology within these principles indicates that the program helps people fulfill important needs such as teaching and guidance in changing destructive thoughts and behaviors, peer support, fellowship in the community, spiritual fulfillment, and the opportunity to flourish while abstaining from the addictive substance or behavior.

They are clearly onto something. While the program may not be for everyone, there is so much goodness in this model that has been life-changing and lifesaving for so many people.

Key Points:

The AA model can be powerful and serves as an example of how we can all learn, share, and grow together. Principles to promote psychological fitness include acceptance of accountability, learning new skills, taking inventory, sharing, reflecting, the empowerment that you can change, being in community and fellowship, believing in a higher power, and teaching and helping others.

CHAPTER 9

LEARNING PARTNERS

Being able to tolerate people who you find to be difficult is also a component of well-being and psychological fitness. I call them learning partners, not difficult people. Just because I find someone to be difficult doesn't mean they are "a difficult person." If I'm irritated with them, it's my problem. We all face learning partners, and we all act as learning partners for others as well. Everyone can be difficult to deal with on occasion.

I have a history of being a bit impatient. While I've worked on this for years and have made progress, I still simply don't like unnecessary waiting. I used to find myself feeling more agitated than I would like to admit, and I'm certain I would frustrate those around me with this tendency.

Years ago, my daughter told me that I had a lot of pet peeves. I wish it wasn't true, but she was right. There were times when I would find essentially harmless or neutral behaviors to be aggravating, especially if they involved movement at a slow pace.

Here are a few: stopping in the middle of an aisle or parking lot to text, holding up traffic, gum-smacking, bad manners in general, chewing food with one's mouth open (my kids call it "chomping"), overtly poor grammar, interrupting, long, unnecessarily detailed stories, socks on the floor, ingratitude, not saying thank you, arrogance, and talking loudly on the phone in a public place.

Regardless of what irritates me, it is my problem to solve. It doesn't matter what others are doing. If I'm annoyed or frustrated, I'm the one that needs to take accountability and deal with it. By the way, it is not lost on me that I am guilty of engaging in these behaviors as well.

Everyone faces people they find to be challenging. Sometimes, they can be avoided. Other times, we have less choice. There is something to be learned from people who frustrate us. Be curious and open to how your encounters can help you grow and increase your self-awareness.

◇◇◇

When another person makes you suffer, it is because he suffers deeply within himself, and his suffering is spilling over. He does not need punishment; he needs help. That's the message he is sending.
—Thich Nhat Hanh, author and monk

◇◇◇

I often need to remind myself and my kids that **hurting** people **hurt** people. Emotionally injured or troubled individuals are apt to be more judgmental and inclined to magnify the faults and short-comings of others. It is also true that we all hurt each other to varying degrees. If we are in a relationship long enough, we will hurt and get hurt, even if we don't intend, mean it, or even realize we've done it. It's the emotionally messy part of being human.

We don't see people's internal wounds; we only observe their behavior and their faults. Conversely, we experience our inner hurts. The following quote is from Roman emperor Marcus Aurelius, who lived in 121–180 A.D.

◇◇◇

When you wake up in the morning, tell yourself: the people I deal with today will be meddling, ungrateful, arrogant, dishonest, jealous, and surly. They are like this because they can't tell good from evil.

◇◇◇

This quote is timeless. Relatable? Probably for many. Difficult people emerge, especially when we are tired, compromised, or over-worked.

Key Point:

Emotional suffering often comes out sideways in behavior.

Challenge:

Extend grace. Assume positive intent. Have compassion. Forgive others even when they don't deserve it. The world will be better this way. Your life will be better this way too.

P.S. This does not mean tolerating abuse, compromising yourself, not standing up, or advocating for what's right. It means not carrying others' suffering or negative behaviors with you unnecessarily.

Key Points

Random Reminders that May Be Pertinent to Your Mental Health Journey

- If you fear judgment, remember people are mostly not thinking about you.
- To avoid disappointment, modify your expectations.
- Know that we will disappoint each other.
- Difficult people can be important learning partners.
- Perceptions vary. You have agency over the perception you create.
- Your thoughts don't need to define you, but your actions do.
- Bad things happen without sufficient reason or explanation too often.
- No one is coming to save you or make you happy. Sometimes, accepting this harsh reality is what you need to get on with it and move ahead.
- You have the potential to change. Focusing only on what you have control over can be a catalyst for action.
- Allowing your inner critic to continuously give you a mental beatdown won't help you.
- Anger is not solved with more anger.
- You have choices and don't need to become absorbed by your thinking, emotions, and reactions.

Chapter 10:
Mental Health in the Workplace

W E NEED TO TALK MORE ABOUT MENTAL HEALTH AT WORK. There are numerous global statistics highlighting the mental health challenges in the workplace. The global economy is estimated to lose $1 trillion per year due to lost productivity caused by mental health challenges such as depression and anxiety.

We spend most of our waking hours at work, so paying attention to working conditions and work lives is relevant. Our working environment has changed in ways impossible to imagine a generation ago.

Once again, the latest technologies and expanded internet access have enabled us to work almost around the clock. This hyperconnected global world has created challenges for people to create work and home life boundaries. Many professionals are finding that work is ever-present.

We are facing a workplace mental health crisis. We are on the precipice of changing the landscape. I see a new frontier of mental health at work, and it involves connection, community, and peer support. Fortunately, there is more understanding that supporting mental health at work has a positive impact on organizational success as well as on employee health in general.

It's important to recognize that there is shared accountability. Organizations can establish the infrastructure to promote mental health, leaders and managers can distribute work and create conditions conducive to mental health, and individuals need to work on their own personal well-being and mental health.

The architecture of organizations can be improved to address the mental health of the workforce. Companies need to build a framework that considers employees' individual needs. We are beyond a one-size-fits-all approach; the needs are greater now. No magic webinar will address the complexity of mental health. We need to develop additional tiers of mental health support at work that are customized, accessible, and flexible.

Employees need more options. At a basic level, we still need increased awareness and the reduction of mental health stigma. People need expanded access to care and resources and psychological safety that provides them with permission to access such services. Upgraded tools, skills, and support to guide employees will be necessary.

Additionally, effective mental health support must be centered on human connection. Being over-dialed into technology has contributed to isolation and loneliness.

It's time for a renewed focus on the humanity of employees and the importance of fostering closeness in relationships. Employees need the community level of support to know they are not the only one who is struggling or languishing. Mental health support needs to have a human connection for purposes of accountability as well.

As in precision medicine, all employees deserve the right dose and level of mental health intervention. They deserve to be offered support that is relevant, useful, and right-sized to their needs. Making inventories available and effective triaging to get the right level of care and support that people need can help.

The commitment to fostering a culture focused on mental health and well-being must come from the top to normalize it and give people permission to seek help, talk about it, utilize resources, and access and promote services. The question is no longer if an organization should address workplace mental health; it is at what level, how, and when.

Many organizations are answering the call by making well-being and mental health a strategic objective.

<u>Organizations can consider the following to promote mental health at work:</u>

- Meet employees where they are. Some need relief from suffering or want to move from being stuck to flourishing. Others are self-actualized and need development offerings accordingly.
- Offer mental health support on demand.
- Provide a menu of options and resources for varying mental health states. Personalize and customize the level of support needed.
- Make resources and tools accessible, available, cost-effective, and user-friendly.
- Expand peer support, employee resource groups, and ally networks.
- Offer assessments/check-ins.
- Provide training: educate managers and leaders.
- Promote leadership vulnerability and self-disclosure.
- Reduce the stigma. Give the topic more attention.
- Balance accountability with compassion. There is no free pass, yet we need to be reasonable about what is being asked of employees.
- Evaluate expectations and work demands fairly.

CHAPTER 10

PSYCHOLOGICAL FITNESS AT WORK

Psychological fitness is foundational to performance, well-being, and effectiveness. The mind's powerful and often invisible role shapes your experiences and behaviors, which impacts how you show up to work.

The benefits of having mentally, psychologically, and emotionally fit individuals are clearly recognized in the world of athletics. Having a healthy mindset and a positive mood contributes to peak performance. Plenty of athletes know what it's like to be in a mental slump and appreciate how it affects their performance.

When you can understand the components of your state of mind, feelings, and thoughts, you can use this to your advantage when it comes to performance, productivity, and effectiveness. Access to psychological resources helps employees manage stress, think more clearly, and connect more effectively with others — all leading to a healthier workplace.

Being psychologically fit opens the door to creativity, more innovative thinking, and problem-solving.

Key Points:

Cultivating your mental health and well-being will help you navigate through the complexity of today's work atmosphere. Leaders and organizations need to invest in the psychological fitness of their employees. Cultivating the well-being and mental health of employees and teams will foster positive work behaviors and output.

Challenge:

Many leaders are well-intentioned yet unsure how to approach the topic. Consider implementing a psychological fitness well-being plan with your team. It is not a binding contract or mental health treatment plan, yet an agreement designed to facilitate healthy conversations between managers and employees.

Psychological Fitness Well-Being Plan

Access the plan in your free psychological fitness guide here: Psychfitguide.com/book.

WORKPLACE FACTORS IMPACTING MENTAL HEALTH

A variety of workplace factors impact employee mental health. Poor communication, micromanagement, low levels of autonomy, excessive workloads, long hours, inequity, and lack of team connection are all examples of organizational challenges. Bullying, negative work behaviors, and harassment are also causes of work-related stress.

Stress is rising. Americans are among the most stressed employees. Work-related stress is estimated to affect at least 83 percent of American workers.

WHAT WILL IT COST ORGANIZATIONS THAT DON'T SUFFICIENTLY ADDRESS WORKPLACE MENTAL HEALTH?

Absenteeism. More employees than ever are taking medical leave to address chronic stress, mental health challenges, and burnout.

Attrition. Employees are demanding more of their employers, and if not satisfied, they'll leave.

Continued burnout.

Loss of high potential talent. Employees have options now, and they aren't afraid to leverage them.

More presenteeism. People who are struggling may be showing up for work, yet not in a fully effective manner, costing productivity and leading to inefficiencies.

Increased health care costs. Costs for health care are nearly 50 percent higher in high-pressure companies

Disengagement. Disengaged workers have higher absenteeism, more unsafe work behaviors, lower productivity, and higher turnover.

Decreased morale. Negativity is contagious, and it only takes a few negative behaviors to spread.

More stress and illness.

RECOMMENDATIONS FOR PROMOTING A MENTALLY HEALTHY CULTURE

Foster community. People want to belong and be a part of something larger than themselves. Remind people of purpose and meaning in the work your organization provides. Ask them what they need. Listen. If you are going to ask, take action. Otherwise, don't ask.

Promote interpersonal connections. Social connections at work produce highly desirable outcomes.

Find a friend and ally at work. Having one friend at work leads to positive work outcomes: improvements in retention and reduction in burnout. Develop multiple alliances. Create a coalition around raising mental health awareness in your workplace.

Show empathy and be present with people. Be intentional in your interpersonal interactions. Reduce interruptions and distractions.

Validate people. Inquire and listen. People want to know they matter and are valued by their boss, employees, and co-workers.

Amy Edmondson of Harvard University has studied the importance of psychological safety at work, consisting of inclusive, humble leaders who encourage their employees to speak up or ask for help. Her research demonstrates how creating an environment of safety leads to better learning and performance outcomes.[260]

Share and self-disclose selectively, with boundaries. It builds trust.

Demonstrate vulnerability. Be authentic and open and acknowledge challenges. Don't pretend to be perfect. There is nothing

helpful about leaders pretending to be perfect and without problems.

Be a giver. Have you had a manager or mentor who went out
of his or her way to help you? You likely remained loyal to them.

Leaders demonstrating a commitment to values aligned with
kindness promote a healthy culture. In Give and Take, Wharton
professor Adam Grant highlights how kindness and generosity
in leadership predict team and organizational effectiveness.[261] Of
course, caring workplace culture will contribute to employee mental health.

As I did the research for this book, I spoke with many experts
on workplace mental health. My intention was to include the data,
yet I quickly realized it was too much. The research will be highlighted in my next project.

Key Point:

When employee well-being isn't considered, it will come
at a cost to the people, as well as the effectiveness of an
organization.

Challenge:

Leaders/Managers: Evaluate workloads. Adjust excessive
demands.

Employees: Do your part to manage your own
psychological fitness and mental health.

Conclusion

Heal yourself, but don't rush
Help people, but have boundaries
Love others, but don't let them harm you
Love yourself, but don't become egotistical
Stay informed, but don't overwhelm yourself
Embrace change, but keep pursuing your goals.[262]
—Yung Pueblo, *Clarity and Connection*

T HE PSYCHOLOGICAL STRAIN OF CURRENT TIMES IS COMING AT A COST TO OUR MENTAL HEALTH, AND WE CAN INSTILL HOPE BY UNDERSTANDING THAT THERE ARE ACTIONS WE CAN TAKE TO PARTIALLY REMEDY IT. Building and enhancing your internal resources will help mitigate the negative effects of worldly stress, uncertainty, and change that is out of your control.

Recognize the more grounded and self-aware you are, the better you can activate your potential, show up as a better you, and leverage opportunities for growth. I hope this book has reminded you how your emotional state is not at the mercy of your environment. You have some agency over your mental health, regardless of where you fall on the well-being continuum.

This book offers mental health tonic—a menu of options, ideas, and tools to help you make customized changes in your life. You are in more control of your internal resources than you think.

As the alchemist of your own life, find the right blend, mix, and integration of practices to best serve your mental health. Self-pre-scribe what will help you get through the episodic nature of life. The more you invest in your own psychological capital, the more you can help others.

Psychological fitness is the enhancement of cognitive, psychological, and behavioral abilities to improve life. You can train to optimize psychological and mental fitness just like training physical fitness.

This book offers frameworks and foundations, theories, relevant research, quotes, and suggestions on how to apply the concepts to make progress. By taking the time to read this book, you have already enhanced your overall mental health because psycho-education — learning about well-being — enhances well-being, and action metabolizes fear.

◇◇

If you want momentum, you'll have to create it yourself, right now, by getting up and getting started.
—Ryan Holiday, bestselling author

◇◇

Influential psychologist William James reminds us that action doesn't guarantee happiness, but there is no happiness without action. To experience real CHANGE, now is the time to turn intentions into action.

While it is tempting to hope for a miraculous elixir that will provide pleasure, achievement, and success, it doesn't exist. Our fast-paced, immediate-focused culture has conditioned us to seek cheap and short paths to improvement, yet this is misleading us.

The reality can contribute to a perpetual state of disappointment and unnecessary distress if we aren't careful. If you want to achieve anything of significance in life, determination, training, and hard work are required.

Understanding that hardship and doing the internal work can't be fully circumvented will accelerate your progress. You need to train, manage your energy, emotions, and thoughts, and learn what levers to adjust so you can enhance your mental health. Play an active role in shaping your perception and cultivating a constructive, healthy mindset.

The work is finding just the right blend of acceptance and letting go, exertion and recovery, tension and ease, stretch and release, learn and contemplate, ground and adapt, reflection and action, flex and focus, etc.

Water skiing was a passion of mine growing up. It was the ultimate flow experience and can be metaphorical for navigating through life and responding to your circumstances.

As you learn to ski, you need to concentrate closely on body mechanics, especially when getting up out of the water. Your arms need to be straight, legs bent, skis together, and have a strong core. You must find just the right tension as the boat pulls you up. If you pull the rope in too hard, you'll fall backward. If you pull yourself up too hard, the momentum will cause you to fall forward. You need just enough finesse and tension to let the boat lift you out of the water. After you get the hang of it, it happens more automatically, yet you still need to pay attention.

Once you're up, you adapt to the conditions, managing your speed and direction by keeping balance. You need to respond to the speed of the boat, the size of the waves, and the angle your ski approaches the wake. If the lake is smooth and calm, and you can speed across the wake, when it's windy and the lake is choppy, you need to just hang on and not fall.

It reminds me of the episodic nature of life and the importance of preparing for turbulent conditions. You are preparing for adversity by building your psychological fitness.

XX

Happiness is not the absence of problems;
it's the ability to deal with them.
—Steve Maraboli,
military veteran and global philanthropist

XXXXXXXXXXXXXXXXXXXXXXXXXXXXXXXXXXXXXXXXXXXXXXXXXX

You are unique, and there is no one else like you. My hope is that this book has provided you with food for thought, practical suggestions and interventions, inspiration, and motivation.

My intention is to share psychoeducation, bring awareness to mental health, and provide a menu of practices to help you build psychological fitness.

From here, you will decide how to make changes that will impact your life in a positive way. Begin right now, no matter where you are. Don't wait for optimal conditions to take action. Life is challenging and messy; train, so you're ready to respond in the face of your circumstances.

Challenge:

Focus on how you show up for life, not what life gives you.
Focus on what you bring to life, not what life brings to you.
Focus on how you show up to relationships, people, and
work, not what they do for you.

I have offered evidence-based interventions to help you develop the mental capacity you'll need to deal with life's messiness.

My hope is that it has helped you understand how to achieve, prosper, and make progress while maintaining emotional equilibrium. My desire is that you have gained an increased awareness of the power of your thinking, emotional experience, and your ability to self-regulate.

I challenge you to take small steps. Developing insight, learning new ideas, and discovery isn't enough. The information must be applied, reflected upon, and revised.

Action generates momentum. Consider the practices and suggestions for internal maintenance as well as preventative measures to avert future decline, which include nourishing and replenishing yourself.

I hope this book arms you with additional psychological supplies and assets to help handle the hard stuff and manage your inner life.

Heal and help each other. Do it together. Find an accountability partner, form a book club, and assemble a group so you can grow and transform together. Personal growth is best done when blended in both solitude and community. Leveraging the power of relationships promotes and accelerates behavior change. Accelerate your personal growth by engaging in shared learning.

Just like physical fitness, training done in community fuels growth.

◇◇◇

The whole is greater than the sum of its parts.
—Aristotle

◇◇◇

I believe in the power of engaging small groups to accelerate change and development, regardless of the topic. Individuals have been informally gathering for centuries, sharing challenges, conducting a review of the day, and learning together what they can do better tomorrow.

The camaraderie and fostering of the community are self-reinforcing and provide benefit to all who are participating.

A peer forum is an inner circle of people who meet regularly with a common purpose, offering opportunities for sharing, education, learning, and connecting. It involves engaging in thoughtful conversation, learning from each other, and developing together. Common topics could include leadership development, faith development, or personal growth in general.

Doing individual personal development work is important, yet small group settings provide another level of benefit and can complement one-on-one work. Being involved in a group provides a support network, reciprocity, intimacy, education, and accountability partnerships. It offers the opportunity to teach, learn, and help others. It allows one to tap into the collective genius of others. Insights generated in a small group setting can be even more nuanced and impactful.

Since loneliness and isolation are at an all-time high, this format is timely. People are desperate for more meaningful connections. The bonding that can take place in a peer forum is powerful and rewarding.

For peer groups to be effective, here are a few suggestions for optimal conditions: establishing confidentiality, commitment to sharing and being vulnerable, nurturing an atmosphere of trust, being willing to support and help others, psychological safety, and permission to be brave. In small groups, there is no room for criticism, judgment, or giving advice; rather, the focus should be on empathizing, being present, active listening, and sharing lived experiences.

Learning how to build psychological fitness and elevate your mental health in a peer forum will enhance your results and prove to be a worthwhile investment.

Key Point:

Participating in small group settings can accelerate, foster, and enhance personal growth and change.

Challenge:

Consider starting or joining a peer forum to progress and strengthen your psychological fitness. More on this in the What's Next section.

◇◇

What we reach for may be different, but what makes us reach is the same.
—Mark Nepo, author and poet

◇◇

We are all interdependent. Separate selves, yet together on the journey. Mark Nepo describes aspen trees in the forest as being like us. Above ground, trees appear separate, yet their roots are interconnected below the ground, reinforcing their strength, vitality, and growth. The interconnection allows the trees to better withstand the impact of the elements. [263]

You have increased your self-awareness, and psychological fitness training will equip you to better handle stressors and uncertainty in your life. It's a journey, not a destination, and you are taking control of your inner resources. Do the internal work necessary to create the changes you want to see in your life.

CHAPTER 10

◇◇

The only person you are destined to become is the person you decide to be.
—Ralph Waldo Emerson

◇◇

Consider doing the work, like visiting a gym for mental health. Remember, the training isn't supposed to be easy. Changing behavior can be difficult. Choosing is exhausting too.

My all-time favorite passage from Theodore Roosevelt:

◇◇

It is not the critic who counts, not the man who points out how the strong man stumbles or where the doer of deeds could have done them better. The credit belongs to the man who is actually in the arena, whose face is marred by dust and sweat and blood; who strives valiantly; who errs, who comes short again and again because there is no effort without error and shortcoming; but who does actually strive to do the deeds; who knows great enthusiasms, the great devotions; who spends himself in a worthy cause; who at best knows, in the end, the triumph of high achievement, and who at the worst, if he fails, at least fails while daring greatly, so that his place shall never be with those cold and timid souls who neither know victory nor defeat.

◇◇

If you are doing the work on yourself, **you are in the arena.** Remember, **you can achieve and perform with ease**. They are not mutually exclusive.

To end on a message of **hope**…

Let's accompany each other,

so the hard things aren't as hard...

and let's **lift** each other up.

CHEERING FOR YOU!

◇◇◇

Go forth and set the world on fire.
—St. Ignatius of Loyola

◇◇◇

What's Next?

ONGRATULATIONS! I want to extend my appreciation for spending your time reading this book. Hopefully, by now, you have learned something to help you build your psychological fitness. You have plenty of options available; what you do with it is up to you.

My crusade: Advance mental health awareness, so talking about mental health and psychological fitness is just as mainstream as physical fitness. **Join me.**

I'd like to leave you with potential calls to action. Promote mental health awareness in your communities, share with a friend, engage in more outreach, and check in with each other.

Review and final challenge: Change happens best in small groups. Learning, reflecting, and applying new practices together amplifies the likelihood of positive outcomes and progress. It's more effective because everyone is attempting to change in a structured environment together. What we understand about change is if you work with a partner, it's more apt to stick.

I'm going to suggest it again because I know it works. Engage in the practices suggested in this book together in the community, bring it to your book club, start a book club, develop a peer forum, or invite friends to participate with you on the journey toward enhanced mental health and psychological fitness.

Let's train together. If you are serious about advancing your mental health, please consider participating in a self-study psychological fitness course to accompany this book or joining a psychological fitness training group. You can learn more and sign up for waiting lists here: psychfitguide.com/group.

Acknowledgements

SOMEONE TOLD ME NOT TO WORRY ABOUT THIS SEC-TION SINCE NO ONE WILL READ IT. That surprised me because I always read acknowledgments pages. It touches me to witness gratitude and the impact people have had on authors' lives. Even though so many people were committed to supporting me during this project, it goes way beyond a book.

It isn't even about the book. I wish I could write a whole book on my gratitude for so many who have influenced me in my life. I have been blessed with too many to recognize in this tiny section, so I'll just mention a few.

I mentioned my mom, Marjean DeCesare, in the dedication of this book, who, ever since her passing, continues to inspire me. Her life was a model of love, kindness, and service to others. I'd also like to acknowledge my dad, Ron DeCesare, who has always believed in me and is my greatest fan and champion. My parents taught us the values of family, generosity, faith, education, and humility, to name a few.

I hit the jackpot in the parent and family department. My brothers, Brian and Jeff, have also been anchors and a consistent source of love, support, and presence in my life. I had no sisters growing up, but I have been blessed in my adult life to have sisters-in-law that I adore and who have lifted me up — Ruby, Cosette, Sarah, Tammy, and Dawn.

An extra special thanks to my husband Bill (aka Dollar Bill), who has loved, tolerated, and supported me every day, no matter what. Today, we celebrate our 24th wedding anniversary, and I appreciate the meaningful life we have created together. I'm grateful for his understanding and appreciation of my dedication to doing the work I love.

We managed to raise (and are still raising) two sons and three daughters. Our kids are amazing human beings, despite our parenting imperfections. Stephen, Sophia, AJ, Josie, and Lisa bring me joy that is impossible to describe; words don't begin to capture it. They have been involved, supportive, encouraging, and patient with me through this book project. All that I do, I do with them in mind.

Thank you to my extended family and my besties, whose support, love, and encouragement have been integral in my life, especially during the last four and a half years since losing my mom. I greatly appreciate and cherish the DeCesare and McShane families, who also supported the promotion of this passion project.

Thank you to my publisher, Trevor Crane, the Epic Author team, and the Epic Influence peer group. I've learned so much, and you all have encouraged me to push way outside my comfort zone through this process.

My deepest thanks to my clients who trust me in sharing intimate details of their lives. It requires courage and vulnerability. You truly inspire me. I learn something valuable from all of you. I feel deep gratitude every single day for having the privilege to do this work.

Lastly, I want to thank all the scientists, researchers, and thought leaders referenced in this book. I leaned heavily into offering quotes, data, and studies to build on the credibility and genius of others in the field of psychology. I hope you found the information helpful.

I look forward to more connecting, community, and goodness that can come from this book.

About the Author

D R. KAREN DOLL is a licensed psychologist, consultant, coach, and #1 international bestselling author. At the intersection of personal well-being and professional development, she collaborates with industry-leading organizations and coaches high-achieving professionals. Her mission is to help people thrive, enhance well-being, and optimize leadership skills at every phase, from burgeoning new entrants to accomplished senior leaders.

She has been committed to mental health awareness and helping organizations address workplace mental health throughout her 25-year career. Her expertise has been featured on NBC, FOX, and Medium.com and shared with the United Nations.

Karen and her husband Bill live in Edina, Minnesota, with their five children. Favorite moments are time together at their family lake cabin. You can contact her at buildingpsychologicalfitness@gmail.com. Find her on **LinkedIn** and at drkarendoll.com.

Endnotes

1. Spira, Jonathan B. *Overload!: How too Much Information is Hazardous to Your Organization.* John Wiley & Sons, 2011.

2. World Health Organization. *"Burn-out an "occupational phenomenon": International Classification of Diseases. 2019."* World Health Organization, Geneva, Switzerland (2019).

3. Deloitte, L. L. P. "Workplace burnout survey." (2018).

4. Thompson, William W. "National and State Trends in Anxiety and Depression Severity" *Centers for Disease Control and Prevention.* (October 8, 2021). https://www.cdc.gov/mmwr/volumes/70/wr/mm7040e3.htm

5. Shields, Amy. "US Experienced Highest Ever Combined Rates of Deaths Due to Alcohol, Drugs, and Suicide During the COVID-19 Pandemic." Well Being Trust. (May 24, 2022). https://wellbeingtrust.org/press-releases/u-s-experienced-highest-ever-combined-rates-of-deaths-due-to-alcohol-drugs-and-suicide-during-the-covid-19-pandemic/.

6. Robert Half. 2019. *"Survey: 96% Of Managers Say Their Staff Are Experiencing Some Degree of Burnout."* Survey: 96% Of Managers Say Their Staff Are Experiencing Some Degree of Burnout. August 20. https://press.roberthalf.com/2019-08-20-Survey-96-Of-Managers-Say-Their-Staff-Are-Experiencing-Some-Degree-Of-Burnout.

7. Boyd, Danielle. "Workplace Stress." *The American Institute of Stress.* (April 13, 2022). https://www.stress.org/workplace-stress.

8. Qualtrics, X. M. "The Other COVID-19 Crisis: Mental Health." Available at: https://www.qualtrics.com/blog/confronting-mental-health/ (accessed May 28, 2020)

9. Harris, Dan, Jeffrey Warren, and Carlye Adler. *Meditation for Fidgety Skeptics: a 10% Happier How-to Book.* Spiegel & Grau, 2018.

10. de Mello, Anthony. "The Death of Me", p. 151 in *Awareness: The Perils and Opportunities of Reality.* 1992.

11.   https://www.who.int/data/gho/data/major-themes/health-and-well-being

12. Allport, Gordon Willard. *Personality: A Psychological Interpretation.* Henry Holt and Company, NY, 1937.

13. Travis, J. W. "The wellness/illness continuum." *Mill Valley, CA:* J.W. Travis, 1972.

14. Soots, L. (n.d.). *Flourishing. Positive Psychology People.* Retrieved from: http:///www.thepositivepsychologypeople.com/flourishing.

15. Seligman, Martin E. P. *Flourish: A Visionary New Understanding of Happiness and Well-being.* Atria Books, 2012.

16. Keyes, Corey LM. "Mental illness and/or mental health? Investigating axioms of the complete state model of health." *Journal of Consulting and Clinical Psychology* 73, no. 3 (2005): 539.

17. APA. n.d. American Psychological Association (APA). https://www.apa.org.

18. Hawes, Mariah T., Aline K. Szenczy, Daniel N. Klein, Greg Hajcak, and Brady D. Nelson. "Increases in depression and anxiety symptoms in adolescents and young adults during the COVID-19 pandemic." *Psychological Medicine* (2021): 1-9.

19. World Health Organization. "Live life: an implementation guide for suicide prevention in countries." (2021).

20. Kola, Lola, Manasi Kumar, Brandon A. Kohrt, Tobi Fatodu, Bisola A. Olayemi, and Adeyinka O. Adefolarin. "Strengthening public mental health during and after the acute phase of the COVID-19 pandemic." *The Lancet* 399, no. 10338 (2022): 1851-1852.

21. Accenture. n.d. "It's all of us - Research." Accenture. https://www.accenture.com/_acnmedia/pdf-90/accenture-tch-its-all-of-us-research-updated-report.pdf. Brassey, Jacqueline, Arjen van Witteloostuijn, Csaba Huszka, Tobias Silberzahn, and Nick van Dam. "Emotional flexibility and general self-efficacy: A pilot training intervention study with knowledge workers." PloS one 15, no. 10 (2020): e0237821.

22. Kahneman, Daniel. "Maps of bounded rationality: Psychology for behavioral economics." *American Economic Review* 93, no. 5 (2003): 1449-1475.

23. Ryan, Richard M., Veronika Huta, and Edward L. Deci. "Living well: A self-determination theory perspective on eudaimonia." *Journal of Happiness Studies* 9, no. 1 (2008): 139-170.

24. Diener, Ed, and Robert A. Emmons. "The independence of positive and negative affect." *Journal of Personality and Social Psychology* 47, no. 5 (1984).

25. Diener, Ed, Ed Sandvik, and William Pavot. "Happiness is the frequency, not the intensity, of positive versus negative affect." In *Assessing Well-being*, pp. 213-231. Springer, Dordrecht, 2009.

26. Vaden, Rory. *Take the Stairs: 7 Steps to Achieving True Success.* Penguin, 2012.

27. Mangels, Jennifer A., Brady Butterfield, Justin Lamb, Catherine Good, and Carol S. Dweck. "Why do beliefs about intelligence influence learning success? A social cognitive neuroscience model." *Social Cognitive and Affective Neuroscience* 1, no. 2 (2006): 75-86.

28. Gladwell, Malcolm. "Most likely to succeed." *The New Yorker* 15 (2008): 36-42.

29. Robson, Sean. "Psychological fitness and resilience: A review of relevant constructs, measures, and links to well-being." *Rand Health Quarterly* 4, no. 1 (2014).

30. Tolle, Eckhart. *The Power of Now: A Guide to Spiritual Enlightenment.* New World Library, 2004.

31. Cherniss, Cary, Melissa Extein, Daniel Goleman, and Roger P. Weissberg. "Emotional intelligence: what does the research really indicate?" *Educational Psychologist* 41, no. 4 (2006): 239-245.

32. Eurich, Tasha. "What self-awareness really is (and how to cultivate it)." *Harvard Business Review* (2018): 1-9.

33. Seligman, Martin EP, and Gregory McClellan Buchanan, eds. *Explanatory style.* L. Erlbaum, 1995.

34. Seligman, Martin EP, Tayyab Rashid, and Acacia C. Parks. "Positive psychotherapy." *American psychologist* 61, no. 8 (2006): 774.

35. Bandura, Albert. "Guide for constructing self-efficacy scales." *Self-efficacy beliefs of adolescents* 5, no. 1 (2006): 307-337.

36. Hickman, Steven. n.d. "Mindful Self-Compassion | MSC." Chris Germer. https://chrisgermer.com/mindful-self-compassion-msctm/.

37. Rockman, Patricia, and Vinny Ferraro. 2016. "Why Self-Compassion is the New Mindfulness." Mindful.org. June 22. https://www.mindful.org/self-compassion-new-mindfulness/.

38. Leary, Mark R., Eleanor B. Tate, Claire E. Adams, Ashley Batts Allen, and Jessica Hancock. "Self-compassion and reactions to unpleasant self-relevant events: the implications of treating oneself kindly." *Journal of personality and social psychology* 92, no. 5 (2007): 887.

39. Neff, Kristin. *Self-Compassion: The Proven Power of Being Kind to Yourself.* HarperCollins, 2015.

40. Neff, K. D., & Beretvas, S. N. "The role of self-compassion in romantic relationships. Self and Identity." *Self and Identity* 12 (1) (2012): 78-98.

41. Neff, K. D., & Pommier, E. "The relationship between self-compassion and other-focused concern among college undergraduates, community adults, and practicing meditators." *Self and Identity* 12 (2) (2012): 160-176.

42. Rockliff, Helen, Paul Gilbert, Kirsten McEwan, Stafford Lightman, and David Glover. "A pilot exploration of heart rate variability and salivary cortisol responses to compassion-focused imagery." (2008).

43. Heffernan, Mary, Mary T. Quinn Griffin, Sister Rita McNulty, and Joyce J. Fitzpatrick. "Self-compassion and emotional intelligence in nurses." *International journal of nursing practice* 16, no. 4 (2010): 366-373.

44. Kelly, Allison C., David C. Zuroff, and Leah B. Shapira. "Soothing oneself and resisting self-attacks: The treatment of two intrapersonal deficits in depression vulnerability." *Cognitive Therapy and Research* 33, no. 3 (2009): 301-313.

45. Magnus, Cathy MR, Kent C. Kowalski, and Tara-Leigh F. McHugh. "The role of self-compassion in women's self-determined motives to exercise and exercise-related outcomes." *Self and identity* 9, no. 4 (2010): 363-382.

46. Germer, Christopher. *The Mindful Path to Self-Compassion: Freeing Yourself from Destructive Thoughts and Emotions.* Guilford Press, 2009.

47. Neff, Kristin D., and Christopher K. Germer. "A pilot study and randomized controlled trial of the mindful self-compassion program." *Journal of Clinical Psychology* 69, no. 1 (2013): 28-44.

48. Segal, Zindel V., John D. Teasdale, J. Mark Williams, and Michael C. Gemar. "The mindfulness-based cognitive therapy adherence scale: Inter-rater reliability, adherence to protocol and treatment distinctiveness." *Clinical Psychology & Psychotherapy* 9, no. 2 (2002): 131-138.

49. Chiesa, Alberto, and Alessandro Serretti. "Mindfulness-based stress reduction for stress management in healthy people: a review and meta-analysis." *The Journal of Alternative and Complementary Medicine* 15, no. 5 (2009): 593-600.

50. Shapiro, Shauna L., Kirk Warren Brown, and Gina M. Biegel. "Teaching self-care to caregivers: Effects of mindfulness-based stress reduction on the mental health of therapists in training." *Training and education in professional psychology* 1, no. 2 (2007): 105.

51. Neff, Kristin D. "The development and validation of a scale to measure self-compassion." *Self and identity* 2, no. 3 (2003): 223-250.

52. Deci, Edward L., and Richard M. Ryan. "The" what" and" why" of goal pursuits: Human needs and the self-determination of behavior." *Psychological Inquiry* 11, no. 4 (2000): 227-268.

53. Pink, Dan. "The puzzle of motivation." *TED Global 2009* (2009).

54. Vohs, Kathleen D., and Roy F. Baumeister, eds. *Handbook of self-regulation: Research, theory, and applications.* Guilford Publications, 2016

55. Kaufman, Scott Barry. *Transcend: The New Science of Self-Actualization.* Penguin, 2021.

56. Ames, Carole, and Russell Ames. "Goal structures and motivation." *The Elementary School Journal* 85, no. 1 (1984): 39-52.

57. Locke, Edwin A., and Gary P. Latham. "Building a practically useful theory of goal setting and task motivation: A 35-year odyssey." *American Psychologist* 57, no. 9 (2002): 705.

58. Locke, E.A. & and Latham, G.P., *A Theory of Goal Setting and Task Performance.* Prentice Hall, 1990.

59. Goggins, David. *Can't hurt me: Master your mind and defy the odds.* 2021.

60. Achor, Shawn. *The Happiness Advantage: The Seven Principles of Positive Psychology that Fuel Success and Performance at Work.* Random House, 2011.

61. Lama, Dalai, Desmond Tutu, and Douglas Carlton Abrams. *The Book of Joy: Lasting Happiness in a Changing World*. Penguin, 2016.

62. Pressfield, Steven. *Turning Pro: Tap Your Inner Power and Create your Life's Work*. Black Irish Entertainment LLC, 2012.

63. Molden, Daniel C., and Carol S. Dweck. "Finding" meaning" in psychology: a lay theories approach to self-regulation, social perception, and social development." *American psychologist* 61, no. 3 (2006): 192.

64. Dweck, Carol S. *Mindset: The New Psychology of Success*. Random House, 2006.

65. LePera, Nicole. *How to Do the Work: Recognize Your Patterns, Heal from Your Past, and Create Your Self.* Harper Collins Publishers, 2021.

66. "Stress in America™ 2020: A National Mental Health Crisis." American Psychological Association. https://www.apa.org/news/press/releases/stress/2020/report-october.

67. American Psychological Association. n.d. "Resilience." American Psychological Association. https://www.apa.org/topics/resilience.

68. Selye, Hans. "The stress syndrome." *The American Journal of Nursing* (1965): 97-99.

69. Le Fevre, Mark, Jonathan Matheny, and Gregory S. Kolt. "Eustress, distress, and interpretation in occupational stress." *Journal of Managerial Psychology* (2003).

70. Sanders, Robert. "New evidence that chronic stress predisposes brain to mental illness." *Berkeley News* 11 (2014).

71. Jazaieri, Hooria, Ihno A. Lee, Kelly McGonigal, Thupten Jinpa, James R. Doty, James J. Gross, and Philippe R. Goldin. "A wandering mind is a less caring mind: Daily experience sampling during compassion meditation training." *The Journal of Positive Psychology* 11, no. 1 (2016): 37-50.

72. Mills, H., N. Reiss, and M. Dombeck. "Stress reduction and management: Types of stressors (eustress vs. distress)." (2018). www.mentalhelp.net/articles/types-of-stressors-eustress-vs-distress/.

73. Lazarus, Richard S., and Susan Folkman. *Stress, Appraisal, and Coping*. Springer publishing company, 1984.

74. Sapolsky, Robert M. "Social status and health in humans and other animals." *Annual Review of Anthropology* (2004): 393-418.

75. Sapolsky, Robert M. *Why Zebras Don't Get Ulcers (3rd ed.)*. New York, 2004.

76. Nagoski, Emily, and Amelia Nagoski. *Burnout: The Secret to Unlocking the Stress Cycle*. Ballantine Books, 2020.

77. McGonigal, Kelly. *The Upside of Stress: Why Stress Is Good for You, and How to Get Good at It*. Penguin Publishing Group, 2016.

78. Robertson, Ian. *The Stress Test: How Pressure Can Make You Stronger and Sharper*. Bloomsbury Publishing, 2016.

79. Ratey, J. J., and R. D. Hagerman. *SPARK Your Brain*. The Eric Yang: Houston, TX, USA, 2008.

80. Stubbs B, Vancampfort D, Rosenbaum S, Firth J, Cosco T, Veronese N, Salum GA, Schuch FB. " An examination of the anxiolytic effects of exercise for people with anxiety and stress-related disorders: A meta-analysis." *Psychiatry Res.* 249 (2017): 102-108.

81. Heisz, Jennifer. *Move the Body, Heal the Mind: Overcome Anxiety, Depression, and Dementia and Improve Focus, Creativity, and Sleep*. Harvest, 2022.

82. Savitz J, Drevets WC, Smith CM, Victor TA, Wurfel BE, Bellgowan PS, Bodurka J, Teague TK, Dantzer R. "Putative neuroprotective and neurotoxic kynurenine pathway metabolites are associated with hippocampal and amygdalar volumes in subjects with major depression." *Neuropsychopharmacology* 40 (2) (2015): 463-71.

83. Rebar, Amanda L., Robert Stanton, David Geard, Camille Short, Mitch J. Duncan, and Corneel Vandelanotte. "A meta-meta-analysis of the effect of physical activity on depression and anxiety in non-clinical adult populations." *Health Psychology Review* 9, no. 3 (2015): 366-378.

84. Harvey, S.B., F.R.A.N.Z.C.P., Ph.D., Overland, S. Ph.D., Hatch, S.L. Ph.D., Wessely, S., F.R.C.Psych., M.D., Mykletun, A. Ph.D., Hotopf, M. F.R.C.Psych., Ph.D. "Exercise and the Prevention of Depression: Results of the HUNT Cohort Study." *The American Journal of Psychiatry* 175 (1) (2017): 28-36.

85. Wapner, Jessica. 2020. "Vision and Breathing May Be the Secrets to Surviving 2020." Scientific American. November 16. https://www.scientificamerican.com/article/vision-and-breathing-may-be-the-secrets-to-surviving-2020/.

86. Salzberg, Sharon. *Lovingkindness: The Revolutionary Art of Happiness.* Shambhala, 2018.

87. Fredrickson, Barbara L., Michael A. Cohn, Kimberly A. Coffey, Jolynn Pek, and Sandra M. Finkel. "Open hearts build lives: positive emotions, induced through loving-kindness meditation, build consequential personal resources." *Journal of Personality and Social Psychology* 95, no. 5 (2008): 1045.

88. Lembke, Anna. *Dopamine Nation: Finding Balance in the Age of Indulgence.* Penguin Publishing Group, 2021.

89. Lieberman, Daniel Z., and Michael E. Long. *The Molecule of More: How a Single Chemical in Your Brain Drives Love, Sex, and Creativity--and Will Determine the Fate of the Human Race.* BenBella Books, 2019.

90. Keen, Sam. *Fire in the Belly: On Being a Man.* Bantam, 2010.

91. Olson, Kristine, Christine Sinsky, Seppo T. Rinne, Theodore Long, Ronald Vender, Sandip Mukherjee, Michael Bennick, and Mark Linzer. "Cross-sectional survey of workplace stressors associated with physician burnout measured by the Mini-Z and the Maslach Burnout Inventory." *Stress and Health* 35, no. 2 (2019): 157-175.

92. Maslach, Christina, and Michael P. Leiter. *The Truth About Burnout: How Organizations Cause Personal Stress and What to Do About It.* Wiley, 2000.

93. Jha, Amishi P., Anthony P. Zanesco, Ekaterina Denkova, William K. MacNulty, and Scott L. Rogers. "The Effects of Mindfulness Training on Working Memory Performance in High-Demand Cohorts: a Multi-study Investigation." *Journal of Cognitive Enhancement* 6, no. 2 (2022): 192-204.

94. Minear, Meredith, Faith Brasher, Mark McCurdy, Jack Lewis, and Andrea Younggren. "Working memory, fluid intelligence, and impulsiveness in heavy media multitaskers." *Psychonomic Bulletin & Review* 20, no. 6 (2013): 1274-1281.

95. Ophir, Eyal, Clifford Nass, and Anthony D. Wagner. "Cognitive control in media multitaskers." *Proceedings of the National Academy of Sciences* 106, no. 37 (2009): 15583-15587.

96. Goleman, D., and R. Davidson. *Altered Traits: Science Reveals How Meditation Changes Your Mind, Brain, and Body.* Avery, 2018.

97. Leroy, Sophie, Aaron M. Schmidt, and Nora Madjar. "Interruptions and task transitions: Understanding their characteristics, processes,

and consequences." *Academy of Management Annals* 14, no. 2 (2020): 661-694.

98. Thomas, Maura. *Attention Management: How to Create Success and Gain Productivity—Every Day.* Vol. 1. Sourcebooks, Inc., 2019.

99. Aguilar, Mario I. *The 14th Dalai Lama: Peacekeeping and Universal Responsibility.* Routledge India, 2020.

100. Gorman, Thomas E., and C. Shawn Green. "Short-term mindfulness intervention reduces the negative attentional effects associated with heavy media multitasking." *Scientific Reports* 6, no. 1 (2016): 1-7.

101. Mrazek, Michael D., Michael S. Franklin, Dawa Tarchin, Phillips, Benjamin Baird, and Jonathan W. Schooler. "Mindfulness training improves working memory capacity and GRE performance while reducing mind wandering." *Psychological science* 24, no. 5 (2013): 776-781.

102. Harris, Dan, Jeff Warren, and Carlye Adler. *Meditation for Fidgety Skeptics: A 10% Happier How-To Book.* New York: Spiegel & Grau, 2017.

103. Newport, Cal. *Deep work: Rules for Focused Success in a Distracted World.* Hachette UK, 2016.

104. Honoré, Carl. *The Slow Fix: Solve Problems, Work Smarter and Live Better in a World Addicted to Speed.* Knopf Canada, 2013.

105. Kahneman, Daniel, Dan Lovallo, and Olivier Sibony. "Before you make that big decision." *Harvard Business Review* 89, no. 6 (2011): 50-60.

106. Morrison, Alexandra B., and Amishi P. Jha. "Mindfulness, attention, and working memory." In *Handbook of Mindfulness and Self-Regulation*, pp. 33-45. Springer, New York, NY, 2015.

107. Kasser, Tim, and Kennon M. Sheldon. "Time affluence as a path toward personal happiness and ethical business practice: Empirical evidence from four studies." *Journal of Business Ethics* 84, no. 2 (2009): 243-255.

108. Ben-Shahar, Tal. *Happier: Learn the secrets to daily joy and lasting fulfillment.* Vol. 1. New York: McGraw-Hill, 2007.

109. Giurge, Laura M., Ashley V. Whillans, and Colin West. "Why time poverty matters for individuals, organizations, and nations." *Nature Human Behaviour* 4, no. 10 (2020): 993-1003.

110. Schulte, Brigid. *Overwhelmed: How to Work, Love, and Play When No One Has the Time.* Macmillan, 2015.

111. Dembe, Allard E., and Xiaoxi Yao. "Chronic disease risks from exposure to long-hour work schedules over a 32-year period." *Journal of Occupational and Environmental Medicine* 58, no. 9 (2016): 861-867.

112. WHO. 2021. "Long working hours increasing deaths from heart disease and stroke: WHO, ILO." WHO | World Health Organization. May 17. https://www.who.int/news/item/17-05-2021-long-working-hours-increasing-deaths-from-heart-disease-and-stroke-who-ilo.

113. Irvine, William B. 2009. *A Guide to the Good Life: the Ancient Art of Stoic Joy.* Oxford University Press, USA.

114. Kahneman, Daniel, Edward Diener, and Norbert Schwarz, eds. *Well-being: Foundations of Hedonic Psychology.* Russell Sage Foundation, 1999.

115. Lembke, Anna. *Dopamine Nation: Finding Balance in the Age of Indulgence.* Penguin, 2021.

116. Lieberman, Daniel Z., and Michael E. Long. *The Molecule of More: How a Single Chemical in Your Brain Drives Love, Sex, and Creativity--and Will Determine the Fate of the Human Race.* BenBella Books, 2018.

117. Bloom, Paul. *The Sweet Spot: The Pleasures of Suffering and the Search for Meaning.* HarperCollins Publishers, 2022.

118. Evans-Wentz, Walter Y. *Autobiography of a Yogi.* Self-Realization Fellowship, 1993.

119. Wilson, Timothy D., David A. Reinhard, Erin C. Westgate, Daniel T. Gilbert, Nicole Ellerbeck, Cheryl Hahn, Casey L. Brown, and Adi Shaked. "Which would you prefer-do nothing or receive electric shocks!." *Science* 345, no. 6192 (2014): 75-77.

120. MacLeod, Ken. n.d. "Exhilarating if flawed, Colin Wilson helped open my mind." Aeon. https://aeon.co/essays/exhilarating-if-flawed-colin-wilson-helped-open-my-mind.

121. Quindlen, Anna. "Doing nothing is something." *Newsweek* 139, no. 19 (2002): 76-76.

122. Russell, B. "The Conquest of Happiness. By ES Ames." *Ethics* 41, no. a (1930).

123. Keller, Gary, and Jay Papasan. *The One Thing: The Surprisingly Simple Truth Behind Extraordinary Results.* Bard Press, 2013.

124. Kofman, Fred. *Conscious Business.* Sounds True, 2013

125. Didion, Joan. "On keeping a notebook." *Slouching Toward Bethlehem* (1968): 131-141.

126. Babin, Leif, and Jocko Willink. *Extreme Ownership.* Pan Macmillan Australia Pty, Limited, 2018

127. Kessler, R. C., Aguilar-Gaxiola, S., Alonso, J., Benjet, C., Bromet, E. J., Cardoso, G., Degenhardt, L., de Girolamo, G., Dinolova, R. V., Ferry, F., Florescu, S., Gureje, O., Haro, J. M., Huang, Y., Karam, E. G., Kawakami, N., Lee, S., Lepine, J. P., Levi. "Trauma and PTSD in the WHO World Mental Health Surveys." *European Journal of Psychotraumatology* 8 (5) (2017): 1353383.

128. Van der Kolk, Bessel. *The Body Keeps the Score: Brain, Mind, and Body in the Healing of Trauma.* Penguin Books, New York, 2014.

129. Rinpoche, Sogyal, and Sogyal. *The Tibetan Book of Living and Dying.* Edited by Patrick Gaffney and Andrew Harvey. HarperCollins, 1992.

130. Dalai Lama, H. H., and H. Cutler. *The Art of Happiness: A Handbook for Living.* New York: Riverhead,1998.

131. Neff, Kristin D., and Katie A. Dahm. "Self-compassion: What it is, what it does, and how it relates to mindfulness." In *Handbook of Mindfulness and Self-Regulation*, pp. 121-137. Springer, New York, NY, 2015.

132. Tedeschi, Richard G., and Lawrence G. Calhoun. "Posttraumatic growth: conceptual foundations and empirical evidence." *Psychological Inquiry* 15, no. 1 (2004): 1-18.

133. n.d. "Reach Forgiveness of Others — Everett Worthington." Everett Worthington. http://www.evworthington-forgiveness.com/reach-forgiveness-of-others.

134. Irvine, William B. *A Guide to the Good Life: The Ancient Art of Stoic Joy.* Oxford University Press, 2008.

135. Billingsley, Gaelen. *The Marble Game: Therapeutic Metaphors for Life.* 2016.

136. Brown, Brené. *The Gifts of Imperfection: Let Go of Who You Think You're Supposed to Be and Embrace Who You Are.* Simon and Schuster, 2010.

137. Hill A.P. & Curran T. "Multidimensional Perfectionism and Burnout: A Meta-Analysis." *Personality Social Psychological Review* 20 (3) (2016): 269-88.

138. Snowdon, David A. "Healthy aging and dementia: findings from the Nun Study." *Annals of Internal Medicine* 139, no. 5_Part_2 (2003): 450-454.

139. Siegel, Daniel J. *Mindsight: The New Science of Personal Transformation.* Bantam. 2010.

140. Pennebaker, James W. "Writing about emotional experiences as a therapeutic process." *Psychological Science* 8, no. 3 (1997): 162-166.

141. Pennebaker, James W., and Evans, J.F. *Expressive Writing: Words that Heal: Using Expressive Writing to Overcome Traumas and Emotional Upheavals, Resolve Issues, Improve Health, and Build Resilience.* Idyll Arbor, Incorporated, 2014.

142. Burton, Chad M., and King, L.A. "The health benefits of writing about positive experiences: The role of broadened cognition." *Psychology and Health* 24, no. 8 (2009): 867-879.

143. Harris, D. Warren, J. & Adler, C. *Meditation for Fidgety Skeptics: A 10% Happier How-To Book.* New York: Spiegel & Grau, 2017.

144. Brewer, Judson. *Unwinding Anxiety: New Science Shows How to Break the Cycles of Worry and Fear to Heal Your Mind.* Penguin, 2022.

145. Leaf, Caroline. *Cleaning Up Your Mental Mess: 5 Simple, Scientifically Proven Steps to Reduce Anxiety, Stress, and Toxic Thinking.* Baker Books, 2021.

146. Proffitt, Dennis, and Drake Baer. *Perception: How Our Bodies Shape Our Minds.* St. Martin's Press, 2020.

147. David, Susan. *Emotional Agility: Get Unstuck, Embrace Change, and Thrive in Work and Life.* Penguin, 2016.

148. Barrett, Lisa Feldman. *How Emotions are Made: The Secret Life of the Brain.* Mariner Books, 2018.

149. Gross, James J. "The emerging field of emotion regulation: An integrative review." *Review of General Psychology* 2, no. 3 (1998): 271-299.

150. Gallwey, W. Timothy. *The Inner Game of Tennis: The Ultimate Guide to the Mental Side of Peak Performance.* Random House, 1997.

151. David, Susan. "Three Ways to Better Understand Your Emotions." https://hbr.org/2016/11/3-ways-to-better-understand-your-emotions.

152. Brown, Brené. *Atlas of the Heart: Mapping Meaningful Connection and the Language of Human Experience.* Random House, 2021.

153. Gunaratana, Bhante. *Mindfulness." Voices of insight: Teachers of Buddhism in the West Share Their Wisdom, Stories, and Experiences of Insight Meditation,* ed. Sharon Salzberg. Boston: Shambhala Publications, 1999.

154. Salzberg, Sharon. *Real Happiness, 10th Anniversary Edition: A 28-Day Program to Realize the Power of Meditation.* Workman Publishing Company, 2019.

155. Hanson, Rick. *Hardwiring Happiness: The New Brain Science of Contentment, Calm, and Confidence.* Harmony, 2016.

156. Lyubomirsky, Sonja. 2008. *The How of Happiness: A Scientific Approach to Getting the Life You Want.* Penguin Press.

157. Lyubomirsky, S., Schkade, D., Sheldon, K. Pursuing Happiness: The Architecture of Sustainable Change. *Review of General Psychology* 9 (2) (2005): 111–131.

158. Sheldon, K. M., & Lyubomirsky, D. "Achieving Sustainable New Happiness: Prospects, Practices, and Prescriptions." In P. A. Linley & S. Joseph (Eds.), *Positive Psychology in Practice* (pp. 127–145). John Wiley & Sons, Inc., 2004

159. Lyubomirsky, Sonja. *The How of Happiness: A Scientific Approach to Getting the Life You Want.* Penguin Press, 2008.

160. Achor, Shawn. *The Happiness Advantage: The Seven Principles that Fuel Success and Performance at Work.* Virgin, 2011.

161. Lomas, T., Hefferon, K. & Ivtzan. *Applied Positive Psychology: Integrated Positive Practice.* Sage, 2014.

162. Keyes, C. L., Fredrickson, B. L., & Park, N. "Positive psychology and the quality of life." In K. C., Land, A. C., Michalos & M. J. Sirgy (Eds.). *Handbook of Social Indicators and Quality of Life Research.* Dordrecht: Springer, 2012. 99-112.

163. Macaskill, Ann, and Andrew Denovan. "Assessing psychological health: The contribution of psychological strengths." *British Journal of Guidance & Counselling* 42, no. 3 (2014): 320-337.

164. Sin, N. L., & Lyubomirsky, S. "Enhancing well-being and alleviating depressive symptoms with positive psychology interventions: A prac-

tice-friendly meta-analysis." Journal of Clinical Psychology, 65 (5) (2009): 467-487.

165. Parks, A. C., & Schueller, S. *The Wiley Blackwell Handbook of Positive Psychological Interventions.* West Sussex, UK.: John Wiley & Sons, 2014.

166. Parks, A. C., & Biswas-Diener, R.T. B., Kashdan & J. V., Ciarrochi (Eds.). "Mindfulness, acceptance, and positive psychology: The seven foundations of well-being Oakland, CA: Context." In *Positive Interventions: Past, Present, and Future,* 140-165. Oakland, CS: Context Press, 2013.

167. Seligman, Martin E. P. 2012. *Flourish: A Visionary New Understanding of Happiness and Well-being.* Atria Books.

168. Forgeard, M. J., Jayawickreme, E., Kern, M., & Seligman, M. "Doing the right thing: Measuring wellbeing for public policy." *International Journal of Wellbeing* 1 (1) (2011): 79-106.

169. Kern, M., Waters, L., Alder, A., & White, M. "Assessing employee wellbeing in schools using a multifaceted approach: Associations with physical health, life satisfaction, and professional thriving." *Psychology* 5 (6) (2104): 500–513.

170. Center for Healthy Minds. n.d. Center for Healthy Minds: Home. https://centerhealthyminds.org/.

171. Rashid, Tayyab, and Martin E. P. Seligman. *Positive Psychotherapy: Clinician Manual.* Oxford University Press, 2018.

172. Coursera/Yale University. n.d. https://www.coursera.org/learn/the-science-of-well-being.

173. Lyubomirsky, S., King, L., and Diener, E. "The benefits of frequent positive affect: Does happiness lead to success?" *Psychological Bulletin* 131 (6) (2005): 803.

174. Thoreau, H. D. Walden or Life in the Woods. (Original work published 1854). New York, NY: Barnes & Noble, 1993.

175. Mao GX, Lan XG, Cao YB, Chen ZM, He ZH, Lv YD, Wang YZ, Hu XL, Wang GF, Yan J. "Effects of short-term forest bathing on human health in a broad-leaved evergreen forest in Zhejiang Province, China." *Biomed Environ Sci.* 25 (3) (2012): 317-24.

176. Soga M, Evans MJ, Tsuchiya K, Fukano Y. "A room with a green view: the importance of nearby nature for mental health during the COVID-19 pandemic." *Ecol Appl.* 31 (2)(2021): 2248.

177. Weir, Kirsten. 2020. "Nurtured by nature." *American Psychological Association*. April 1. https://www.apa.org/monitor/2020/04/nurtured-nature.

178. Bratman, G, Anderson, C.B., Berman, M.G., et. al. 2019.

179. Nature and mental health: An ecosystem service perspective." *Science Advances* 5 (7). https://www.science.org/doi/10.1126/sciadv.aax0903.

180. Gidlow, C. J., Randall, J., Gillman, J., Smith, G. R., & Jones, M. V. "Natural environments and chronic stress measured by hair cortisol." *Landscape and Urban Planning* 148 (2016): 61-67.

181. Berman, M. G., Kross, E., Krpan, K. M., Askren, M. K., Burson, A., Deldin, P. J. & Jonides, J. "Interacting with nature improves cognition and affect for individuals with depression." *Journal of Affective Disorders*, 140 (3) (2012): 300-305.

182. Bratman, G. N., Daily, G. C., Levy, B. J., & Gross, J. J. "The benefits of nature experience: Improved affect and cognition." *Landscape and Urban Planning*. 138 (2015): 41-50.

183. White, M.P., Alcock, I., Grellier, J., Wheeler, B.W., Hartig, R., Warber, S.L., Bone, A., Depledge, M.H. & Fleming, L.E. "Spending at least 120 minutes a week in nature is associated with good health and wellbeing." *Sci Rep* 9 (2019): 7730.

184. Cartwright, B., White, M.P., & Clitherow, T.J. "Nearby Nature 'Buffers' the Effect of Low Social Connectedness on Adult Subjective Wellbeing over the Last 7 Days." *Int. J. Environ. Res. Public Health* 15 (6) (2018): 1238.

185. Largo-Wight E, Wlyudka P, Merten J, Cuvelier E. "Effectiveness and feasibility of a 10-minute employee stress intervention: Outdoor Booster Break." *J Workplace Behav Health*. 32 (3) (2017): 159-171.

186. Atchley, R. A., Strayer, D. L., & Atchley, P. "Creativity in the wild: Improving creative reasoning through immersion in natural settings." *PloS one* 7 (2012): 12.

187. Hartig, T., Mang, M., & Evans, G. W. "Restorative effects of natural environment experiences." *Environment and Behavior*, 23 (1) (1991): 3-26.

188. Faber Taylor, A., & Kuo, F. E. "Children with attention deficits concentrate better after walk in the park." *Journal of Attention Disorders* 12 (5) (2009): 402-209.

189. Kaplan, R., & Kaplan, S. *The Experience of Nature: A Psychological Perspective.* UK: Cambridge University Press, 1989.

190. Stokols, D., & Altman, I. *Handbook of Environmental psychology (Vol. 2).* New York, NY: Wiley, 1987.

191. Gifford, R. *Environmental Psychology: Principles and Practice.* Colville, WA: Optimal Books, 2007.

192. Orwell, R. L., Wood, R. L., Tarran, J., Torpy, F., & Burchett, M. D. "Removal of benzene by the indoor plant/substrate microcosm and implications for air quality." *Water, Air, and Soil Pollution.* 157 (2004): 193-207.

193. Nadkarni, N., P. Hasbach, T. Thys, E. Gaines, and L. Schnacker. "Impacts of nature imagery on people in severely nature-deprived environments." *Frontiers in Ecology and the Environment.* 15 (2017): 395-403.

194. Nadkarni, N., L. Schnacker, P. Hasbach, T. Thys, and E. Gaines. "From orange to blue: how nature imagery affects inmates in the "Blue Room"." *Corrections Today.* 79 (2017): 36-41.

195. Van Hedger, S.C., Nusbaum, H.C., Clohisy, L. et al.. "Of cricket chirps and car horns: The effect of nature sounds on cognitive performance." *Psychon Bull Rev* 26 (2019): 522–530.

196. Schertz, K. & Berman, M. "Understanding Nature and Its Cognitive Benefits." *Current Directions in Psychological Science* 28 (5) (2019).

197. Gascon, M., Zijema, M., Vert, C., White, M. & Nieuwenhuijsen, M.J. "Outdoor blue spaces, human health and well-being: A systematic review of quantitative studies." *International Journal of Hygiene and Environmental Health* (8) (2017): 1207-1221.

198. Bryant, F. B., & Veroff, J. *Savoring: A New Model of Positive Experience.* Erlbaum Associates, 2007.

199. Emmons, Robert A. *Thanks! How the New Science of Gratitude Can Make You Happier.* Houghton Mifflin Company, 2007.

200. Emmons, R.A., Crumpler, C.A. "Gratitude as a human strength: Appraising the evidence. *Journal of Social and Clinical Psychology.*" 19 (1) (2000): 56-69.

201. Iodice, J.A., Malouff, J.M. & Schutte, N.S. The Association between Gratitude and Depression: A Meta-Analysis. *International Journal of Depression and Anxiety* (4) (2021): 1.

202. Seligman, M. E. P.& Steen, T. T., Park, N., & Peterson, C. "Positive psychology progress: Empirical validation of interventions." *American Psychologist* 60 (2005): 410-421.

203. Fox, G.R., Kaplan, J., Damasio, H., Damasio, A. "Neural correlates of gratitude. Frontiers in Psychology." 6 (1) (2015): 1491.

204. Frijda, N. H. *The Emotions.* Cambridge, UK: Cambridge University Press, 1986.

205. Fredrickson, B. L. "What good are positive emotions?" *Review of General Psychology* 2 (3) (1998): 300-319.

206. Folkman, S. "Positive psychological states and coping with severe stress." *Social Science & Medicine,* 45 (8) (1997): 1207-1221.

207. Langer, E., & Rodin, J. The effects of choice and enhanced personal responsibility for the aged: A field experiment in an institutional setting. *JPSP* (1976): 191-198.

208. Kim, E.S., Kawachi, I., Chen, Y. et. al. "Association Between Purpose in Life and Objective Measures of Physical Function in Older Adults." *JAMA Psychiatry* 74 (10) (2017): 1039-1045.

209. Kim, Eric S., Strecher, V.J. & Ryff, C.D. "Purpose in life and use of preventive health care services." *Proceedings of the National Academy of Sciences* 111 (46) (2014): 16331-16336.

210. Csikszentmihalyi, M. *Flow: The Psychology of Optimal Experience.* New York, NY: Harper & Row Publishers, 1990.

211. Caddick, N., Smith, B. & Phoenix, C. "The effects of surfing and the natural environment on the well-being of combat veterans." *Qual Health Res* 25 (1) (2015): 76-86.

212. Loehr, James E. and Tony Schwartz. *The Power of Full Engagement: Managing Energy, Not Time, Is the Key to High Performance and Personal Renewal.* Free Press, 2005.

213. Loehr, James E., Jim Loehr, and Tony Schwartz. *The Power of Full Engagement: Managing Energy, Not Time, Is the Key to High Performance and Personal Renewal.* Free Press, 2005.

214. The Happiness Lab. n.d. "Laurie Gets a Fun-tervention (Part One) | The Happiness Lab with Dr. Laurie Santos." Accessed June 20, 2022. https://www.pushkin.fm/podcasts/the-happiness-lab-with-dr-laurie-santos/laurie-gets-a-fun-tervention-part-one.

215. Price, Catherine. *The Power of Fun: How to Feel Alive Again*. Random House Publishing Group, 2021.

216. Snyder, Charles Richard. *The Psychology of Hope: You Can Get There From Here*. Simon and Schuster, 1994.

217. 2020. "Russell Wilson: My secret to staying focused under pressure." TED. June 16. https://www.ted.com/talks/russell_wilson_my_secret_to_staying_focused_under_pressure?language=en.

218. Dunfield K. A. "A construct divided: Prosocial behavior as helping, sharing, and comforting subtypes." *Frontiers in Psychology* 5 (958) (2014).

219. Lawton, R.N., Gramatki, I., Watt, W. & Fujiwara, D. "Does Volunteering Make Us Happier, or Are Happier People More Likely to Volunteer? Addressing the Problem of Reverse Causality When Estimating the Wellbeing Impacts of Volunteering." *Journal of Happiness Studies* 22 (2021): 599–624.

220. Thoits, P.A. & Hewitt, L.N. "Volunteer Work and Well-Being." *Journal of Health and Social Behavior* 42 (2) (2001): 115-131.

221. Binder, M. & Freytag, A. "Volunteering, subjective well-being and public policy." *Journal of Economic Psychology* 34 (2013): 97-119.

222. Tift, Bruce. *Already Free: Buddhism Meets Psychotherapy on the Path of Liberation*. Sounds True, 2015.

223. Singer, Michael A. *The Untethered Soul.* New Harbinger Publications, 2007.

224. Brach, T. *Radical Acceptance: Embracing Your Life with the Heart of a Buddha.* Bantam Books, 2004.

225. Irvine, William B. *A Guide to the Good Life: the Ancient Art of Stoic Joy.* Oxford University Press, USA, 2009.

226. Pink, D.H. *The Power of Regret: How Looking Backward Moves Us Forward.* Penguin Publishing Group, 2022.

227. Ware, B. *The Top Five Regrets of the Dying: A Life Transformed by the Dearly Departing.* Hay House, Inc., 2012.

228. Levin, Jeff, and Jeffrey S. Levin. 2002. God, Faith, and Health: Exploring the Spirituality-Healing Connection. Wiley.

229. Moreira-Almeida, A., Neto. F.L. & Koenig, H.G. "Religiousness and mental health: a review." Brazilian Journal of Psychiatry 28 (3) (2006): 242-250.

230. Miller, Lisa. The Awakened Brain: The New Science of Spirituality and Our Quest for an Inspired Life. Random House Publishing Group, 2021.

231. Kendler KS, Gardner CO, Prescott CA. Religion, psychopathology, and substance use and abuse; a multimeasure, genetic-epidemiologic study. Am J Psychiatry 154(3) (Mar 1997) :322-9. doi: 10.1176/ajp.154.3.322. PMID: 9054778.

232. Benson, Herbert, and Miriam Z. Klipper. The Relaxation Response. Edited by Miriam Z. Klipper. HarperCollins, 1976.

233. Zanesco, A.P., King, B.G., MacLean, K.A. et al. Cognitive Aging and Long-Term Maintenance of Attentional Improvements Following Meditation Training. J Cogn Enhanc 2, 259–275 (2018). https://doi.org/10.1007/s41465-018-0068-1.

234. Duhigg, Charles. The Power of Habit: Why We Do What We Do in Life and Business. Random House Publishing Group, 2012.

235. Vieten, Cassandra, Helané Wahbeh, B. Rael Cahn, Katherine MacLean, Mica Estrada, Paul Mills, Michael Murphy et al. "Future directions in meditation research: Recommendations for expanding the field of contemplative science." PloS one 13, no. 11 (2018): e0205740.

236. Grinberg-Zylberbaum, J., and J. Ramos. "Patterns of interhemispheric correlations during human communication." International Journal of Neuroscience 36 (1987): 41-53.

237. Turkle, Sherry. Alone Together: Why We Expect More from Technology and Less from Each Other. Basic Books, 2017.

238. Joiner, Thomas. Lonely at the Top: The High Cost of Men's Success. Palgrave Macmillan Trade, 2011.

239. Harvard University. n.d. Harvard Second Generation Study. https://www.adultdevelopmentstudy.org/.

240. Mineo, Liz. 2017. "Over nearly 80 years, Harvard study has been showing how to live a healthy and happy life." Harvard Gazette. April 11. https://news.harvard.edu/gazette/story/2017/04/over-nearly-80-years-harvard-study-has-been-showing-how-to-live-a-healthy-and-happy-life/.

241. Baumeister, R. F., & Leary, M. R. "The need to belong: Desire for interpersonal attachments as a fundamental human motivation." *Psychological Bulletin* 117 (3) (1995): 497–529.

242. Gere, J., & MacDonald, G. "An update of the empirical case for the need to belong." *Journal of Individual Psychology*, 66 (1) (210): 93–115.

243. Holt-Lunstad J, Smith TB. "Social relationships and mortality." *Social and Personality Psychology Compass* 6 (2012): 41–53.

244. The Atlantic. 2017. "John Cacioppo on How to Combat Loneliness." The Atlantic. April 6. https://www.theatlantic.com/health/archive/2017/04/how-loneliness-begets-loneliness/521841/.

245. Goldstein, Weissman-Fogel, I., Guillaume Dumas & Shamay-Tsoory, S.G. "Brain-to-brain coupling during handholding is associated with pain reduction." *Proc Natl Acad Sci* U S A 115 (11) (2018): E2528-E2537.

246. Schnall, S., Harber, K.D., Stefanucci, & Proffitt, D.R. "Social Support and the Perception of Geographical Slant." *J Exp Soc Psychol* 44 (5) (2008): 1246–1255.

247. Cigna. n.d. "Loneliness in America." Cigna Newsroom. https://newsroom.cigna.com/loneliness-in-america.

248. World Happiness Report. 2021. "Social Connection and Well-Being during COVID-19 | The World Happiness Report." World Happiness Report. March 20. https://worldhappiness.report/ed/2021/social-connection-and-well-being-during-covid-19/.

249. Watkins, Mary. *Mutual Accompaniment and the Creation of the Commons.* Yale University Press, 2019.

250. Stanford University. n.d. "Center on Stress and Health - Stanford University School of Medicine | Stress Health Center | Stanford Medicine." Stanford Medicine. Accessed June 21, 2022. https://med.stanford.edu/stresshealthcenter.html.

251. Sepúlveda-Loyola, W., Rodríguez-Sánchez, I., Pérez-Rodríguez, P., Ganz, F., Torralba, R., Oliveira, D. V., & Rodríguez-Mañas, L. "Impact of Social Isolation Due to COVID-19 on Health in Older People: Mental and Physical Effects and Recommendations." *The Journal of Nutrition, Health & Aging* (2020): 1–10.

252. Martino, J., Pegg, J. & Frates, E.P. "The Connection Prescription: Using the Power of Social Interactions and the Deep Desire for Con-

nectedness to Empower Health and Wellness." *Am J Lifestyle Med* 11 (6) (2017): 466–475.

253. Venniro, M., Zhang, M., Caprioli, D., Hoots, J.K., Golden, S.A., Heins, C., Morales, M., Epstein, D.H, & Shaham, Y. "Volitional social interaction prevents drug addiction in rat models." *Natural Neuroscience* 21 (11) (2018): 1520-1529.

254. Taylor SE, Cousino Klein, L. Lewis, B.P., Gruenewald, T.L., Gurung, R.A.R. & Updegraff, J.A. "Biobehavioral Responses to Stress in Females: Tend-and-Befriend, Not Fight-or-Flight." *Psychological Review* 107 (3) (2000): 411-429.

255. Taylor, SE. "Tend and Befriend Theory." In *Handbook of Theories of Social Psychology*,. Chapter 2. London, England: Sage Publications, 2012.

256. Aaron, A., Melinat, E., Vallone, R.D. & Bator, R.J. "The Experimental of Generational Closeness: A Procedure and Some Preliminary Findings." *Personality & Psychological Bulletin* 23 (4) (1997): 363-377.

257. Eisenberger, Naomi I. "The pain of social disconnection: examining the shared neural underpinnings of physical and social pain." Nature reviews neuroscience 13 (6 (2012): 421-434.

258. Cohen, S., Janicki-Deverts, D., Turner, R.B., & Doyle, W.J. "Does hugging provide stress-buffering social support? A study of susceptibility to upper respiratory infection and illness." *Psychological science* 26 (2) (2015): 135-147.

259. Grewen, K.M., Anderson, B.J., Girdler, S.S. & Light, K.C. "Warm partner contact is related to lower cardiovascular reactivity." *Behav Med* 29 (3) (2003): 123-30.

260. Edmondson, Amy C. *The Fearless Organization: Creating Psychological Safety in the Workplace for Learning, Innovation, and Growth.* Wiley, 2018.

261. Grant, Adam. *Give and Take: A Revolutionary Approach to Success.* Penguin Publishing Group, 2013.

262. Pueblo, Yung. *Clarity & Connection.* Andrews McMeel Publishing, 2021.

263. Nepo, Mark. *More Together Than Alone: Discovering the Power and Spirit of Community in Our Lives and in the World.* Atria Books, 2018.